THE BUSINESS
OF PUBLIC
SPEAKING

THE BUSINESS
OF PUBLIC
SPEAKING

FOR EXECUTIVES, CONSULTANTS, AUTHORS, AND TRAINERS

HERMAN HOLTZ

JOHN WILEY & SONS

New York • Chichester • Brisbane • Toronto • Singapore

Library of Congress Cataloging in Publication Data:

Holtz, Herman.
    The business of public speaking.

    Bibliography: p.
    Includes index.
    1. Public speaking—Vocational guidance.   2. Lectures
and lecturing—Vocational guidance.   I. Title.

PN4098.H65   1985   808.5′1′023   84-25732
ISBN 0-471-87991-6

Printed in the United States of America

10   9   8   7   6   5   4   3   2   1

*To
Sherrie
for many things*

PREFACE

"I could leave a rich widow," responded Menachem Begin, then Prime Minister of Israel, when lecture-agent Harry Walker promised him $15,000 a night on what has been called the "chicken and peas circuit"—lecturing for fees.

Harry Walker, an old friend of Begin's, numbers among the notables he books for lectures such luminaries as ex-Presidents Gerald Ford and Jimmy Carter, former Secretary of State Henry Kissinger, TV interviewer Barbara Walters, and others who command fees ranging even higher than the promised $15,000 per speech.

Based in New York City, where he maintains his offices, Harry Walker is an especially successful and prominent vendor of public speakers, and he probably focuses even more than other lecture agents on the noted and the notorious—those who often command handsome speaking fees much more because their names are "bankable" (audiences are more curious to see and hear them in person) than because they are especially good speakers. (Such is the power of publicity.) Nevertheless, he is the operator of only one of many hundreds of lecture bureaus and other agencies for public speaking engagements. In fact, speakers are supplied by convention- and conference-management firms, by entertainment and theatrical booking agents, and by many others for whom the booking of public speakers is only one of many activities. (Do you want to know where those famous names and faces are when you don't see them on the tube or on the big screen? They are busy making speeches and entertaining people at trade shows, conventions, and other business events. On one occasion, for example, when I delivered a seminar on government marketing at a national convention of the Land Improvement Contractors of America, the obligatory luncheon speaker was none other than the well-known comedian Henny Youngman.)

According to the press, such leading lights of our civilization as Henry Kissinger, Alexander Haig, Paul Harvey, and Dan Rather can command $20,000 or more for a speech, whereas such lesser luminaries as Dick Cavett, Milton Friedman, and Barbara Walters command "only" $12,000 to $15,000, and those who cast even fewer lumens, such as David Brinkley, William F. Buckley, Jr., Betty Ford, and numerous others of this reduced luminescence, must settle for only $10,000 or thereabout. The atmosphere and the asking price change with the recency of the fame and other factors that bear on how curious potential listeners are to see and hear the Great Person. Fame is fleeting, as is well known, and those who manage to achieve fame or infamy must strike swiftly, while they are yet on the pages of the daily and weekly press, if they wish to reap the full benefits.

On the other hand, you need not wait until you are a "name" to join those who are rewarded for the words they utter on the platform. The fact is that almost anyone who wishes to be a public speaker can do so, and can even earn money doing so. Isaac Asimov, that superprolific writer of scientific/technical fiction and nonfiction, speaks frequently and commands substantial fees for so doing. However, sophisticated and celebrated figure that he is today, he was equally naive when he was first asked to speak— before he was so well known—before a group of strangers: He was stunned to discover that he was actually to be paid for being so honored! He relates that he felt almost guilty of fraud in accepting money for speaking, especially as he began to command fees far greater than he had earlier thought possible, even after discovering that speakers do get paid.

Many thousands of individuals speak publicly at various gatherings and convocations. By far the majority do so without specific compensation, other than possible career or business benefits. And probably a great many people do not even suspect that one can make a profitable career of public speaking without being notable or notorious, or even that it can be a profitable facet of one's career. The many books and training courses on how to speak publicly rarely touch on speaking as a career activity—on how to speak profitably. (This is not one of those books on the art of being a great speaker, although you may find a few tips on speaking methodologies, if you pay close attention. There is an abundance of books that teach the art of speaking well, including a few that are recommended in these pages, written by people who are far more experienced and more qualified as public speakers than I, and therefore far more qualified to teach others how to speak well.)

In addition to those who command such large fees for their appearances and those who speak publicly without being paid fees, there are those for whom public speaking is their profession or part of their income-producing professional activities. For every Art Buchwald, Gordon Liddy (of Watergate notoriety), or other public figure who commands large speaking fees because of fame or infamy, there are thousands of speakers who command relatively modest fees—perhaps "only" $1000, $2000, or $3000 per speech—which they earn because they have something to say that audiences want to hear, and they know how to present their material professionally. These are the real backbone of the public speaking profession. It is on them that all those lecture agents depend to create and sustain the markets for public speaking.

In short, public speaking is a rather large business for those who act as the agents and arrange the bookings, and a profitable profession for those who make a profession of speaking for fees. And the market continues to expand, for several reasons. Some literary agencies, for example, have taken to acting as agents for writers who are willing to venture into the lecture circuit. And many organizations, including business corporations, associations, and other for-profit and nonprofit organizations maintain internal lecture bureaus, supplying speakers from their own staffs, without charge, as a public service which enhances their own images and promotes their own marketing—provides excellent PR, that is. (Of course, that latter one is the exception to the rule, as far as fees and profits—at least, direct profits—are concerned, but it does reflect the growing popularity of public speaking.)

On the other hand, not everyone who commands fees for speaking publicly is a true professional speaker, no matter the size of the fee nor the frequency of appearances on the platform. Nor does it relate to how "well" or how entertainingly the individual speaks. In addition to such entertainers as Henny Youngman and other show-business figures who are invited to speak at conventions and banquets, many others are invited to speak (and are paid appropriate fees) because they are in lines of work or professions that are of interest to others.

This latter class of paid public speaker, then (those whose names are not known to the general public, although they may be well known within their own professional or career circles) consists of individuals who may be full-time professional speakers, as many are; or they may be busily engaged in some special field, but devoting a significant portion of their time and effort to appearances on the platform. They may be writers, artists, architects, musicians, composers, engineers, scientists, military professionals, physicians, association executives, consultants, or active careerists in any of thousands of other fields, as many professional speakers are. (Dottie Walters, herself a well-known veteran of the speaker's platform, operator of her own lecture bureau, and publisher of the popular speakers' journal, *Sharing Ideas!*, estimated that probably not more than 10 percent of those who speak professionally for fees do nothing else but speak professionally. The other 90 percent have other business interests and activities, although speaking is a major element in the career/business/professional activities of a large portion of that 90 percent.)

The main orientation and purpose of this book is to make you aware of public speaking as a profession—a *paid* profession—or as a business enterprise, if you prefer to regard it in that light, open to anyone who is willing to work at entering this field and work hard at succeeding in it. But note that you do not have to make public speaking your sole or even main career activity, although many do; you may very well opt to make it one of your career activities, to supplement other work you do, such as consulting or writing.

In fact, public speaking for profit is an almost perfect complement to a great many other professional activities, and a great many professional speakers are, indeed, also consultants, writers, and executives in many fields. In fact, not only does public speaking complement other professional and business careers nicely, but the combined activities are usually mutually supportive: each contributes to the success of the other.

It is therefore my goal not to teach you how to speak, but to make you aware that public speaking can be a rewarding career or part of your career, and to show you how to enter this world of paid public speaking and achieve success in it. What you need for success, contrary to what you may have always believed, is neither a great speaking voice nor a great deal of special training, helpful though they may be. Nor do you need special talent, whatever that may be. (Does anyone really know?) But there are three things you do need for success there: (1) You do need to have something to say—something to say, that is, that is worth your listeners' time to listen to, something that a large number of people will want to hear, something that you believe strongly, even passionately, in. That means also knowing what you are talking about; to know your subject well and be able therefore to present it with some authority. (2) You need to understand this field of paid public speaking—*professional* public speaking, that is. And, (3) you need true dedication: perseverance, patience, practice, courage, spirit, enthusiasm, optimism, sincerity, and integrity. Those are the things that count, far more than any natural talents of any kind.

That first need—something to say and mastery of your subject—is something you must bring with you, something you already have or can get somewhere by intensive research and study.

That second requirement—knowledge and understanding of the field of paid, professional public speaking—is what I plan to help you acquire in the pages that follow. I will lay out a regimen of work for you, because I can help point you in the right direction—however, you have to take all the steps on your own.

As for that third requirement—that dedication and all those characteristics listed as part of the necessary dedication—that can come only from within you. I will try here to inspire you without gilding the lily—no false promises. But you have to want to succeed in the public speaking profession/business enough to make the total commitment to it.

HERMAN HOLTZ

Silver Spring, Maryland
March 1985

ACKNOWLEDGMENTS

Like most authors of how-to-do-it and where-to-find-it books, I sought and got help from a great many gracious people, experts in their field and eager to help others. Acknowledgment here is little enough reward for their unselfish efforts and many contributions. Very special thanks to all the following, many of whose names will be found mentioned again in these pages, and to many, many others whose contributions are freely acknowledged.

Doc Blakely	Dan T. Moore
Art Fettig	Bob Orben
Mike Frank	Mike Podolinsky
Lou Hampton	Nido Qubein
Will Jordan	Fran Slotkin
M.R. "Kop" Kopmyer	Dottie Walters
Ed Larkin	Dave Yoho
Bob Montgomery	

H.H.

CONTENTS

Rewards and merit are not necessarily related. For some it's show biz—almost. The famous. The infamous. The unfamous. Sponsors and clients. A few statistics typifying the field. But you do not have to be a "big name," either. Who finds the clients? The agent–client relationship. Can one become a celebrity on the platform? How does the ordinary individual enter this field?

The inevitability of public speaking. Speaking occasions. Conferences and conventions. Who sponsors conventions? The typical convention/conference program. Occasions dictate kinds of speakers. Local organizations and occasions. The broad basis for all associations. How special is the common interest? Who manages associations?

PART 2   CREATING THE PROFESSIONAL SPEECH

Content versus presentation. Fear, the first hurdle. What is the true fear? Reducing the exposure. The least stressful speaking situation. Barriers and shields. Diffusing the focus. Style and preparation. Organization. Delivery.

The greatest secret of success. Body language.

Some tips on success. Humor is highly salable. What is a professional speaker?

PART 3 THE BUSINESS OF SPEAKING

lishers. Book publishing as an information industry. What are these information books? The
economic realities of articles versus books.
Querying book publishers: the proposal. Some
basic publishing lore. Some book publishing economics. Direct-response marketing. Creating
and selling your own products. The cooperative
book. On creating cassette tapes and albums.
Other self-publishing. Seminars. Producing
printed materials. Word processors.

PART 4   MARKETING

What is marketing? Some basic principles of selling. How this relates to marketing. How this relates to selling your speaking services. Marketing
and sales methods. Agents and brokers. Lecture
bureaus and their role. Costs of being represented: fees and commissions. Should you sign
with a bureau? Some beginning tactics in self-
marketing. Finding opportunities to speak. First
steps in preparation. Content. Style. Choosing
style and content. Content versus delivery. Making the market matches. Market analysis worksheet. Creating speaking opportunities. Still,
you do not necessarily have to work for nothing.
Guesting at seminars. A few case histories.
Showcases. Other events and opportunities.

The product. The buyer. Packaging. A case history. One major marketing tool: good mailing
lists. The direct-mail package. Special alternatives. How to write a sales letter. What is an ab-

straction? Motivators: what are they? Self-interest is the prime motivator. Fear and greed. The worry item. Applying this to your own marketing. The meaning of need. What you need. The letter. The brochure. Photographs. Audition tapes. Press releases. Why the need for "sales appeal." How to get releases published. Where to send releases. Get yourself written about. Radio and TV interviews. The sales close. Proposals and proposal writing. The cover letter. The letter proposal. Don't wait to be asked. Don't make sales; make customers. How to follow up engagements.

THE BUSINESS
OF PUBLIC
SPEAKING

PART 1

THE PROFITS IN
PUBLIC SPEAKING

Public speaking may not be humankind's oldest profession, but it is certainly one of our oldest activities, prominently in evidence in the oldest records found.

CHAPTER 1

THE MANY REWARDS OF PUBLIC SPEAKING

Not all public speakers are motivated by money.

WHY PEOPLE MOUNT
THE PLATFORM

Some people get paid in coin—and quite handsomely, in many cases—for orating from the platform for an hour or two, or even more. In fact, there are many thousands of individuals who derive all or most of their income from that activity. But there are many others who speak publicly without pay, but not without profit. For there are other kinds of profits in public speaking than the coin of our economic system.

Aside from the direct reward of speaker's fees or income deriving from paid attendance, here are some of the other reasons and occasions which bring speakers to the public platform:

☐ Prominent individuals who are specialists or experts in some field of great interest to the public at large sometimes agree to speak without fee as a public duty—altruistically, that is. (There are those who are motivated by other considerations than direct, personal gain.)

☐ Individuals active in their associations—especially office holders and officials of trade groups, professional societies, and perhaps other kinds of associations—are frequently called upon to address the membership on matters of concern to the association and the members thereof.

☐ Executives of important or prominent organizations are expected, in a kind of *noblesse oblige*, to be available to make speeches when asked to do so as a matter of civic duty or its industrial equivalent. They tend to consider it something that "goes with the territory," and in the interests of their organizations, if not their direct personal interests.

☐ In a parallel of the above, public officials, both elected and appointed, are expected to sacrifice their time and make such speeches to various groups, when invited to do so.

☐ Many companies operate internal speakers bureaus, as part of their public relations programs, and make speakers available on request—even go to considerable trouble and expense to announce the availability of speakers free of charge.

☐ Many government agencies make speakers available on request, in precisely the same manner, again as a duty owed the public who pay their salaries and support their organizations.

☐ Individuals, especially professionals who, for whatever reason, cannot use conventional advertising, often leap at every opportunity to speak publicly, as a substitute for paid advertising. (A very good substitute, often far better in the results it produces than paid advertising would be.)

☐ Many young professionals and executives grasp every opportunity to speak publicly as an image-building (hence career-enhancing) activity, particularly at prestigious conferences and conventions.

☐ Many people run free seminars, miniseminars, and lectures as direct marketing promotions. The Evelyn Wood organization, for example, does this, offering free sample lessons in speed reading to draw prospects to whom they can then make full sales presentations.

☐ Speaking publicly to groups on some subject in which you have chosen to specialize may confer on you a mantle of special authority—that is, while some people are asked to speak on a subject in which they are regarded as expert and especially authoritative, it works in reverse, too: Speaking often and everywhere on a subject imparts a reputation, eventually, as an expert and authority, and there are those who have benefited in this way, whether by design or by serendipity.

☐ Finally, there are those who seek to make a career of speaking publicly for fees and are trying to gain experience and visibility to establish both some relevant experience and competence, and a set of speaking credentials. Experienced professionals advise the hopeful newcomer to the field to do just that—to seize every possible opportunity to speak publicly, and not to worry about earning fees while gaining experience. The accumulating experience is fee enough, they reason, for the apprentice.

Probably they are right, for public speaking is a highly rewarding field to those who make good in it, whether they speak for actual fees or for other kinds of rewards. In this book we are concerned primarily with public speaking as a direct income-producing activity, whether as a full-time profession or as a part-time activity, and whether a moonlight activity—carried out in spare time by those employed in regular jobs—or one activity of self-employed individuals for whom public speaking meshes well with their other work. This is not to slight those who wish to speak publicly in pursuit of some of those other goals and purposes mentioned, but merely to make our orientation and general objective crystal clear.

In this first part we'll explore the fee-paid speaking field generally. Later, in other parts, we'll probe several other major aspects and vistas of public speaking as an income-producing activity.

THE WORLD OF PAID
SPEAKING

Few outside the world of paid speaking know anything about the public speaking profession—perhaps not even that it exists.

A BRIEF INTRODUCTION TO THIS
SPECIAL WORLD

If you did not read the preface you may have missed a major point of this book, but even if you did read the preface, the point is worth repeating and stressing here:

This is not a book on how to "speak well," but a book on how to speak profitably. It is a book about the world of paid speaking, and how to enter and succeed in that world.

Not a great deal has appeared in the press about this world of paid public speaking. Perhaps that is ironic because so many public speakers are writers also, but few appear willing to tell others about their own professions—at least, not about how to become successful professional speakers.

In 1982 the weekly newsmagazine *U.S. News & World Report* reported that speaking fees had leaped as much as 30 percent over the previous year, also revealing that satirist Art Buchwald draws $25,000 for each of about 25 speaking engagements each year, and estimated that President Ronald Reagan had earned some $2 million in lecture fees over the two years prior to his election.

Many others earn far less per engagement—lesser lights are estimated to earn from $2000 to $5000 for each talk—but many speak frequently, as often as 300 times a year, allegedly.

There are a few periodicals covering the field—*Talent*, a quarterly publication of the International Platform Association; *The Executive Speaker*, a monthly newsletter; and *The Toastmaster*, a slim monthly magazine published by Toastmasters International, Inc. All of these deal with the art of public speaking, none with the business side of speaking for pay. There is one periodical, however, that does cover that side of public speaking. It's a bimonthly magazine, titled *Sharing Ideas Among Professional Speakers*. It's published by Dottie Walters, herself an accomplished and experienced public speaker, operator of her own lecture bureau, and publisher of books for speakers, as well as of her periodical. (More information about this later.)

WHERE DO PROFESSIONAL
SPEAKERS COME FROM?

It has been noted here already that just about anyone can become a successful professional speaker. For some, the route to success in public speaking is one traversed only with deliberate intent and planning. For others the route to public speaking is almost inevitable because they are in careers that are relevant to public speaking—even require the individual to do some speaking. The following individuals are almost "naturals" for the dais because of their regular careers, and a great many public speakers come from these fields and backgrounds:

Writers, all kinds—novelists, columnists, journalists, and others
Politicians and public officials at all levels
Consultants, all kinds
Prominent professionals, all fields—medicine, engineering, law, other
Association officials
Clergymen
Prominent executives of large corporations and other organizations

WHERE ARE PAID SPEAKERS IN
GREATEST DEMAND?

There are many places to speak: Colleges and universities hire speakers regularly. Conventions and conferences include many speeches and seminars. Every luncheon and dinner banquet requires speakers. Corporations hire speakers to conduct seminars and make other training, consciousness raising, and inspirational presentations. Business meetings galore are held daily all over the country—all over the world, for that matter, and many speakers travel in foreign countries to make their presentations. Cruise directors often book interesting public speakers to serve as part of their programs. And producers of seminars often hire "outside" speakers.

Once, years ago, in an era before all the modern forms of entertainment and information—radio, and TV, for example—many lecturers performed for the general public, speaking at the local town hall or auditorium, and charging an admission fee. Individuals paid to hear lecturers speak on a variety of subjects because the subjects were entertaining and informative, and attending lectures was a form of recreation, much like going to the theater. A big-game hunter, for example, might speak on the subject of his adventures and probably bring along a set of lantern slides to illustrate his talk.

Some talks of this nature are still offered today, usually sponsored by associations and other institutions. But despite the many talks sponsored by and held in the facilities of colleges, universities, and other such organizations, by far the majority of lectures today are sponsored by professional and business organizations for business purposes. The vehicles for these presentations are seminars, conventions, conferences, symposia, and other such gatherings of people with mutual professional and business interests.

As a speaker on such occasions you may be called upon to speak after lunch or dinner, as one of a panel, or as a solitary presenter. You may be asked to speak for an hour, a half-hour, several hours, or even all day (in the case of seminar presentations). You may be in demand because you have certain exclusive information to offer, because you have a reputation as an outstanding expert in your field, because you have an especially interesting presentation, perhaps because you have a novel and interesting viewpoint to offer on certain subjects, or because you are a wit and a generally entertaining speaker.

HOW MUCH CAN A SPEAKER EARN?

You can earn a good bit of money, if you can keep busy—keep a full calendar of speaking dates. Even at the relatively low speaker's fee of $500, a busy schedule will reward you handsomely in dollars. But there are other rewards than the pecuniary ones. There is, for example, that one-of-a-kind reward of applause from an appreciative audience, and from people who approach you later, individually, to tell you how much they enjoyed hearing you and how valuable they thought your presentation was.

Many—probably most—speakers do not depend entirely on their fees for their income. Most speakers become writers, as many writers become speakers, and many speakers also become their own publishers and sell their books and newsletters at their own speaking engagements in those "back of the room sales" so well known to professional speakers. That, in fact, is an important part of their income-producing activity, for many speakers. Some speakers, especially seminar producers, also record their presentations on audio cassettes and sell the cassettes. And many speakers organize their own seminars, to which they charge individual admission fees, and earn profits on top of the fees they pay themselves for speaking at their own seminars.

IT'S NOT ALL SKITTLES AND BEER

There is a downside to this, too. Full-time, professional speakers spend a great many lonely nights away from home in Holiday Inns. They eat a lot of chicken a la king (banquet food) for dinner. They rush around a great deal, struggling to get taxis and catch airplanes, pleading with hotel clerks who have lost or never received their reservations, and they often have to ponder, after waking up in the morning, to remember what town—perhaps even what state—they are in.

HOW DO SPEAKERS GET THEIR BOOKINGS?

Some speakers work through booking agencies exclusively, while some do all their own booking. Most, probably, use a combination of the two methods and often register with more than one lecture bureau.

Some speakers have a single presentation they offer, while others have several different ones they can deliver, and a few have many different ones, or have a single one but change it frequently. (It is important to have more than one presentation, preferably of interest to the same kinds of audiences, if you want to be invited back. But there are exceptions to this too.)

Speaking, like consulting, is so diverse a profession that it is most difficult to generalize about it without pointing to many exceptions. And, like consultants, some speakers specialize, while others generalize. For example, there are those who present seminars only, and they are likely to travel widely and do the same seminar over and over. There are others who prefer to do only the after-dinner speech or other relatively brief presentations. Some speak only to business groups, while others speak primarily to consumer groups or community groups, or other groups of lay people. And some are professionals who speak only to their own professional peers (e.g., before professional societies and similar gatherings).

WHAT DO PAID SPEAKERS SPEAK ABOUT?

The subjects on which lay speakers hold forth are the most diverse aspect of the field, representing near-infinity in number. But as a means for getting a "handle" on the subject, the talks can be divided into several general groups:

Humor

Consciousness-raising and other "positive thinking" presentations

Business and professional topics

It is hardly necessary to point out that the last-named category is by far the broadest and most diverse, as well as the most in demand. And it is not difficult to identify, even in that broad and diverse category, the one kind of topic that is most in demand and most often presented: A large portion of the business presentations are of information and instruction that will help the listeners win more business success, especially in sales and marketing fields.

EXAMPLES

In my own case, I speak most often about that field in which I consult and about which I have written a great deal: how to write winning proposals in pursuit of contracts, especially government contracts. (But sometimes I am asked to speak on how to become a successful independent consultant.)

In the case of several other people I know, they speak about sales and marketing methods, techniques which will help the listeners sell more effectively.

To a large degree, positive thinking presentations approach that target too, helping individuals become more effective marketers and salespeople because their general outlook and attitude has become healthier.

But it isn't all sales/marketing oriented. There are lectures and seminars on contract administration, coping with legal requirements in various businesses and professions, improving office systems, using word processors, finding tax shelters, coping with stress, managing time more effectively, being a more efficient executive, stopping smoking, and an almost limitless list of subjects, most of them with business and career implications and applications.

WHAT IS THE ATTRACTION OF
LECTURES AND SEMINARS?

Somehow, although one might be able to buy a book for perhaps $20 that would include far more detailed information than a speaker can present in an hour or two, many people will opt for the lecture, and even pay far more for that than they would for the book. Why? Probably for several reasons:

☐   Not everyone likes to read. For some, reading is almost a lost art. Somehow, for many, listening is easier than reading. Probably this is because listening is essentially passive, whereas reading is essentially active.

☐   Some people find that they simply cannot learn a subject by only reading about it, no matter how detailed the reading material. They need "live" presentation and a classroom atmosphere.

☐   Some people want to be able to ask questions, hold discussions, and seek detailed explanations about many points—not only want to, but find it necessary to, if they are to get the full benefits of the information.

☐   Finally, there are many individuals who can't endure the essentially solitary and lonely nature of studying a book or a self-study program, but need the sense of belonging to a group with mutual problems, needs, and interests.

In my own case, despite my several books on the subject of government contracts and, especially, on proposal writing, many people far prefer to attend my seminars on proposal writing, even if they have already read my books. (Of course, no one can anticipate all possible questions, when writing a book, and I do get questions at my seminars which touch on points not explained in detail in my books.) In fact, many find the books most helpful as a follow-up to the seminar.

JUST WHAT IS A SEMINAR?

Not all lectures and seminars are "how-to" presentations, and it would be misleading to suggest that they are, even if a great many of them fall into that category. Most are learning experiences, but not necessarily how-to learning—not formal or even informal training, that is. In fact, in its classical sense, the seminar is a small group studying a subject at some graduate level, usually a highly specialized subject. However, the original meaning of the term has been greatly extended in the modern business world, and almost any training session consuming from one-half day to not more than one week of exclusive and intensive focus on a single, special subject area is today referred to as a seminar, with appropriate fees for attendance—usually on the order of $100 to $300 per day per attendee. And it is a major business, with many organizations specializing in—even devoted exclusively to—seminar development and presentation. (One Washington, D.C. organization alone does some $6 million or more per year in seminars.)

WHO ATTENDS SEMINARS?

There are, in general, two types of seminars and seminar attendees, in at least one sense—the sense of who pays the registration fees to attend the session. In that sense, there are sessions which induce organizations to send their employees (and pay for their registration), and there are those which motivate individuals to pay for their own registrations and attendance.

The question revolves around who the principal beneficiary of the seminar is, the individual as an individual, or the organization as the employer of the individual.

In the pages to come we will explore these and many other questions and aspects of this fascinating and diverse world of paid public speaking, which is today as far removed from the itinerant lecturer of yore—of that almost legendary Chautauqua lecture, for example—as today's microchip portable radio is from the scratchy crystal set of several generations ago.

THE FAMOUS, THE UNFAMOUS, AND THE INFAMOUS

In many ways, paid public speaking resembles show business, but is not nearly as difficult a profession to break into and succeed in.

REWARDS AND MERIT ARE NOT
NECESSARILY RELATED

There is about as much justice and injustice in the field of paid public speaking as there is in most fields, and especially as much as there is in show business. In fact, paid public speaking bears a great deal of resemblance to show business in a great many ways, including the justice and injustice of the relationships between abilities and rewards. And in many ways paid public speaking appears to be part of show business.

This similarity is especially apparent with respect to who is accepted most readily into the fraternity of paid public speakers, and who reaps the greatest rewards from making public presentations: As in show business, fees are based primarily on "name," and that means appeal or the capability of the name for arousing interest of the kind that commands large fees—on the "box office" of the name, to put it into Hollywood vernacular. In fact, a great many of those who have managed to win fame or notoriety, permanent or fleeting, do not mount the speaker's platform on their own initiative: In a great number of cases the individual has not even thought to exploit the prominence, and in any case public speaking is perhaps the last thing that would have occurred to some of these individuals as a smart next move. But aggressive and alert entrepreneurs who operate lecture bureaus swiftly seek out the famous and the infamous with tempting offers, as they explain how, with their representation, one looming large in the public eye can earn tidy fees for doing little more than making appearances.

FOR SOME IT'S SHOW BIZ—
ALMOST

For the professional entertainer, the similarity to show business is especially striking—in fact, such appearances *are* show biz, as surely as though they were offered in a theater or night club, and probably easier to book, as well. Many entertainers who make only occasional appearances on the large or small screens, or even in cocktail lounges and dinner theaters, are sustained in the meantime by appearances on lecture platforms. Others, who are not exactly a real part of show business, such as humorists and raconteurs, are in a somewhat ambivalent position, not really professional entertainers, and yet called upon primarily for entertainment, rather than information or instruction.

THE FAMOUS

Even more difficult to define are the roles of those who are summoned to the dais primarily as the consequence of their having arrived at the status of being well known to the public at large for whatever achievements may have brought them fame of some sort. These fall into different classes—those whose "name" is the result of worthy achievement that suggests they have knowledge, experience, and ideas that are worth hearing about, and who might even be good speakers; those who might be entertaining by having some deliciously scandalous stories to tell—inside gossip; those who are merely well known because they are principals in highly publicized lawsuits or criminal trials, or even sensational scandals; and others whose appeal is strictly that of idle curiosity—to see, for oneself, what the newspapers, magazines, and TV news have been reporting on and prattling about.

Examples of such types are very much in evidence: Among the well-known names and faces summoned to the platform to receive respectably large speaking fees have been such figures as Henry Kissinger, Art Buchwald, Jimmy Carter, Norman Mailer, John Kenneth Galbraith, Norman Vincent Peale, Jesse Jackson, William Safire, and Pat Buchanan, and if you do not recognize some of these names, that illustrates how fleeting fame may be. In fact, some of these names are hardy perennials, whose appeal survives, year after year so that they can go on speaking regularly. Others can command speaking fees only for a short time, while the public remembers them.

THE INFAMOUS

There are many who, while perhaps not exactly infamous, enjoy a notoriety that is not a reflection of great achievement but is related to some infamy, directly or indirectly. Gordon Liddy, for example, when released from prison (to which he had been committed as a result of conviction arising out of his Watergate activities and refusal to testify) became almost a cult figure, for a time. He wrote a book and intensively toured the lecture circuit—colleges, primarily. It was, of course, not the literary event of the year to hear Gordon Liddy speak; it was more of a carnival or circus atmosphere.

But one does not necessarily have to be or have been the chief figure in infamous events; merely being connected with them in such a way as to gain a great deal of publicity is often enough to arouse the curiosity of the public to want to see and hear the individual in person. Who today remembers Elizabeth Ray, the secretary who couldn't type and who was the notorious paramour of U.S. Congressman Wayne Hays in a Washington scandal of a few years ago?

THE UNFAMOUS

For every famous name—celebrity—who tours the lecture circuits, there are dozens who are not famous or who, at best, enjoy a much lesser form of fame. You may or may not recognize the name Ray Bradbury, although he is a rather well-known writer of science fiction, well known to aficionados of that genre of fiction, or Scott Armstrong, a former astronaut, who gained at least temporary prominence in the space program. Here are those and others whose names you may or may not recognize, who speak on college campuses and elsewhere:

Scott Armstrong (former astronaut)
Ray Bradbury (science fiction writer)
Shirley Chisholm (U.S. Congresswoman)

George Gilder (economist, writer)

Hamilton Jordan (former chief of staff to President Jimmy Carter)

Moorhead and Louisa Kennedy (Moorhead was one of hostages held in Iran)

Coretta Scott King (widow of Martin Luther King)

Patrick Leahy (Senator)

Fran Leibowitz (best-selling author)

Arthur Miller (noted playwright)

Ralph Nader (consumer activist)

Edwin Newman (journalist, commentator)

Beverly Sills (star of opera)

Jack Anderson (columnist, investigative reporter)

Jeane Dixon (psychic, seer)

Robert J. Dole (U.S. Senator)

Malcolm S. Forbes (publisher *Forbes* magazine)

Heloise (columnist: "Hints From Heloise")

Doug Henning (magician)

Kitty Kelley (author)

James J. Kilpatrick (columnist, TV commentator)

George Plimpton (author)

Liv Ullman (actress)

Richard Valeriani (noted journalist, commentator)

Victor Borge (musician, humorist)

Henry J. Heimlich (physician, inventor of "the Heimlich maneuver")

Arthur J. Goldberg (distinguished jurist and diplomat)

Hal Holbrook (actor)

Art Linkletter (radio-TV personality)

Carl Sagan (scientist and author)

George Will (columnist, author, TV commentator)

John Denver (actor, singer)

Harry Blackstone (magician)
William Safire (columnist, author)

SPONSORS AND CLIENTS

Colleges and universities are among the many organizations who engage speakers. Here are a few recorded not long ago as such sponsors:

Hamline University
Washington University
Foothill College
Johns Hopkins University
Eastern Michigan University
Luther College
LaSalle College
Mental Health Association
Whitman College
International Society of Weekly Newspaper Editors
St. Mary's College
Rock Valley College
Eastern Iowa Executive Club
Northern Indiana Sheet Metal Contractors Association
Cuyahoga Community College
Drury College
Southern Connecticut State College
Green River Community College
Lakeland Community College
San Joaquin Delta College
Meridian Junior College
University of North Carolina

(This is not to suggest that speakers are invited to speak mostly by colleges, but colleges and universities are a prime market for speakers.)

A FEW STATISTICS TYPIFYING
THE FIELD

Most of the presentations run about an hour, although there are many exceptions to this—there's nothing especially magic about one hour as a time standard. Fees vary widely among these, the lesser stars of the galaxy, and have little or nothing to do with any standard for excellence, as far as it is possible to determine. And while there is no doubt that "name" exercises a great deal of influence, the relationship is not on any precise scale. Hamline University, for example, paid Scott Armstrong $1000 plus expenses for his 90-minute presentation, whereas Foothill College paid Ray Bradbury $2000, and LaSalle College paid George Gilder $4000, including expenses. Edwin Newman, on the other hand, commanded $5000 plus expenses from Whitman College, although Ralph Nader was paid $3500, expenses included, by Southern Connecticut State College.

BUT YOU DO NOT HAVE TO BE A
"BIG NAME," EITHER

For those whose names are less familiar to us, the situation is even more checkered and unpredictable: Carey Connell Sutton appeared at several colleges for a $600 fee, but Dorothy Debolt was paid $1900 by Luther College for her 80-minute talk, Robert O. Muller talked for two hours, also showing a one-hour film, and was paid $2800 plus expenses by Drury College, and George Sheehan spoke at Whitman College for a fee of $2750, expenses included.

You can see, then, that it is hard to draw any hard and fast rules from specific examples, because there are so many variables—the speaker, the topic, the client, the agent, and miscellaneous circumstances.

WHO FINDS THE CLIENTS?

Not all these speakers worked through agents. Some were booked by well-known lecture bureaus, but some booked "direct"—made their own bookings, that is. In a review of 32 recent bookings, it turns out that nearly one-half (14) of the bookings were made directly. And even that is not a full picture because some of the speakers operate their own lecture bureaus, in addition to being speakers themselves and, of course, usually handle their own bookings. Still, well over 200 speakers bureaus remain in existence, and this provides some indication of the robust health of the speaking profession.

THE AGENT–CLIENT RELATIONSHIP

The professional writer who uses an agent generally has an exclusive agreement with that agent: the agent will be the writer's sole representative in selling the writer's work to publishers, and the writer will not deal directly or sell directly to a publisher. Performers in show business also have exclusive agreements with agents. Professional speakers, however, are usually represented by agents, such as lecture bureaus, on a nonexclusive basis, with or without a formal written agreement. Most "sign" (register their names, credentials, and availability, even if not executing a formal written agreement or contract) with one or more agencies on a nonexclusive basis and also seek out their own bookings. One exception is the celebrity speaker who is too busy to attend to marketing, travel, and the many other details of a busy speaking schedule, and therefore turns the entire thing over to an agent to handle, the latter acting as manager, as well as agent.

Edward Larkin, president of the Speakers Guild, Inc. (Sandwich, Massachusetts), when asked about this, says, "Most do not sign exclusive agreements unless they are so busy with their primary career (politics, broadcasting, etc.) that they need someone to manage their schedule and deal with a large amount of inquiries."

D. Michael (Mike) Frank, himself a public speaker and agent (Speakers Unlimited, Columbus, Ohio), states: "90 percent sign nonexclusive agreements. It is not in anyone's best interest to sign exclusively unless (1) the bureau can guarantee an amount to the speaker of what the speaker wants to net for the year, and/or (2) the speaker is in such a position that they flat don't want any hassles with contacts."

Fran Slotkin, president of Lecture Consultants, Inc. (Mineola, New York) and publisher of the quarterly newspaper *The International Speakers Gazette* and the annual *Corporate Guide to Effective Programming, A Directory of Speakers, Consultants and Performers,* agrees that only celebrity speakers tend to sign exclusive agreements.

James Keppler, President of Keppler Associates (Washington, D.C.) takes a somewhat different view, pointing out that an agency is not likely to press hard in selling its nonexclusive clients, since it owes its allegiance to those speakers with whom it has exclusive contracts. (It is obviously also in the agency's own interest to work hardest for those speakers they represent exclusively.) He suggests that while agencies do sometimes handle clients with whom they do not have exclusive agreements, such clients rarely sign agreements at all, exclusive or nonexclusive.

In some cases, the agency chooses to specialize in exclusive representation—actually, overall management of the individual's speaking career—and handles only those it can represent exclusively. In some cases, the speaker pays a fee for the services. And in some cases the agency guarantees the speaker some minimum income, in such case undertaking a risk and possible loss if the agency fails to book the speaker often enough to meet the guarantee out of commissions. (This is what Mike Frank referred to, in his observations about nonexclusive representation.) Obviously, no agency wants to enter into an agreement with a guarantee of this sort unless the speaker is of such prominence and in such demand that there is little doubt that an ample number of bookings can be achieved.

CAN ONE BECOME A CELEBRITY ON THE PLATFORM?

There is a temptation here to paraphrase Shakespeare's Malvolio in *Twelfth Night* ("Some are born great, some achieve greatness, and some have greatness thrust upon 'em"), and point out that some are born to prominence, some achieve it, and some have it thrust upon them. Probably no one comes to true fame—national prominence, that is—strictly as a result of platform appearances. Most celebrity speakers achieved their celebrity status elsewhere—as politicians and officials, as performers, as artists, as writers, as educators, as criminals, as theologians, as scientists, as leaders of one sort or another, and as one of those involved by fate in some circumstance that brought them to some high level of visibility. Performances on the platform can extend, prolong, and even enhance that public image; it has and does for many people, such as many of those who first came to public attention as a result of close association with the White House during some administration, and who might very well have otherwise remained able but not particularly noted college professors, economists, writers, journalists, administrators, accountants, and practitioners of whatever other professions they sprang from to their politically inspired fame.

For some of these individuals, public speaking has not only paid direct dividends in satisfying fees, but has furthered their main careers by the prominence one can gain on the public platform, less than that of speaking from the White House, of course, but more than the obscurity of a long-since-gone Administration.

One the other hand, if we define "celebrity" in less demanding terms than those of national prominence, professional speakers can gain a certain celebrity status within the milieu of their own career activities. People such as Norman Vincent Peale and Zig Ziglar, for example, are exceedingly well known (do, in fact, enjoy celebrity status) for their talks, for their books, and for their ideas, but their several activities are usually so closely interrelated that it is nearly impossible to say which is the principal activity and which the ancillary ones. Are they writers who speak? Speakers who write? Philosophers who speak and write? Or does it really matter?

HOW DOES THE ORDINARY
INDIVIDUAL ENTER THIS FIELD?

To be inspired once again by the idea expressed by Shakespeare's Malvolio, some speakers are virtually "born" that way—have some natural, almost instinctive need to speak publicly. Some deliberately seek out opportunities to speak—choose to speak as a career or important segment of their career activity. And some, such as those already mentioned in earlier paragraphs, are propelled by circumstances into speaking careers—have it thrust upon them by circumstance and alert lecture agents.

As we proceed through these pages, we'll look at how a number of professional speakers arrived at that career state. But let's review here the story of Dottie Walters, who has become a very well-known figure among professional speakers and others connected with the field. Whether hers is a typical case or not—if there is, truly, such a thing as a typical case—it is a case that implies lessons worth learning about an indomitable human spirit.

We'll meet Dottie Walters several times in these pages because she occupies a prominent position in the field as a speaker, as a lecture agent, as a publisher of literature on the subject, and as an entrepreneur generally within the field. By her own accounts, she never started out to become a speaker nor had any vision of the field at all, although she had been an enthusiastic high school journalist. But, as a Depression days' child whose father deserted the family, she certainly got a firsthand acquaintanceship with poverty. Later, married and the mother of two tots, she was to renew the acquaintanceship, when a postwar recession devastated her family again. Reacting with the imagination and courage she has always shown, Dottie made a deal with the local newspaper to buy space for a shoppers' column (in which she proposed to sell space to local businesses), and began speaking to local organizations to promote her column and her sales of space to others. The light went on in her head when one of her customers, impressed and inspired by what Dottie had to say, asked what she would charge to speak to his employees. In that instant Dottie became a professional public speaker.

You might say that Dottie falls into that class of having public speaking thrust upon her by circumstance and an interested customer, but Dottie had a great deal to do with it, too, recognizing in a flash opportunity and having the courage to seize it unhesitatingly. And if you will watch for this, you'll find it a major factor in a great many success stories. Opportunity does not knock once; it knocks frequently. But we must listen for it and recognize the knock.

CHAPTER 4

ARE THERE DIFFERENT TYPES OF SPEAKERS?

We are all speakers of one sort or another, although most of us do not speak professionally: Speech is as natural to the human race as is walking upright and using implements. But we are many different types of individuals, and we speak on many different kinds of occasions for many different purposes.

THE INEVITABILITY OF PUBLIC SPEAKING

Every group of humans everywhere in the world developed a language of their own, evidently at an early stage in their development, and even those who shared a common language developed a variety of dialects and regional expressions. Nothing, not even walking upright, so characterizes humans as our affinity for oral communication—for speech. And so it is not surprising that, as it has been observed, by far the bulk of the information most of us acquire is borne to us orally—by speech—in spite of the great amount of reading most of us do also. This is true in the acquisition of formal education, which consists largely of many lectures and explanations delivered by teachers. But it is also true of our learning experiences in everyday life, as we listen to radio and TV, to tapes, and to others in direct face-to-face conversation and in telephone conversation. The act of speaking is, in fact, perhaps our most frequent activity in general. And this is a human trait that transcends all conditions and situations. We humans find in speech a great many utilities—an instrumentality for business uses, for education, for social amenities, for recreation, and even for pure entertainment. Small wonder, then, that public speaking has become a popular career specialty: it was inevitable. But if it was inevitable that public speaking became a career field in itself, it was also inevitable that it became a diverse career field, with many variables. There are variables in speaking occasions, in speaking specialties, and in speaking styles, for example.

SPEAKING OCCASIONS

One of the most common types of speaking occasions is the formal meal—dinners and luncheons (and sometimes banquets) attended by large groups of people for social and business purposes. Such occasions almost invariably have one or more speakers, usually after the meal. And often there are several speakers at such occasions, one being the main speaker, introduced by speakers who precede the main speaker. Frequently, these speakers are members of the sponsoring group—a professional or trade association, for example—responsible for the occasion. Quite often they are guest speakers, who may or may not be professional, paid speakers. They may be humorists, specialists of one sort or another, public figures who are prominent on either a national or local scale, officials, or of some other genre.

Because of the nature of the occasion, especially if the occasion is a business luncheon of some sort, the speeches tend to be considerably shorter than they might be under other circumstances. It is not too unusual for a speaker to talk for an hour or two on some occasions, but it would be fairly unusual for a luncheon or after-dinner speaker to take that much time, especially if there are several speakers on the program.

On other occasions, when an audience has gathered in an auditorium especially to hear some speaker, it is more likely that the speaker will take up an hour or two, after being introduced by someone who speaks for only a few minutes in making the introduction. (It is customary for a main speaker to be introduced on all occasions, and if there is a roster of speakers, each usually introduces the next one.)

CONFERENCES AND CONVENTIONS

One of the busy activities in the United States is the holding of conferences, conventions, trade shows, and similar convocations of people with some mutual interest that draws them together in an annual event. A great many people attend at least one convention each year, and some people attend several. In fact, there are many people whose professions demand that they attend many of these annual gatherings. Marketing executives in many fields, for example, find it necessary to attend an annual gathering of some sort virtually every month of the year.

Conventions—using that term generically, to refer to all such gatherings as those referred to here—constitute almost an industry in the United States, supporting several periodicals, many professional speakers, companies devoted to managing such events under contract, suppliers of related materials and supplies (signs, exhibit furniture and fixtures, printers, and others), and a few other businesses and individuals. The professional speaker must develop and maintain an awareness of these activities.

WHO SPONSORS CONVENTIONS?

Americans are enthusiastic organizers of groups with related interests—trade associations, professional societies, clubs, community groups, and other such organizations. (The advent of the personal computer, for example, gave rise rapidly to computer clubs, which are growing in number steadily, usually bound by something more than a common interest in personal computers. Many are based on being owners of a given make and/or model of computer, such as the Morrow series, the Apple, the IBM PC, the Radio Shack TRS-80, and others.) There are many thousands of associations in the United States, a considerable number having national status. That is, they have a national headquarters (many of them in Washington, D.C. because their interests are closely related to government activities), and they have members throughout the United States. Also, they may or may not have local chapters throughout the United States; some associations do, but others do not, although probably the majority of national associations do have local chapters.

Large associations tend to have national conventions, almost without exception. And most of these include an "exhibit hall" or trade show, where manufacturers and suppliers of many kinds pay for booth space and set up exhibits, staffed by salespeople. In fact, these trade shows or exhibits are invariably a popular highlight of the show.

Associations are not always formed of people with common business or professional interests. There are many associations of people with common personal interests. War veterans, for example, have several national associations, of which the American Legion is probably the largest, and which has probably the largest convention of veterans every year.

A convention or trade show may be sponsored, however, by sundry other organizations and interests: *Training* magazine, for example, sponsors a well-attended annual convention devoted to training and consulting professionals. Some colleges and universities sponsor "job fairs" annually. Communities—state and local governments, that is—sponsor trade shows to promote local industry and attract investors. And federal government agencies have often sponsored symposia and conferences, especially in new and important fields, such as alternate energy sources and environmental protection.

THE TYPICAL CONVENTION/ CONFERENCE PROGRAM

Conventions are always occasions for many speeches. Most conventions include a general convocation in a main auditorium or meeting hall early in the program where someone makes what is referred to as a "keynote" address or speech. This is supposed to set the tone for the entire convention, and the invitation to make the keynote address is considered quite an honor. This honor is most often accorded either a high official of the sponsoring organization or someone else of prominence and prestige, such as a public official or a high-placed executive, depending on the nature of the situation.

Conventions have various sessions, depending on the size, scope, and duration of the convention. A large convention (which may be called a "conference") is likely to last an entire week and have separate sessions in small meeting rooms each day, as in the case of the annual Training/Consulting conference (referred to earlier) held in New York the first week of December each year. The main feature of that program, in fact, is the large roster of three-hour seminars held throughout the week. (At the same time, the exhibits and demonstrations are always a popular feature, and there are always a great many booths and attendees in the Exhibit Hall too.)

There are four major—almost obligatory—events and features of most large conventions: (1) the opening keynote speech; (2) exhibits (booths in a separate hall); (3) the many special sessions (seminars, plenary sessions, meetings of "SIGs"—special-interest groups—within the association, and other "breakout" groups and meetings); and (4) a formal banquet, often with an awards ceremony, held near the close of the convention. Sometimes there are other, usually minor events, such as wine and cheese parties and prize drawings. Too, many conventions are marked by company "hospitality suites." These are rooms or suites of rooms reserved by companies, in which they receive guests, offer refreshments, distribute literature, exhibit products, and discuss attendees' needs and desires vis-à-vis the company's services and products. These are especially to be found at annual convocations which do not include formal exhibit halls or trade shows, and especially those which last for several days and, therefore, invariably have many out-of-town guests staying for several nights.

OCCASIONS DICTATE KINDS OF SPEAKERS

This alone—the nature of the programs and activities in conventions, conferences and other occasions—illustrates that there are different needs for speakers, and that dictates the need for different types of speakers. The seminar, for example, is a training or at least an information session, whereas a luncheon or after-dinner speaker may very well be a humorist or inspirational speaker, engaged entirely to entertain or otherwise to furnish a diversion. The seminar speaker must therefore be an expert of some sort, and even a trainer, and speak as an expert passing on information to attendees. The after-dinner speaker, on the other hand, may be a public official, an officer of the organization sponsoring the occasion, a professional entertainer or speaker or an expert of some sort. It is likely, however, that an after-dinner or luncheon address will be a light one, as compared with a seminar presentation, and will generally include a bit of humor, congratulations, awards, farewell speeches by those concluding terms of service to the organization, and often a good bit of "inside" humor, which only those familiar with the association or the industry it represents will fully appreciate.

LOCAL ORGANIZATIONS
AND OCCASIONS

Most cities and towns have at least one local association, perhaps a chapter of some national association, for example. And it is a fairly rare city or town that does not have at least one business-persons' group, such as a Lions or Rotary club. These organizations have meetings, usually on a regular basis, and they have luncheons and other special occasions. The interests of these groups, like the interests of the larger associations (of which they may be part), related usually to their industry, profession, or other common factor. But whereas national conventions tend to concern themselves to a large extent with the association itself, at the local organization and local chapter level the members' concerns are usually focused exclusively on their career and business interests. And if the organization is purely a local one—the Paducah Employment Agencies Association, for example—the interest will center entirely on matters concerning the local area—the Paducah area, in this case—or on other matters only as and if they have a direct effect on the local situation.

THE BROAD BASIS FOR ALL
ASSOCIATIONS

Associations are founded on common interests, of course, which are the basis for associating themselves with each other. However, the most basic common interest that will be found in all associations is this: The members believe that they can and will benefit from association with others having the same interests. Each member belongs to the association for a selfish motive: the benefits to be derived from joining forces. Some associations work hard at influencing legislation, a reason for so many associations maintaining their national headquarters in Washington, D.C. In general, all work at providing to members services the members would not be able to provide for themselves individually—publications, training, legal counsel, and a library, to name a few. An association exists to serve its members (even though most associations urge members to serve the organization), and if that service falters or declines in quality and quantity, members will soon leave the organization. It is, of course, those programs provided members—including good speakers provided by the management of the association—that constitutes a large part of that service to members.

HOW SPECIAL IS THE COMMON INTEREST?

An association may be founded on some fairly narrow or highly specialized common interest, such as the Household Goods Carriers, or it might be a rather general one, such as the National Canners Association. But inevitably, there is some duality or even plurality of interests; it's unavoidable. An organization of canned food manufacturers, for example, might have a variety of related interests because there may be, in that association, people connected with the canned food industry in a variety of ways and capacities. For example, the association's membership might include some or all of the following:

Marketing directors
Production managers
Accountants
Wholesalers and distributors (of canned foods)
Shipping executives
Advertising managers
Purchasing agents

The common interest here is canned foods, and while the marketing director may be interested in learning something of production methods, his or her principal interest is in whatever is latest and greatest in selling canned foods. Moreover, the companies represented may differ widely, too, in many ways, and include some or all of the following as accurate descriptors:

Canners of dog food only
Canners of vegetables only
Canners of snack foods, nuts, and candy
Canners of meat products
Canners of fruits only
Manufacturers of food canning supplies and machines

Again, their interests will differ considerably, and an address that will have something for everybody in it must be one that transcends these differences of interests.

Too, a great many of the members of any trade association are likely to belong to at least one other association. The canned food marketing director is likely to belong also to an association of people who are professional marketers of one sort or another, for example. But he or she may also belong to several other associations, not necessarily all related to business or career interests.

On the other hand, while some associations are broad in their scope—across an entire industry, for example—others are relatively narrow and specialized. Here, to illustrate this, are the names of a few of the national associations whose names reflect the focus and interests of the organization:

Association of Plaintiffs Trial Attorneys
Adjutants General Association of the U.S.
American Association of Homes for the Aging
Air Traffic Control Association
American Institute of Architects
National Association of Black Manufacturers
Brick Institute of America
National Candy Wholesalers
National Cigar Leaf Tobacco Association
Dairy and Food Industries Supply Association
Direct Mail Marketing Association
Independent Terminal Operators Association
Music Educators National Conference

National Rifle Association
Screen Printing Association

WHO MANAGES ASSOCIATIONS?

Large associations have salaried staff, including a usually rather well-paid chief executive, and a program manager. (There is, in fact, an association of association executives!) The latter, often known as a program manager, is responsible for the agendas for various events, and usually does the hiring of speakers, although if the association retains a conference-management firm, the latter may hire speakers or, at least, recommend speakers.

Small associations—those local chapters and local associations alluded to earlier—are a different matter entirely. Because they are small groups, often with limited funds, many of these do not pay speakers—not even nominal honorariums. Still, some professional speakers will agree to address such groups because they believe that this serves other interests of theirs or because they feel an obligation to support local community activities. The "other interests," however, can be any of the following, at least:

☐ If you sell books or tape cassettes, you may be able to make a few sales to individuals. (Check in advance, however, if you plan to sell at the back of the room, and be sure that you will be permitted to do so.)

☐ The publicity or exposure you get from this may be good advertising for you in whatever you do. (Or even helpful in winning job offers, if that is a goal.)

☐ If you are not experienced in speaking, the practice you get can be helpful.

PART 2

CREATING THE PROFESSIONAL SPEECH

Some speakers have the good fortune to have natural attributes and talents that make them great speakers, while others work hard to be accomplished performers on the platform. But all who do perform well and succeed as speakers, even those with those wonderful natural instincts, work hard throughout their careers at polishing their skills and their presentations—at being true professionals, that is.

CHAPTER 5

TIPS ON SPEAKING

No matter how easily public speaking comes to some, as compared with others, it is not a natural talent; it must be (and can be) learned. And what one has learned another can learn. Let us start learning here and now.

CONTENT VERSUS PRESENTATION

After you have heard many speakers you tend to classify them into types, by their personal characteristics and by the nature and characteristics of their presentations and general performances. Some years ago, a group of technical writers at RCA Service Company in New Jersey were permitted to attend a series of free lectures on technical writing, given at nearby Rutgers University by three of the senior editors in the organization. At the end of the course, they were asked to make out evaluation forms, expressing their opinions of the course and the instructors. They thought that the course was excellent, and the instructors were rated thus:

1. _____ put us to sleep.
2. _____ kept us laughing.
3. _____ taught us something.

All three of these instructors were quite competent and knew their subject well enough. In fact, all three instructors covered the subject quite well, but the students came away with the impression that only the third instructor was truly effective. In fact, the third instructor, while capable enough, was by far the least experienced of the three. The first instructor was undoubtedly the most experienced general writer/editor, and easily the most knowledgeable editor about grammar, composition, and sundry other relevant subjects. The second one was a highly experienced writer and was easily the most experienced in electronics and technical publications. But the third instructor managed the best balance of content *and* presentation, neither boring the students with an excess of tedious detail, nor distracting them with excessive frivolity, so that they were convinced that they had learned most effectively in his sessions—that his overall performance was the most effective in helping them learn what he had to offer in his classes.

Speakers ought to be judged on both content and presentation, but unfortunately they often are not, and speakers who are better at making interesting and even entertaining presentations than they are at offering information of real value have no difficulty in gaining approval and succeeding as speakers. In fact, if you were forced to choose between the two, as a professional speaker, you would do well to choose excellence in presentation, rather than in content. If listeners enjoy your presentation—your performance, that is—they are hardly conscious of whether the content of your presentation was of any great substance or value. But the reverse is not true: the most valuable content will not salvage a poor presentation.

This does not mean that you should not be the master of your subject; far from it. Being master of the subject—truly an authority—is a great asset in many ways, although it still does not relieve you of the need to be a good presenter; you must be that too. But let's look at some of the obstacles to effective presentations that people, especially beginners at speaking, commonly encounter.

FEAR, THE FIRST HURDLE

Probably the biggest problem newcomers to public speaking face is fear. The fear that many people have of facing an audience is almost a phobia with some. The mere prospect of standing before a large group produces physical symptoms:

   Your throat is dry
   Your palms are moist
   Your stomach is fluttery
   You're on the verge of nausea
   You struggle for breath
   Your feet are lead weights

Why all this fear? What terrible things can happen to you up there on that platform? What fate worse than death awaits you there?

Probably there are many ways to describe and account for the basis of that fear: Lack of self-confidence. Poor self-image. (Don't many of us secretly harbor one of those?) Fear of failing. Fear of appearing inadequate. Fear of appearing the fool. Fear of embarrassment. A man worries about whether his tie is straight, his hair combed neatly enough, his ensemble in good taste and in style. A woman also worries about her makeup, hair, clothes, probably even more than a man does.

WHAT IS THE TRUE FEAR?

In many ways those are all the same fear, or at least all are directly related to each other, and all are true enough explanations. But the foregoing definitions are not very helpful because they are not good definitions of the problem. They are, rather, identifications of symptoms. A problem definition is not a definition of the true problem unless it contains within itself the suggestion, or at least the seeds of a solution to the problem. One way of explaining that fear, a way that does suggest or lead to a solution, is this: The fear that so many have of the speaker's platform is the fear of being naked before the spectators—not literally without clothes, of course, but exposed, defenseless, and vulnerable—because all eyes are upon the speaker, and the ball is entirely in the speaker's court. For the moment, at least, the speaker is the whole show, and must "carry" it all. And to the uninitiated, that is a fearsome challenge. In fact, it is remarkable that anyone ever summons the courage to mount the platform alone for the first time.

If that latter is a true definition of the problem, it should suggest or point the way to a solution. And it does. There are no direct ways of overcoming those physical symptoms and those terrible fears of failing, but there are ways of coping with those feeling of vulnerability before an unsympathetic audience. (No matter how sympathetic the audience actually is, the neophyte speaker can't help but feel that the audience is hostile.)

REDUCING THE EXPOSURE

The reason for that feeling of being exposed is that the speaker is (presumably) the single focal point of all attention: the audience's eyes are fixed on the speaker's mouth, face, hands, clothing. But the important thing is not whether the speaker is indeed the focal point of all that attention—perhaps even critical attention—but the fact that the speaker believes this to be so. Ergo, whether the remedy results in actually diluting and diverting that focus of attention or not is not important. What is important is that something persuade the speaker to believe so—to *feel* less naked, less exposed, and less *alone* there on the platform. It is traumatic to feel yourself to be alone when you are under stress. And therein lies the direct approach to reducing the apprehensions of speakers. There are several ways of accomplishing this.

THE LEAST STRESSFUL SPEAKING SITUATION

Probably the ideal way to have your first public speaking experience, if you can arrange it, is sitting down behind a table as part of a panel of at least three people and preferably more, and not even making a prepared presentation, but responding to questions or making contributions to general discussions. There are four major factors that lessen the stress here—that virtually eliminate that feeling of vulnerability:

1. You are seated, which is far more reassuring than standing.
2. You are behind a table, which serves you as a barrier or shield.
3. You are not alone, but are sharing the splendid misery with others.
4. You speak casually, informally, and for only as long as you wish.

Given all that armor, you can afford to relax and enjoy being in the public eye, for you are only a relatively small part of the show, almost a spectator yourself. If you can arrange to do this a few times, it will help you gain a bit of confidence for the next step. However, even if you cannot arrange this, the principle is the same: do whatever is possible to reduce your exposure by utilizing any shields or barriers you can and gain some relief from being the whole show yourself. This is not a matter of chance, as being a member of a panel would normally be, but is something you can arrange as a basic condition of any speaking engagement. Normally, you are asked what your requirements are, and so you can arrange things to make it easy on yourself.

BARRIERS AND SHIELDS

A table is always a good shield, and there are some speakers who sit behind a small table on the dais, even when speaking alone, presumably because they must have recourse to their papers while they speak. Or they may sit on a chair, on the dais, as an alternative. (Many professional speakers might consider this to be an unprofessional way to function as a public speaker—sitting, when you are speaking alone, rather than standing, as most speakers do—and perhaps it might not "sit well" with others, too, unless there is some fairly obvious reason for the arrangement. Consider this contingency when specifying your requirements.)

Another alternative is a lectern of some sort, that special altar-like piece of furniture with a sloping surface upon which to rest your notes and papers, and which permits you to find something to do with your hands (always a problem, otherwise, if you are nervous and self-conscious on the platform). Standing behind the lectern is a help to many for the same reason that sitting behind the table helps. Of course, it also serves the useful and practical purpose of serving as a convenient place to lay out your notes and other necessary papers.

DIFFUSING THE FOCUS

The other problem, one which is equally important, is that of being the sole and entire focus of attention while speaking. Anything you can do to relieve that disturbing distinction should help greatly. And there are several things you can do that will divert attention from your mouth and person to other things.

Presentation Aids

There are many presentation aids you can use to help with your presentation. Not only will these give you a relief from speaking and give you the comfort of focusing the audience's attention elsewhere than on your person, but the change of pace is beneficial in stimulating and maintaining audience interest: they are less likely to become bored when they can be diverted by movies, slides, transparencies, posters, models, demonstrations, and other things that represent a change of pace.

Handouts

For some kinds of presentations, handouts—material distributed to everyone in the audience—are appropriate. These can be typewritten pages, printed brochures, novelties, samples, or almost anything else. Discussing these diverts the audience's attention to the handout, which relieves the pressure on you as the speaker.

Audience Participation

For some kinds of sessions, such as meetings and seminars, audience participation is appropriate, and the speaker—and leader, in this case—poses problems, supervises exercises, conducts critiques, invites questions, and leads discussions.

STYLE AND PREPARATION

This chapter began with the a discussion of content versus presentation, and stressed the need to be completely professional—articulate and polished—in presentation. But this is not to say that content is of no importance, and it is particularly not to say that being the absolute master of your subject is of no importance. Quite the contrary, any doubts you have about the completeness of your preparation for speaking and/or your mastery of the subject contributes directly to your fears. You have enough natural apprehension about speaking publicly without adding to it by doubts as to your command of your subject. It is essential that you be completely prepared, although that means different things to different speakers, as you'll discover in a moment.

What Is Style?

Learning how to speak professionally is not a·matter of simply aping those who appear to do the job well. You need to be you, to develop your own style, the one that works best for you. In fact, you will eventually discover a style that is the *only* one that will work well for you, a style that is your own *natural* style. That is the style you are or should be looking for. But remember, too, that there are many who will suggest "rules" to you, perhaps even rules they believe to be ironclad, but those rules are not necessarily for you. Every case is an individual case, and different from the others. You need to discover what "rules" work for you, whether others think they are good rules or not. And you'll discover, before long, that most speakers conform to one of the following four general styles of presentation:

1. Reads a speech directly from a written manuscript, looking up from time to time, perhaps with expression, but usually with a rather mechanical delivery.
2. Recites a speech which appears to have been carefully memorized, word for word, also with a rather mechanical delivery or with fairly obvious rehearsed gestures.
3. Speaks informally, apparently extemporaneously, under the obvious guidance of detailed outline or voluminous set of notes, with what at least appear to be spontaneous gestures and inserted remarks.
4. Appears to be completely extemporaneous, with no outline or notes in view, with what appears to be an entirely spontaneous, good-humored, and enthusiastic delivery.

A celebrity speaker or someone with unchallenged authority, such as an eminent and acknowledged expert in some field, can get away with reading a speech mechanically from the lectern because his or her eloquence and other skills as a speaker are not on trial. But few people will ever want to hear you read a prepared speech, and that is not being a professional speaker, of course. And to recite what is obviously a memorized speech is essentially the same thing, even though you can keep your eyes on the audience throughout your speech.

Many speakers resort to notes, while speaking. In some cases this is merely to ensure that they do not fail to cover all the important points they wish to make, especially when they are delivering a rather lengthy talk. However, most professional speakers use notes as unobtrusively as possible, if they use them at all.

What Is Preparation?

Being or appearing to be completely extemporaneous, knowing your subject so well, and being so thoroughly prepared that you do not even require notes is by far the best style, if you can manage it. You probably will not be able to do so immediately, nor would you want to give up the little bit of insurance—security— of having a heavily detailed set of notes before you the first few times you face an audience alone. But it's a good target to aim for as an eventual goal.

The only way to realize that goal is to either have a completely memorized presentation and be a good enough actor to make it appear to be spontaneous or to be so much the master of the subject that you can, in fact, speak for hours on the subject extemporaneously. Trying to bluff—to pretend to be extemporaneous—is hazardous; you will probably be tripped up eventually, when some circumstance compels you to depart from your memorized script. The most fluent and successful speakers tend to be those who know their material well, but can speak extemporaneously without difficulty because they are truly knowledgeable about their subject and thus very much in command.

Preparation is more than memorizing your material, studying your notes, and rehearsing your presentation; it is being the complete master of your material. What you present should be only a tiny fraction of the knowledge you have about the subject, *and you should feel that that is a fact.* Nothing can lend you more confidence, give you more self-assurance, and make you feel more in command and invulnerable than that awareness of your mastery and authority in the subject.

This latter factor of your own mental set has a great deal to do with how effectively you present your material. Still, despite the importance of being in command of your subject and the benefits of spontaneity, there is more, far more, to a good presentation. The quality of a presentation depends heavily on other factors, especially the effectiveness of the organization and the quality of your delivery.

ORGANIZATION

In casual conversation, some of your friends are quite well organized when they relate a story or discuss a viewpoint, while others are quite disorganized, and make listeners quite impatient. One common problem is that people of this latter class take forever to get to the point, but even worse, they give no hint of what that point is to be. Instead, they deliver a long and usually unnecessary preamble; digress frequently into unrelated or, at best, only remotely related subjects; and even forget themselves what their original point was to be. The opposite extreme is that of the person who gets straight to the point, and makes the point most clearly.

Some General Truths About Organization

Some public speakers are like that. They and their materials are not organized. They appear not to even know what their main point is, as they ramble on and on about some subject. Even when they have interesting or entertaining styles of delivery, you find yourself growing impatient to discover what the point of it all is. And if their delivery is an uninspired one, you begin to wonder when there will be a propitious moment to escape from the room.

Being well organized demands first that you know where you

want to go—what main point or thesis and what subordinate, supporting points you are trying to establish. Unless you have a clear idea of these in advance, you are not likely to make them clear to your audience. For example, in presenting seminars on writing winning proposals for government contracts, my thesis is that a proposal is a sales presentation and must be based on some well-defined and well-thought-out strategy, if it is to be a winner. The main point is that it is both necessary and possible to find the right strategy for each proposal. Supporting points establish the several kinds of strategy (technical, cost, and presentation) and how to build each, with explanations of how to determine what the proper or effective strategies are to be for different circumstances. Even speaking extemporaneously to some degree, because my audiences vary somewhat in their specific interests, I make this a consistent theme. The audience is introduced to the theme and main point early, and thus understands at all times where we are going in our discussions.

Establishing the thesis and/or main point early identifies the destination of your presentation: it lets the audience know where you are headed and establishes a theme of sorts. Some speakers, such as Norman Vincent Peale, use as a thesis the proposition that "positive thinking" leads to happiness and success in life. And it has become so popular an idea that many speakers have adopted it in principle. Some utilize that principle on a broad basis to argue that it is the desirable approach to life generally, while others pursue it as the main point of a more specialized application, such as salesmanship or entrepreneurmanship.

What Is Your Mission?

Every presentation has two goals: One is the rhetorical goal—proving the thesis or main point. But there is another goal you must have clearly in mind before you can organize your material and construct an effective presentation: you must know what you are trying to do with your presentation—why you are there on the platform. There are at least these possible reasons for your presence—the things you are expected to do to or for your listeners:

Entertain

Enlighten

Inspire

Argue

Train

Logically, you would build your material differently for each case. For example, if you are to train your listeners in something or other, as compared with simply enlightening them about something, your material should challenge them periodically, and try to compel them to think, instead of simply presenting the information, point by point. Or if you are there to entertain—and this does not mean necessarily to amuse, but simply to be an interesting speaker—you don't want to tax their minds at all, but give them the information in easy-to-digest form. You must have a clear sense of mission, in short, and organize your material for an effective presentation that is appropriate to your mission.

DELIVERY

A great many speakers succeed almost entirely on the basis of delivery. A speaker who happens to have natural charisma, an impressive dramatic style, an engaging personality, and/or other attributes that make for powerful delivery, can get by quite well with information and messages that are considerably less than earthshaking in their importance and meanings. The great leaders of the world have almost always displayed some of these traits in making their speeches, and they have swayed and led millions of people even when what they had to say was largely nonsense. However, while it is true that many speakers enjoy certain of these qualities as natural talents or as instinctive impulses, many have simply learned how to exhibit some of these traits in making their speeches. It is possible to learn how to do so. There are several things you can learn to do which will make for a powerful delivery, no matter what the content is. (However, for some purposes, such as political haranguing, the delivery may be as important as or even more important than the content.)

Enthusiasm

Enthusiasm is a contagious emotion, and the enthusiastic speaker manages to imbue an audience with it. Nothing is more effective, perhaps, in sparking up a delivery than obvious zest exhibited by the speaker.

We vain humans like to imagine that we are entirely rational, thinking creatures who are motivated entirely or almost entirely by logic. In fact, we often refer to those who exhibit or indulge their emotions freely as animals. But the fact is that almost all of us are motivated far more by emotions and emotional needs than by reason and logic. So it is not surprising, in the face of this, that most people respond more easily to emotional appeals than to rational appeals. Every good marketer and salesperson knows this. Or should. And every speaker is a salesperson: As a speaker you must sell yourself and what you have to say. Your success in doing this is a mark of your success as a speaker. The polished speaker knows how to appeal to emotions.

Like spontaneity, it is difficult, if not impossible, to fake enthusiasm. Somehow, unless you happen to be a superb actor, the audience soon senses your lack of enthusiasm, even if you try to feign it. But, on the other hand, you can easily fail to display enthusiasm by simply being inhibited, even though you do feel deeply about your subject. You may believe earnestly that what you are saying is both true and valuable, and you may be the most dedicated of people to your cause, but inhibition is misread easily enough as a lack of enthusiasm. It is quite difficult for a listener to be stirred by what appears to bore the speaker.

How to Display Enthusiasm

The signs of enthusiasm are many. It shows up in your voice, in your face, in your eyes, in your gestures. If you want your audience to become animated and to share your own zeal for what you are saying, let them see your own enthusiasm. Wave your arms freely, when it will accentuate a point. Lower your voice and whisper or hiss. Raise your voice and shout. Let your eyes flash. Grin. Make faces. Laugh. Groan. Use a mocking tone or mimicry when appropriate. Stride rapidly around the dais. Strike the lectern to add emphasis. Point excitedly to people. Write major points on the blackboard, or even on thin air, on an imaginary blackboard. Be inventive, as though you were playing charades, but be vocal too. Act out parts to strike points home firmly. Ask demanding, challenging questions. Ask rhetorical questions. (Questions that do not require an answer, but are actually statements, in question form for emphasis.)

Watch what happens when you do this. Watch the audience light up and come to life. They will grin with you, groan with you, laugh with you. And if you keep at them, they'll make even more direct responses by volunteering answers to your questions, even to the rhetorical ones.

Audience Warm-up

Some speakers do an audience warm-up to get them in a receptive and responsive mood. They'll ask the audience to stand up and stretch, perhaps tell a joke or two, single out a few people to direct specific remarks to or ask specific questions of. Or they will say something such as, "How many of you are retired?" or something else that is appropriate to the situation and will ask the audience to be less passive and do something active.

Of course, many speakers have a funny story or two to tell, sometimes as the opener, for an audience warmup. Dave Yoho, a dynamic and well-known speaker who lives in the Washington, D.C. area, uses the fact of his Washington residence as an opener to draw a laugh and relax his audience. He explains that he comes from Washington, D.C. and offers to enlighten his audience about life in Washington. He remarks, among other things, that when challenged by holdup men with "give me your money or I'll blow your brains out" Washingtonians do not give up their money. That's because, explains Yoho, you don't need brains in Washington, but you really can't get along there without money.

On Being a Bob Hope

Dave Yoho is an experienced and quite expert speaker, and he can tell humorous stories effectively, as can many other professional speakers. But don't be deceived: it is not easy to be humorous, and there are not many more deadly and embarrassing silences than that which falls over an auditorium or meeting room when the speaker tries to be Bob Hope and lays an egg. Trying to be a stand-up comedian is much more difficult than it appears to be. It's much easier to fall on your face—"die," as show business people put it—than to be a hit. Certainly you should not try to be humorous when you are still green at public speaking and are not yet in full command—or do not feel yourself to be in full command. Being funny probably requires even more self-confidence and command of the dais than does speaking in general.

More importantly, it is totally unnecessary to be humorous. For some reason, every neophyte who mounts the platform believes that it is necessary to buy one of the many collections of funny stories for public speakers and sprinkle one's presentation with a few of those funny stories. But that is a totally false idea. Your audience did not come to the hall to hear a comedian. At least, they do not expect you to be a comedian. Moreover, it is hazardous. Not only do you run the risk of falling on your face and producing one of those awkward silences that embarrass both the speaker and the audience, but you run the risk of offending people in the audience. So many funny stories are told at someone else's expense, based on ethnic identities, physical characteristics, or other such factor that there are few stories that are absolutely foolproof in this respect.

If you cannot resist the temptation to try your hand at stand-up humor, and insist on rushing in despite the risks, at least follow a few simple rules which may help:

1. If someone needs to be the butt of the joke, make it yourself. Make yourself the fool or the klutz who did something stupid and funny.

2. Try to tell the story to a large audience. The larger the audience, the better the chance someone will begin the laughter. (Frequently, the laughter is contagious, and people

often do not decide whether your story is funny until they
see how some of the others respond.)

3. Learn to *wait* a few moments after telling a story. Often the
    appreciation of the story and the laughter follow only after
    a pause. Timing is everything, in this respect; if you hurry
    on, you may step on your own lines and kill the punchline.
    (Remember how Jack Benny, the master of timing, waited
    for the audience to catch up after he said something
    funny?)

Eye Contact

One of the most important things for a speaker to remember is to
make eye contact with the audience. There are some people who
advise singling out some individual with whom to establish and
maintain eye contact. Unfortunately, if you do that, you are likely
to make that individual feel most uncomfortable. Far better, I believe, to make eye contact with many people in your audience—
with all of them, if possible, before your session is over, but only
for a few minutes each. Singling people out for eye contact, one
by one, assures them of your interest in speaking directly to each
and every person in the room, but it also helps you judge how you
are coming across—whether, for example, you are drawing smiles
when you want to draw smiles, and frowns when you want frowns.
It enables you to know when the pace is lagging and when you
have touched on a topic or point of great interest. It's the source
of your feedback, the basis on which you can evaluate your own
delivery and adjust it, too, if necessary.

But let's go on and see just what some of the experienced
professionals, the experts, have to say about it.

LET THE EXPERTS
BE HEARD

Not surprisingly, surveying the experts—experienced professionals—produces certain themes and ideas over and over about how
to be a true professional on the platform. One thing they make clear
is that while there may be such a thing as the "born speaker," most
professionals become good speakers by *learning* the techniques
and methods.

THE GREATEST SECRET OF SUCCESS

It is quite evident, after listening to what a great many experienced speakers and speakers' agents have to say, that the most important secret of success on the platform is to be a celebrated person. If your celebrity is great enough, success is all but certain. That failing—if you are unfortunate enough to be an ordinary, little-known citizen—you will have to go to work and learn all the arts and artifices of speaking well. For there are many do's and don'ts in public speaking—right and wrong ways of doing it—as there are in most things. But the experts offer many ideas and tips to help others learn.

BODY LANGUAGE

Gerhard Gschwandtner, publisher of the bimonthly tabloid *Personal Selling Power*, reports in his training program, "The Languages of Selling," the results of scientific research establishing that in speaking only seven percent of emotional content—feelings and attitudes—are conveyed to others by words alone. The remaining 93 percent, reports Gschwandtner, is the result of one's tone of voice and nonverbal communication, 38 and 55 percent, respectively.

That 55 percent communicated nonverbally refers to one's posture, gestures, and facial expressions, but especially to posture.

The No-Nos

By now, probably everyone who has had even the briefest of instruction in making onstage appearances has been taught that hands in pockets or folded behind oneself is the most basic of no-nos. Fidgeting and shifting from one foot to the other self-consciously is as bad. Those are the hallmarks of the rankest amateurs in the art of making public appearances of any kind, speaking or otherwise. Perhaps a bit less obviously, but equally wrong the experts assure us, are these postures or gestures while speaking:

The Jewelry Fidgeter.   Playing with your rings, turning and sliding them up and down your fingers.

Praying.   Holding your hands folded in front of you, as though in prayer.

Authority.   Keeping your arms folded across your chest.

Fiddling.   Playing with a ring of keys, a microphone cord, or some other toy.

Adam and Eve.   Keeping your hands clasped at full length before you, in a kind of fig leaf effect.

The Leaner.   Leaning against a wall, the lectern, or some other object.

The Thinker. Stroking your chin, massaging your neck, scratching your head, or other such motions.

What is wrong with all of these is that they are giveaways. When one or more of these dominate your posture and gestures, it demonstrates that you are a neophyte speaker and ill at ease: like most neophytes at public appearance, you are excessively conscious of your hands and don't know what to do with them. (On the other hand, doing one of these things occasionally and for a moment only does no particular harm.)

The Yes-Yesses

You should, in fact, do with your hands whatever comes naturally—unconsciously, that is. There is absolutely nothing wrong with letting your arms and hands simply hang at your side, while your two feet are planted firmly, spread naturally, and you are standing perfectly straight and at ease in what some call "the professional speaker's stance." Of course, you are not going to do this for extended periods of time, and if you are speaking for an hour or two—or even longer—you will be shifting about frequently, of course, but you should be returning to the natural stance then.

Good speakers, and especially speakers who are truly enthusiastic about what they are saying, can't help but make gestures, emphasizing points by stabbing the air, turning a palm upward, raising both hands to heaven, and by numerous other gestures. Those are natural, unconscious, instinctive gestures—or should be. They are the natural and unplanned movements and gestures of a speaker who is enthusiastic about the subject and concentrating on imparting ideas and information. They are effective when they are motivated sincerely. (If they are deliberate, contrived, and carefully rehearsed they are not sincere and don't belong in the presentation.) But their effectiveness is diluted when they are overdone, and frequent return to that professional speaker's stance—feet slightly apart and firmly planted, body straight and upright, and hands at sides—is necessary. We are told by the experts that all those gestures should begin from the side. That stance reflects your self-confidence and helps inspire the listeners' confidence in what you say, as the sincere and natural gestures emphasize certain points and help the audience identify the major points you want to make. (These are the speaker's equivalent of the headlines, exclamation points, and other devices used in print to help the writer emphasize points and the reader understand what the major points are.)

Constance Yambert

a speech coach and active member of the National Speakers Association in the Los Angeles area, quite agrees with all of this and explains her approach as one of advocating using action in three ways: facial action, which refers to facial expressions; voice action, which refers to inflection and volume; and physical action, which refers to gestures and moving about the dais a bit. She remarks that we are conditioned out of these things as children, to a large extent, when we are admonished not to "make faces," not to "fidget," not to shout, and so on. As adults, if we want to be good speakers, we have to learn to do these things all over again, as natural motions and gestures used by people who are engrossed in their subject and intent on stressing and accenting various points properly.

SOME TIPS ON SUCCESS

A few of the other tips provided by the professionals are passed on as secrets of success in speaking. One of these tips urges the speaker to count three seconds, after being introduced and before beginning to speak, in the meanwhile smiling quietly and confidently at the audience and making eye contact with a few of those seated there.

Another tip urges the speaker to use a similar three seconds of silence at the conclusion of the presentation, before saying, "Thank you," and another three seconds after that before leaving the dais. The rationale for this is that these pauses and confident, friendly smiles impart a distinct air of complete professionalism. The proponents of this assure everyone who will listen that this technique will double the standing ovation given a speaker. (My personal experience suggests that this is true enough: these techniques do somehow propel audiences to greater enthusiasm for the speaker.) However, let's go on and see what a few other experienced and successful professionals have to say about how to be a great speaker:

Dave Yoho

is an "inspirational" speaker and sales consultant, who is often called on to inspire salespeople, a prime market for many speakers. His theme tends to the message that the world is saturated with negativism and that we need to be more positive in all things, but especially in our attitudes, if we want to be more successful and accomplish more. Born with a speech impediment, he worked hard for many years to overcome it, and in so doing became one of the outstanding and most frequently honored speakers in the United States. But Yoho does not credit that with his success, although it undoubtedly made a great contribution and was a spur in his rise to success as a speaker. He says, however, that knowing your audience is by far the most important factor, but that is undoubtedly a bit of his own code signifying a great deal more than those simple words say. Listening to one of his addresses, delivered in his commanding, resonant voice, reveals a great deal of enthusiasm, great emotional content, and a great deal of practical advice offered.

Art Fettig

is an author, as well as a speaker, and one of his books is titled, *How to Hold an Audience in the Hollow of Your Hand*, published by Growth Unlimited, Inc. Among those thousands of words of experience and wisdom he offers a large number of useful tips and suggestions. He speaks, for example, about the importance of "the first two minutes," suggesting that those first two minutes are critical and the speaker can capture the audience and the situation by seven techniques, presented here by quoting from his book (cited earlier) with his kind permission:

1. Respond to your introduction with humor.
2. Present a bit of humor that ties in directly with your audience or the occasion.
3. Show your concern for the comfort or convenience of your audience.
4. Get your audience to join you in applauding something or someone.
5. Compliment your audience with sincerity.
6. Ask your audience a question.
7. Physically invade the territory of your audience.

Fettig reports that he made an important discovery, in discussing his seven techniques with a client whom he had been coaching in public speaking. It suddenly dawned on him, he says, that he had now reached a new plateau in his craft. He had read somewhere, he reports, that speakers progress through several grades, on their way to becoming true professionals, and he now experienced the following revelation: A rookie (speaker) doesn't know, and he doesn't know that he doesn't know (what platform techniques work or why/how they work). A semipro doesn't know, and he knows that he doesn't know. The pro knows, but he doesn't know why. The superstars know and they know why. That is the basis of this book, he says, and calls the book a *sharing process*.

Nido R. Qubein

past president of the National Speakers Association, is one of the superstars of the speaking profession, although he is also well known as a consultant and trainer. Like Dave Yoho, Nido had to overcome a speech problem in becoming the persuasive and successful speaker he is today: he was born elsewhere than the United States and had to learn English as a second language, although he is so fluent in speaking, reading, and writing English today you wouldn't suspect that he was not native to these shores. In fact, inspired by his determination to be an effective communicator, he began speaking to audiences long before he had mastered the English language and in spite of the many unintentional and humorous gaffes he made in his still-broken English.

He publishes cassette albums and manuals and a newsletter, "The Nido Qubein Letter, A Confidential Report for Speakers, Trainers, & Consultants," and like Fettig and a great many other speakers and consultants, he writes a great deal. Of course, he has had much to say on the subject of speaking, including the authoring of a book, *Communicate Like a Pro*, published by Prentice-Hall, and several other books.

Nido makes very much the same point that Art Fettig makes when he says that his first act after being introduced is to get the audience to do something that involves them in his presentation. And he works hard at holding their full attention, he says; if he appears to be losing it, he takes some action immediately to regain it. But most important, he points out, is the need to understand the interests of the audience and gauge their reactions most carefully to guide you in *communicating* with the audience, not simply throwing your words at them. Billed as a motivational speaker, Nido disclaims any ability to motivate anyone, pointing out that everyone does things for their own reasons. At the same time, he is obviously deeply aware of the need for emotional appeal and empathy in communication. *"Poor* communicators say what they think and don't concern themselves with how the audience responds to it," he says. "For them, it's enough that 'It's the truth'! *Average* communicators say what they think," he goes on, "and watch the people respond to it. But the *real pros* in communication check to see what their audiences think and feel," he concludes, "then appeal to those thoughts and feelings."

Nido also makes the point that the good speaker is entertaining, although not necessarily humorous. It includes anything that keeps the audience interested or diverted—good anecdotes, for example, or an interesting "prop" of some kind. But being entertaining includes also being enthusiastic, establishing a rapport with the audience, being obviously sincere, and speaking with spontaneity or apparent spontaneity—without notes, that is. (This advice, heard from other professional speakers, is not in conflict with advice from others that a good speaker always has a descriptive and reasonably detailed outline of his or her presentation. That outline is not a guide to be used while making your presentation, but is useful to program chairpeople or others who have retained you, and is considered by many to be a sign of true professionalism.)

Arch Lustberg

is a former professor of speech and drama at Catholic University, has taught government employees (U.S. Commerce Department) how to testify before Congress, and produced a Broadway play, among other things. He makes at least two major points, that (1) to be a successful speaker, you must persuade the audience to *like* you, above all things, and (2) he states flatly that delivery is more important than content. Among the items he believes to be important are eye contact, use of body language and pregnant pauses for emphasis, an "easy, open" expression on your face, and pausing for deep breaths now and then to relieve stress.

Robert L. Montgomery

who is another well-known professional speaker, has been a radio and television announcer and speaker, is also a professional consultant and trainer, author of several books (like many other professional speakers), and conducts speaker training for the American Management Associations, among his many other activities. (The latter include memory training, management seminars, and positive thinking sessions.) In training speakers Montgomery echoes advice heard from other professionals, including the need to make natural gestures, be thoroughly prepared, move around a little, and take some water and a deep breath or two when you feel nervous.

HUMOR IS HIGHLY SALABLE

One point has been made clear by the experts: Humorists, if they are truly entertaining, are very much in demand. That term "humorist" includes stand-up comedians and comics (comedians tell funny stores and comics do funny things), but includes also those many speakers who evoke chuckles and grins, rather than deep-in-the-belly laughter. It is not necessary to do prat falls or tell hilarious stories to be a successful humorist, and the experts agree that it is dangerous to your career to try to be a show-biz type stand-up comic or comedian. But if you truly have an amused outlook on life generally and can help others see the amusing, lighthearted side of things, you may be a natural as a humorist.

[James] Doc Blakely

is among the best-known professional humorists and has spoken professionally for a number of years throughout the country. He also writes a column, "Pokin' Fun," and has written several books, including a scientific text now used in many colleges and universities, *The Science of Animal Husbandry*. Doc Blakely advises the newcomer to the field to develop and perfect a single great presentation, rather than many mediocre ones. He suggests that to polish your presentation, you should present it at least 100 times to a recording machine before trying to present it to a live audience. Time it to 50–55 minutes, he says, and then pretend that the program chairperson has just asked you to cut your presentation to 20 minutes. He also recommends that you select a subject you are enthusiastic about, and know it so well that you do not need notes.

Bob Orben

is another well-known humorist, writer/editor/publisher of his own jokesheet/newsletter, *Orben's Current Comedy*, and author of the *Orben Comedy Series*, 45 books on humor which are used by most, if not all, professional comedians, comics, and other humorists. He wrote material for Red Skelton, Jack Paar, and Dick Gregory, has also been a speech writer for many prominent business and political leaders, including President Gerald Ford, as well as a speaker himself. One of his rules and bits of advice is to never write or present a joke you wouldn't want your name attached to. And he quite agrees with the observation of E. B. White that humor can be dissected, just as a frog can, but the thing dies in the process. That is to say, humor is part craft and part art.

Carl Kohlhoff

is another professional humorist/speaker who agrees that humor can be dangerous, especially if you use risque material (he enjoins all firmly against it) or make others the butt of your jokes. He favors the one-liners, rather than the lengthier stories, at least partly because the effect of a one-liner failing to draw a laugh is overcome by pressing on with the next one, on the theory that you can tell several one-liners in the time it takes to tell a story, and some of them will draw laughter.

WHAT IS A PROFESSIONAL SPEAKER

Note that all the experts quoted here are professionals—professionals at speaking and professionals, usually, at other activities, such as consulting, training, writing, and entertaining. Nido Qubein, in his monthly publication, *The Nido Qubein Letter* listed these points in defining the professional, and they are presented here with Nido's special permission:

1. A professional person has specialized knowledge and skill that enables him or her to render a valuable service. Do you know many successful speakers who do not have specialized knowledge and skills?

2. Professional people maintain a unique relationship with their clients. People come to them with specific needs and expect them to fulfill those needs.

3. Professionals render services that people are willing to pay for. You might hit the ceiling when you get your doctor's bill, but when you needed treatment, you were willing to pay for the service. Effective speakers can expect to be paid for their services.

4. Professional people are held accountable for the services they render—or fail to render. They are expected to maintain certain standards. And, the professional speakers know that they are accountable to the client-company, the meeting planner, and themselves.

5. And the fifth attribute of professionals is that they have a professional attitude. They know that what they do is vitally important, and they seek to do it to the best of their ability.

It's this simple! If you are going to be a successful speaker, and learn to penetrate your market effectively, you need all the attributes of a professional.

PART 3

THE BUSINESS OF SPEAKING

People mount the platform for a variety of reasons, one of which is that public speaking is their business or a large part of their business. For public speaking is indeed a business, virtually an industry, although it is a little-known one to those not directly involved in it.

CHAPTER 7

WHO HIRES SPEAKERS?

If public speaking is a business, it must have markets, customers who pay public speakers to perform. (For professional speakers are performers, as much as they are anything else.) But performing is not all there is to the business of public speaking. There is more, much more, because speakers are also hired and paid to achieve certain, specific results for entirely practical reasons.

THE PUBLIC SPEAKING MARKETS

Like a great many businesses which are not well known to those not involved in it, the business of public speaking appears to be a completely uncomplicated one. The superficial view, which is the only one most people have of public speaking (if, indeed, they are even aware that it is a business or profession to a great many people) is that speakers are born, not made, and they are paid to stand up and talk for an hour or two. Nor does the average person have any more insight into who the clients are—who hires and pays speakers.

In fact, the clientele to which public speakers sell their services is varied across an entire spectrum, and includes both individuals and organizations. And those two broad categories can be in turn divided into many subcategories. In some cases the mere titling of subcategories suggests the reasons for hiring a speaker; in others the connection is less obvious.

There are four different parameters of interest which we must and will eventually explore to get a full appreciation of the speaking business, and even of the public speaking market—who are the clients who hire speakers. In fact, it is difficult to gain an understanding of any single one of these parameters without examining all four and how they affect each other. And, of course, there are many possible permutations—different combinations—of these elements, for the very term *speaker* has a far more discursive meaning than most people attach to it—more, that is, than that of the guest lecturer or the after-dinner humorist. The four basic parameters are these:

Kinds of clients
Kinds of speakers and speaking services
Kinds of occasions calling for speakers
Fees and sales

KINDS OF CLIENTS

Let's first look at the kinds of clients who hire and pay speakers, and that examination will help you to understand the other parameters—the various kinds of speakers and services they offer, and the fees and sales which constitute their total income base. The beginning of this chapter established that both individuals and organizations become clients of public speakers, but let's look first at organizations retaining speakers for various reasons and occasions, for it is organizations that are, by a great margin, the chief clients for public speaking in all its forms and permutations.

ORGANIZATIONS AS CLIENTS

There are several ways in which we can divide and title organizations that hire and pay speakers. One useful way to make a first separation is to distinguish between nonprofit and for-profit organizations—businesses, that is. Some examples of nonprofit organizations that represent active markets for public speakers are these:

Colleges and universities
Federal, state, and local government agencies
Community groups
Social clubs and associations
Professional societies
Trade associations
Labor unions
Religious or church groups
School groups
Benevolent societies and service organizations
Technical institutes

ORGANIZATIONS GENERALLY

For-profit organizations are commercial and industrial business enterprises, generally speaking, or appurtenances thereto. That latter idea refers to organizations which are of themselves nonprofit, but are supported by and dedicated to the service of for-profit enterprises. For example, some for-profit organizations will separately or in concert with others support a research institute or, at least, a program devoted to research and development or other forward-looking trade activity, as well as a trade association. Trade associations are supported by companies, usually, through dues and sometimes through grants and other efforts to make the association self-supporting, such as seminars and conventions that are designed to produce income for the association, and even other income-producing activities. (e.g., many associations pursue government grants and contracts, and may also win grants from any of the many hundreds of foundations and other such institutions.) Even in small communities, businesspeople often support such nonprofit organizations as Rotary and Lions clubs or other local business groups. In fact, it sometimes becomes rather difficult to draw sharp distinctions between the for-profit and nonprofit organization. But that is not especially important. What is important is to remember that there is a vast diversity of potential clients for all that diversity of services gathered under the umbrella of public speaking.

For-Profit Organizations

There are some 13 to 15 million for-profit organizations—business enterprises, large and small—in the United States, the exact number probably closer to the higher estimate. By far the vast majority of these—some 97 percent—are classified as small businesses by the U.S. Small Business Administration. However, "small" is a relative and subjective term, and many of us would not consider a firm doing $8 million a year or employing 500 employees to be small. (However, the Small Business Administration employs different "size standards" for different industries and so has many definitions of what constitutes a small business. Some of those definitions identify much larger enterprises than these as small businesses.)

In any case, there are a great many industries in the United States—and that term "industry" is used in a rather general sense, to include all fields of trade and commerce—and a large number of substantial enterprises in all these industries. (Government and labor union figures report that a quite large majority of all people employed in the United States are employed by those businesses classified as small.)

The needs of these businesses are many, and those needs afford enterprising professional speakers a great many opportunities for interesting and profitable assignments. Among the opportunities that are available as direct contracts with the assignments from private companies are at least these:

☐ *In-house training projects.* These include seminars and other training sessions in a wide, almost endless, variety of subjects. The following are by no means all the subjects or even classes of subjects covered, but are a small sampling to convey the general idea:

Sales Techniques	Efficient use of time
Motivational	Handling stress
Positive attitudes	Letter writing
Sensitivity training	Public speaking
Office skills	Word processing
Communications	Proposal writing
Interpersonal relations	Telephone manners
In-basket techniques	Purchasing
Contract administration	Managerial methods

These may be conducted as formal training courses or as informal or semiformal seminars. They may be off-the-shelf programs the speaker has readily available, or they may be custom-developed for the client (in which case the program becomes the client's property, but the speaker is also a consultant-contractor, paid suitably for developing the program).

☐ *In-house award dinners/banquets.* Frequently companies conduct their own special dinners and banquets as a company activity. The occasion may be to present the traditional gold watch or other benefits to retiring employees, or for other occasions. One frequent occasion, especially in sales-oriented organizations, is an annual dinner/banquet to honor the top performing sales people and award them bonus checks or other rewards for their outstanding performances. For such joyous occasions, it is not uncommon to bring in professional speakers to entertain and to make suitable speeches in presenting awards.

□ Some companies stage special events that call for presentations by professional speakers. For example, Control Data Corporation (CDC) calls upon several professionals to address their meetings of "OEMs"—original equipment manufacturers—presidents or chief executive officers at the CDC Minneapolis headquarters. (Control Data Corporation sells these OEMs components for their systems, and so offers a variety of technical support services to help them succeed.)

□ Some companies do their marketing through networks of distributors or dealer-distributors, and stage annual convocations, which are occasions for having public speakers make addresses. (And there are companies that stage frequent training sessions, such as seminars offered many times during the year for their distributors and the salespeople employed by their distributors, between annual rallies.) These annual galas—for they generally are galas—tend to include many testimonials from successful dealers, intended to inspire those less successful. In the case of dealer-distributor organizations, such as Amway and similar pyramid-sales organizations, these galas are often also recruiting sessions, designed to add many more dealers, and are therefore held frequently during the year—perhaps continuously—in cities throughout the United States.

INDIVIDUALS AS CLIENTS

The concept of individuals as clients for public speaking is a special case. Of course, no individual pays a speaker to come to his or her home and make a formal speech in the living room or recreation room. However, there are occasions when individuals pay to hear a speaker. On occasion, there are such admission-charged events sponsored and staged by organizations, such as museums and associations, but the more common occasion requiring the individual to pay to hear a speaker is the seminar of the type that individuals (rather than their employers) pay to attend. And there are similar situations, in which the speaker offers training courses, help in abandoning cigarettes or dieting, and other personal help, which are generally summed up as seminars and training. (Of course, such events are not always organized and produced by the speaker, in which case the producer of the seminar or training program is the client.)

WHO ARE THE BEST CLIENTS?

I asked this question of who are the "best" clients—meaning the class of clients who most often hire public speakers—of a number of experienced professionals. Almost without exception they told me that it was not possible to say that any given class of client was better than another. Bob Montgomery, for example, said, "All are best: associations, colleges/universities, corporations, organizations including government agencies. My last three talks in the past week alone have been for the State of Minnesota [Montgomery is a Minnesota citizen], State of Illinois, and IRS Southwestern Conference." Others identified whichever type of client they happen to specialize in or have had the greatest success with. And that might in turn depend on what subject or type of program the speaker happens to specialize in delivering. (eg., the humorist is not very well suited to those markets for seminars and lectures on business subjects, but might be very much in demand on cruise ships and as an after-dinner speaker, whereas the instructor in sales techniques is not likely to get many cruise-ship bookings or after-dinner speeches.)

KINDS OF SPEAKERS VERSUS KINDS OF MARKETS

"Best" markets for your presentations, then, comes down primarily to the question of what kind of speaker you are or what kinds of material you have to present, for there are ample markets for all kinds of public speakers who are truly good at their profession. And looking at the markets from this perspective, in an effort to determine which are the most promising markets for any given speaker, speakers can be classified into these broad categories:

Entertainers

Instructors in specific subjects

Motivational speakers

Experts/authorities in some given field of general interest

Experts/authorities in some given field of specialized interest

Celebrities

Some of these categories tend to merge, in terms of markets. For example, entertainers (i.e., humorists), motivational speakers, experts in some field of general interest, and celebrities might all appeal to the same markets, especially if all are interesting or entertaining speakers. On the other hand, those who are instructors in specific subjects are more likely to be called on to conduct training courses, make instructive presentations, and conduct seminars by business organizations. And those who are experts in specialized fields (i.e., computer technology) are most likely to be in demand for major conferences and relevant seminars and conventions of others in the same field. In my own case, for example, my specialty is proposal writing and other aspects of marketing, especially to government agencies, and I am usually asked to conduct seminars and training courses by business organizations, since there is extremely little entertainment value in what I have to offer the public. Moreover, although the general appeal of my subject is to companies who do business with the government generally, among those companies it is the high-technology organizations, such as computer companies, who are the most frequent clients.

Of course, not every public speaker specializes in some field, nor even lays claim to being an expert or authority of some sort. Nor does every speaker have only a single presentation or a single range of subject matter, so that many professional speakers are equally at home on many platforms—as instructors, as inspirational speakers, and as humorists. And some find, after a while, that they are better suited to, more successful in, and/or happier with some other subject matter or type of address than they started with. So the sales instructor may ultimately become the humorist or the motivational guru. (Humorists appear to be born far more often than they are made. The talent for being humorous, even for telling humorous stories effectively, seems to be far more an unconscious art than a conscious one.)

KINDS OF OCCASIONS VERSUS KINDS OF MARKETS

As you may have already gathered, there are many different occasions that call for the services of professional public speakers. Let's look at a few to get a brief picture of the breadth and diversity of this market:

Conventions

Conventions are usually sponsored and organized by associations, which may be trade associations (associations of companies in some given industry), professional societies (such as the American Psychological Association), or nonbusiness/professional groups, such as the American Legion. (Government agencies and others also may sponsor and promote such gatherings.) The purposes of conventions are many. Nonbusiness groups attending conventions tend to look at the occasion as a kind of vacation at which they can relax, meet old friends again, and generally have a great deal of fun. Business people and professionals attending conventions do so sometimes for much the same reasons, but also because they wish to use the occasion to further their own business/professional interests, "keep up" with what's happening in their industry, make new "contacts," and otherwise satisfy business-professional obligations.

Conventions usually include a number of activities and programs, which of course vary, according to the nature of the sponsoring organization and the individual preferences of the organization's managing committees, but tend generally along the following lines:

◻ A keynote address, generally by some notable, who may or may not belong to the organization sponsoring the convention. This is usually early in the convention and held in a large auditorium, addressing all or nearly all of the attendees.

◻ An exhibit hall, where vendors display what they have to sell, offer demonstrations, give out samples and literature, talk to visitors, and otherwise stage a trade show.

◻ A series of "meetings," held in separate meeting rooms, which may actually be seminars and/or symposia (depending largely on the nature of the organization sponsoring the convention) or may in fact be meetings of "SIGs"—special interest groups. (These are members with interests in specialized areas relevant to the organization overall.)

◻ At least one banquet (sometimes there are special breakfasts, luncheons, and or suppers, too), usually at or near the end of the convention, often with awards.

The banquets of large organizations, and often the luncheons, too, are occasions where paid professional speakers and even professional entertainers are often retained to make presentations of awards, entertain the attendees, and generally lend a professional air to all the proceedings.

The side meetings are often seminars led by professional speakers. The annual Training Conference in New York City, for example, includes literally dozens of such seminars on a variety of subjects related to training and the consulting profession, and they continue throughout the week of the Conference as a major feature of the event.

Frequently conventions stage special entertainments, during the evenings, and may also have special events for spouses who accompany their mates but are not interested in the convention itself, and these may include presentations by professional speakers.

Hospitality Suites

Many companies operate "hospitality suites" in separately rented rooms in hotels where conventions are held, especially when there is no exhibit hall (but sometimes even when there is a trade exhibit.) The idea is to entertain and meet prospective customers, of course, and there is someone in attendance at such suites to greet visitors, chat with them, offer them refreshments, give them literature, and generally do all the things appropriate to wooing the business of prospects and turning them into solid sales leads. In some cases, the separate suite is more of a sideshow or private trade exhibit, in which the sponsoring company sets up samples or models of its line, has a well-stocked and large literature rack, conducts periodic demonstrations, and has several rows of seats for visitors to sit and listen to regularly scheduled presentations by professional speakers.

WHO ARRANGES CONVENTIONS?

Generally speaking, associations arrange conventions, although not always. There are exceptions, as in the case of the annual Training Conference, which is organized, sponsored, and produced by *Training* magazine; and in the case of many other such events, which are sponsored by government agencies. Meeting planners may be professionals at the business, they may be volunteers, or meeting planning may be part of the duties of their jobs or the posts to which they have been elected. Associations tend to have a permanent program official (often a "program chairperson," as in the case of colleges and universities) and/or a special committee to oversee the arrangements for such special events as conventions, including finding and retaining speakers for meetings of all kinds. And, in fact, when the association is one with chapters in many cities, the convention is generally held in a different city each year, and the local chapter in that city becomes the host chapter, responsible for attending to much of the detail and arranging all program events.

On the other hand, there are a great many consultants and convention management companies, who offer services to help others stage conventions, and sometimes even to take over the entire responsibility. And in these cases, the convention-management organization often hires the speakers and even professional entertainers, in addition to selling the exhibit spaces, renting the meeting rooms, printing literature, and attending to all the other myriad details such an effort entails.

It should not be entirely surprising, then, to find some organizations listed both as speakers bureaus and as convention managers, for some organizations provide both services. Some, in fact, are also listed as production companies and/or talent agencies, and book well-known entertainers, along with celebrities, instructors, seminar leaders, and other varieties of public speakers. (Later a reference list will provide the names and addresses of a few of these organizations.)

TRAINING PROGRAMS

Training programs may be formal or informal, may consist of single, even impromptu, meetings and lectures, or may be full courses involving weeks of classes, examinations, and grades, or may fall somewhere between these extremes. Following are some examples and explanations of how the many variations of training courses may come about.

◻ *Seminars.* Most seminars are from one to three days, although there are weeklong seminars and half-day seminars also. Too, a seminar may be a custom or in-house presentation, or it may be open to anyone who wishes to pay the registration fee and attend. Nominally, a seminar is supposed to be a kind of postgraduate course in some highly specialized subject, although few actually are. Generally, seminars are held for those already engaged or employed in some given occupational specialty to help them gather a few new or little-known techniques about their occupation from experts. Usually these techniques are on a specialized subject, such as closing sales, handling stress, writing, and other such skills.

Companies with a large number of employees to be trained will retain seminar presenters to conduct in-house seminars frequently, sometimes on the company's premises, sometimes in an outside facility, such as a hotel, country club, or other establishment offering meeting rooms and other amenities necessary. And it is not at all unusual for these clients to book the seminar repeatedly, to train succeeding groups of people, since seminars by their nature are usually restricted to relatively small groups.

Associations will also retain consultants and professional speakers to present seminars to their members, sometimes at national conventions, as already noted, sometimes as special events, very much along the lines just described for private companies, but with this exception: Companies offering employees an in-house seminar will pay all the costs of the seminar directly, but associations usually require attendees to pay their own individual registration fees and may even realize a profit for the association treasury on the event.

Companies, government agencies, and other organizations also send employees to attend "open registration" seminars (seminars to which everyone is invited to attend, by paying a registration fee, running generally to approximately $200 per day), for which the company pays the fees when it appears that it is in the organization's interests to send the employees.

Some speakers organize and produce their own open-registration seminars, as well as delivering in-house, custom seminars under contract. To do this you must rent a meeting room somewhere, do your advertising—direct mail, media, or both—and handle all the administrative details, of course, and then deliver the seminar, with or without the help of other speakers.

On the other hand, there are organizations who are producers of seminars and who contract with speakers to be seminar presenters on some kind of fee basis, sometimes on a percentage basis or on a fee plus a percentage, if the attendance exceeds some given threshold. Don Dible, author of the long-established and still popular *Up Your OWN Organization!* and other books produces many management seminars every year, some of which he presents himself, but others for which he hires presenters. But he is not alone in this: Some of the many other companies who conduct seminars on the basis of contracting with experts to make the presentations are Federal Publications, based in Washington, D.C.; Dun & Bradstreet, in New York City; United Business Institute, in Maryland; and Performance Seminar Group, in Connecticut.

There are also seminar producers who may or may not deliver some of the presentations personally, but who also retain several people to speak for fees. That is, each speaker is presented as a "guest speaker," usually to make a brief presentation.

☐ *Formal programs.* For-profit companies do not tend to buy long, formal courses of training for the simple reason that these are costly. (There are, of course, many exceptions, such as the Caterpillar company, long noted for its wide-ranging interests in offering training programs to employees.) On the other hand, government agencies will often send employees to courses of several weeks or bring such courses in-house, on government premises.

Proprietary versus custom-designed programs: Such courses may be off-the-shelf—proprietary programs that the customer has learned of in some manner—or custom-designed for the customer, to satisfy some identified need.

The latter—custom-designed training programs—are most costly, and while it is not unheard of for large companies to contract for such courses (e.g., Caterpillar) it is far more often the government agencies who will pay the price for custom development, especially the federal government agencies, many of whom even operate special in-house (sometimes called "inboard") training programs in permanent classroom and lecture facilities.

THE FEDERAL GOVERNMENT MARKETS

The U.S. Government is a major user of training for employees. The U.S. Treasury Department, the U.S. Office of Federal Procurement Policy, the U.S. Postal Service, and the U.S. Labor Department, for example, operate permanent training programs and classroom facilities. In those facilities they present regular courses of study, often courses they have paid to have developed especially for them, but they also present many refresher courses and special courses, which may be proprietaries or may be courses they have had developed especially to meet some detected need. Moreover, they can often also be sold proprietary programs by demonstrating the usefulness of the programs. Training programs in management, writing, leadership, office procedures, and in-basket techniques are among the many popular subjects, and it is not unusual for these organizations to contract for the services of professional speakers who speak on relevant subjects.

The Office of Personnel Management, OPM (the Civil Service Commission, CSC, formerly, before the Carter Administration reorganized it) operates a number of training establishments and conducts a variety of training courses as a service to the other agencies of the federal government. They, too, like the others mentioned here, have regular programs, mostly developed for them, but they also contract with independent public speakers to lecture and present their courses. And they often also order custom courses written for them, or have trainers and lecturers present their own proprietary programs. (Bureaucracy being what it is, however, they may hire a speaker or instructor and call the individual a "consultant," or the service "consulting," according to the policies of the agency or the circumstances of the moment.)

Not all federal agencies utilize these services, and even those who do often find other needs which are not satisfied by the courses offered at these various facilities. And there are, of course, literally thousands of government agencies, when you count all the divisions, officers, administrations, and bureaus within the various Departments and "independent agencies" of the federal government. Here are a few facts and figures to convey some idea of how big the federal government market is:

The federal government, with about 2.8 million employees total (not counting the military establishments, of course) employs some 130,000 government employees as full-time purchasing and procurement personnel, currently spending about $175 billion annually for goods and services purchased on the open market by about 15,000 identified purchasing or contracting offices. (But this does not take into account other government purchasing by offices that are not technically purchasing offices of any kind.) The Office of Federal Procurement Policy operates a permanent school to train contracting officers and related procurement and purchasing personnel, and evidently is unable to keep up with the demand, for there appears to be a continuing shortage of trained

purchasing personnel, especially of contracting officers, negotia-
tors, and other senior procurement personnel.

Important and widespread an activity that training is in federal
government, however, the government agencies utilize speakers
in connection with many other activities, for there are many other
kinds of federal government programs. Federal agencies, for
example sponsor conventions and, especially, conferences and
symposia in many of those specialized fields for which the government has set up programs and/or agencies. The government, acting as sponsor, retains many specialists—consultants, speakers,
and others—to help make these events successful. Some examples
of the kinds of fields referred to here are these:

Energy	Environmental controls
Mental Health	Alcohol and drug abuse
Cancer	Space systems

Like private sector companies and other organizations, government agencies often see benefits for their employees in presentations which are perhaps training, in a specialized sense, but are
not exactly the typical skills training most people think of as training and education. There is acceptance by federal agencies of
motivational, and "positive thinking" presentations, training in
handling stress, sensitivity training, consciousness-raising programs, and other such materials. And even when government
personnel do the training, especially in the case of a custom program developed by a contractor, the contractor must provide a
train-the-trainers program.

Many major procurement contracts awarded to companies to
develop systems and equipment for the government—especially
the military departments—include requirements for orientation
and training programs, and while many of the companies have in-
house staff to handle such requirements, many "go outside" and
hire professional speakers to handle this part of the contract for
them as subcontracts.

There are also some special situations, such as one in which the
National Park Service retained a contractor to dress people in Co-
lonial costumes and stage reenactments of Revolutionary War
events in a national park at Yorktown, Virginia, where the war's

climactic and decisive battle was fought. (The shows were put on for tourists visiting the historic site during the summer months.)

The federal government is also a major producer of films, slide, tape, and filmstrip presentations, and other such audiovisual materials, and often contracts to have such materials developed, both for training and for other purposes. (Many agencies have entire departments for such activities.) For example, some of these are for "educational" purposes, which means to be used by the general public, in schools, in community groups, on radio and TV in "public service announcements," and elsewhere, to deliver messages to the public generally on safety, drug and alcohol abuse, and other subjects of public interest. And some of these materials are prepared with federal funds by federal agencies for the use of state and local governments in their own programs and by anyone else who is interested and wishes to distribute the materials.

STATE AND LOCAL GOVERNMENT MARKETS

Despite the great size of the federal government market—about $175 billion annually—this does not take into account the huge market represented by state and local governments and their purchasing power of some $350 billion annually. To gain some idea of this market, consider these figures: In addition to the 50 states, there are about 3000 counties and 18,000 cities and towns. Each of these, especially the states, has in itself numerous departments, offices, bureaus, and institutions which do some purchasing of their own. Nor does this take into account the thousands of school districts and special districts, which are semi-independent government entities. According to the U.S. Bureau of Census, this totals nearly 80,000 governmental entities in the United States. In the aggregate, this represents hundreds of thousands of potential clients for public speakers.

Each state has a central purchasing organization situated in the state capital. In general terms, these organizations buy very much as the federal government does, under statutes that dictate the purchasing procedures and practices, although with some variations from state to state, of course. In some cases all purchasing must be done through that central facility and organization, even though various state agencies—departments, commissions, prisons, schools, hospitals, and other offices, bureaus, and institutions—may be free to make independent buying decisions; in other cases, many of those agencies may issue their own purchase orders and contracts directly. And in many cases, there are hundreds of these state agencies. There are purchasing offices in most county seats and city halls, too, and some of the larger governmental entities—New York City, for example—have rather large procurement budgets.

COMPANY-BASED GROUPS AND EVENTS

Associations are not the only organizations who have meetings with planned agendas and programs that often include professional speakers. Many companies conduct such programs as the seminars discussed earlier, but sometimes companies sponsor after-hours activities, such as employee associations. Or, even if the company does not sponsor the group directly, employee groups are often based on the fact of being employed in the same company. The Rockwell Management Club is one example of such a group that hires speakers for meetings and other events. But there are also many recreational groups in companies, such as bowling leagues, and these groups have periodic meetings and special events for which they hire speakers.

OTHER LEISURE-TIME ACTIVITIES

Many people belong to groups which represent leisure-time activities, if not actual recreation, such as Men's Clubs associated with religious establishments, and other such organizations, both local and national—and sometimes even international—in scope. Even the local groups have special events for which they hire speakers, but the national and international groups most definitely have needs of this type.

TV AND RADIO

Many public speakers are former or still-active radio and TV announcers, disk jockeys, models, actors, and others in fields closely related to public speaking. Many make transitions from one field to the other, and it works in both directions. Many others work in several fields, holding down a regular job, full- or part-time in radio, TV, or other medium, but doing commercials and/or accepting bookings on the platform, appearing on talk shows or getting themselves interviewed there, and otherwise making the maximum number of public appearances possible—maximizing their "exposure," that is.

Not all of these are paid appearances. Even top-rated professional entertainers are paid only "scale" for appearances on talk shows, and others appear without being paid fees. But many make the appearances because the more prominent they are, the better their chances of getting paid engagements, and the higher their rates, as well.

There are, of course, a variety of miscellaneous opportunities, and we have probed the markets only superficially here, and focused primarily on the paying markets. For the beginner, some of the best advice offered is to speak as often as possible, for minimal fees and even without fees. Many of the top platform performers of today started in precisely that manner, and hardly anyone springs full-blown into the top ranks of public speaking. But in a great many of the markets cited here, there are opportunities for beginners, especially those who are concerned with getting the practice and experience that ultimately transforms the raw, beginning tyro into the smooth, top professional.

CHAPTER 8

FEES, EXPENSES, AND ARRANGEMENTS

The business arrangements you can and cannot, should and should not expect, insist upon, and agree to.

SPEAKING FEES, LARGE AND SMALL

It should not be especially shocking to anyone to learn that Bob Hope today commands a fee of $40,000 plus expenses for himself and entourage, for each appearance, nor that there are a few other marquee-dominating figures (albeit not a large company of others) who also command that much and have equally large entourages of supporters to sustain. On the other hand there are a rather large number of those who can win from $15,000 to $25,000 each time they mount the platform, and there are an even larger population of public speakers who command goodly, even if lesser, sums.

However, this does not mean that a speaker must be famous or even infamous to command at least a quite respectable speaking fee—$2,000, $4,000, and more. Some of these still-well-paid speakers are well-known names and faces—athletes, senators, authors, lesser lights of Broadway and Hollywood, and of the large and small screens—but there are also many recognized stars of public speaking whose names would probably stir not the slightest current of recognition in your brain. They include such names as those of Dan T. Moore, Director General of the International Platform Association and a well-known speaker; Arnold "Nick" Carter, of the Nightingale-Conant Corporation; Lily B. Moskal, businesswoman and real estate broker; and many others from the worlds of business, industry, and the professions—comedy writer Gene Perret, publisher-agent Dottie Walters, TV star/actress Lael Jackson, speaker Mark Victor Hansen, executive Frank Basile, speech and TV coach Lou Hampton, author-publisher Charles Tremendous Jones, and NSA (National Speakers Association) founder Cavett Robert, to mention only a handful of the large population of successful speakers.

WHAT DETERMINES THE FEES?

It's pretty obvious what determines the huge fees commanded by Bob Hope and others of his prominence and stature: if you want

Bob Hope, Art Linkletter, Alexander Haig, Barbara Walters, or others who are well-known public figures, you will have to pay fees that are commensurate with their reputations, recognition factors, entertainment values, and/or demands. But it is "and/or" because each case is different. Bob Hope is a great entertainer, as well as an extremely well-known figure, as is Art Linkletter, but you could hardly call Barbara Walters or Alexander Haig entertainers, despite their well-known names and faces (although some listeners find Haig's ability to rival Eisenhower in mangling syntax at least amusing). But there is also the matter of the speaker's demands—or those of the speaker's agent/manager—and their abilities to sell and to bargain.

One major factor in determining fees is the degree to which the individual is a "draw"—his or her appeal to an audience. Certainly, well-known names and faces tend to draw better than do unknown or little-known names and faces. This has little to do with the ability of the individual as a speaker or as an entertainer. However, if you can combine the two appeals—the well-known name and face and a well-known reputation as an entertainer—it becomes a powerful combination that commands substantial fees, even exorbitant fees, in many cases, arising out of the individual's unreasoning fear. Here is a commonly reported fear of those who have become huge successes, especially in those cases where the success has been almost literally overnight:

Many of those who command fees so huge that they never dreamed they would one day demand and command such sums have the same apprehension: They are still unable to believe that their earning power is real or permanent. They fear that it is all an illusion the public has about them, and that one day suddenly the public will wake up and see their "error." So, they feel, they had better hurry up and "cash in" on the illusion before the public discovers that they are only human and the goose that lays the golden eggs suddenly dies or vanishes mysteriously. That appears to be a fairly common nightmare of those who command large fees, and the reason some of them appear so unreasonable in their demands. They are motivated by fear that they have been the beneficiaries of a monstrous misunderstanding and the "box office" appeal will vanish as suddenly as it arrived.

BOX OFFICE

While probably the majority of public speaking engagements are on the basis of fees paid as an expense of operating an organization—running an association, producing a convention, running a sales meeting, and so on—there are still a number of cases in which the sponsors or promoters expect to recoup the speaker's fees and turn a profit from paid attendances—where the speaker's fee is an *investment*. In the case of many college and university appearances, for example, students pay for registering and attending the sessions, which are sponsored often by student's groups. Here, the "draw" of the speaker becomes a critically important factor because the speaker's name, face, and reputation are stock in trade, items to be sold.

The same thing applies in the case of many seminars, conventions, conferences, fairs, exhibits, author's luncheons, and numerous other events where the speaker (or, at least, the *main* speaker) is expected to be a draw because attendees are paying fees for attending. Washington's National Press Club, for example, has many such occasions, usually with some prominent public figure as guest and main speaker, and *The Washington Post* runs author's luncheons periodically, usually featuring a well-known author, such as Rosalyn Carter, whose fame may or may not be connected with authorship.

ANOTHER KIND OF BOX OFFICE

At least one other factor is that which was touched on in an earlier paragraph: kind of speaker and subjects. And one major factor is the quality of exclusivity. If the speaker has a kind of exclusivity on a subject of great interest, that factor alone bears heavily on the speaker's value and, hence, fees.

That is one reason that the Watergate figures commanded substantial speaking fees while the subject was still in the news and of great popular interest: those people had some genuine "inside information" about the whole affair. That alone enabled them to command big fees, even if they were not especially good speakers.

But of course the subject need not be scandalous, nor even one that has been lately in the news; it may be simply one that captures the imagination of a great many people, and one on which the speaker happens to have some special credentials as an authority of one sort or another.

For example, if you happen to have persuasive credentials as an authority on some kind of dieting that people find appealing, and few people have good information on that, you may very well be able to translate that into handsome speaking fees. Or if you are an expert criminologist or forensic pathologist, you may be able to arouse a great deal of interest in hearing your thoughts on the subject. Or perhaps you know more about vitamins and health than almost anyone, or have some interesting new theories on the subject.

Fortunately—or perhaps unfortunately—you need not necessarily be even a bona fide expert or authority, as long as what you wish to offer appears to be interesting—has its own special kind of appeal—its own box office, that is. As long as you offer a presentation that appeals, you can present it in an interesting fashion, and you appear to have an exclusive or near-exclusive on it, you will probably be well received and well paid.

In short, if *you* are not box office, perhaps you can come up with a subject or presentation that is box office, which is very nearly as good. And what this means, obviously, is that you must work hard at finding both a good subject and an interesting perspective or methodology for presenting it.

THE AVAILABILITY FACTOR

There are some miscellaneous considerations which are not totally unimportant. There is the matter of availability, for example. If you wanted to get Bob Hope to do a show for you next Tuesday night it wouldn't matter what fee you wanted to offer; the overwhelming probability is that he can only be engaged many months in advance. And if experienced professionals are asked to make a presentation on short notice, they may refuse even if they are available, for fear that such ready availability makes them appear to be unsuccessful. Still, there are often opportunities to win engagements by being available to fill in in emergencies, when someone else has been taken ill or some other disaster has struck the program.

AT THE BOTTOM END OF THE FEE SPECTRUM . . .

For all who command large fees there are many others whose fees range from zero dollars to $50, $100, or a few hundred dollars per appearance. This is not an indictment of the speaker or the quality of the speaker's presentations, but is due to one of the following situations:

☐ Some people speak for other rewards than fees.

☐ Some are beginners, willing to work for small fees and even for no fee to gain experience and confidence, while they learn how to speak well.

☐ Some organizations customarily pay no fee (although most will pay expenses, if any are incurred) or only small honorariums. However, frequently even star performers who normally command handsome fees will often agree to speak before these organizations as an act of *noblesse oblige*. (E.g., it may be a fund raiser for some cause the speaker believes worthy of his or her own donation of time and services.)

WHAT KINDS OF FEES CAN *YOU* COMMAND?

Where do *you* fit into this mosaic of fees and values? That is the important question, of course. What can *you* expect to be able to ask for and get?

The answer to that question depends on the same factors we have been discussing: Your experience and ability to make a good presentation, your personal box office, the box office of your presentation, and some miscellaneous factors, such as availability and plain fortune. But there is this consideration, too: Can you plan a presentation that has some of those qualities we have discussed or appeal, while being or appearing to be exclusive? Can you offer something appealing that is not easy to get anywhere else? If you can do this, you can probably bypass many of the harder periods of learning and experience that others must endure.

In my own case, speaking on proposal writing and government marketing, I have a certain degree of exclusivity there because there are simply not that many experts in the subject competing for a place on the platform. On the other hand, it isn't every individual who gives a hang about the subject, so I must seek out those to whom the subject is of interest.

That is another factor determining what kinds of fees you can command, one we'll explore in greater depth in a later chapter.

TYPICAL PRACTICES: ARE THERE ANY?

There is always a great temptation to be influenced by one's own biases and personal experiences in smugly assuring whoever will listen that "this is the way it's always done," thereby trying to set the standard. Were you to ask a number of professional speakers how their fees, expenses, and arrangements are handled, no doubt you would be endowed with much assurance, based on each one's personal preferences, that the procedure presented is the "right way" to do it. And you would then go forth into the speaking world and be utterly baffled to find that most of your own experiences were exceptions of one kind or another to the many "rules" laid down for you as the standard way the professionals operate. For there are probably as many exceptions to any rule you could fashion as there are conformances with that rule.

GETTING PAID

As an example of typical practices, there are those who will assure you that in the professional speaking world the speaker's check is or should be always waiting at the destination and is handed over before the speaker mounts the platform. That has been my experience on occasion—on *rare* occasion. More frequently I have been expected to submit my bill and wait for the accountants to mail my check to me. (But I have found it helpful to be able to hand over an invoice prepared in advance. That speeds up the process, and every once in a while I am pleasantly surprised to get my check before I leave.)

Sometimes advance retainers may be paid, when the agreement is reached, but that appears to be a fairly rare practice for speaking engagements, although not unusual for consulting work. (And many individuals are both speakers and consultants, as well as trainers and writers.)

Of course, a great many practices stem from the speaker's own requests. It is possible to *ask* that your check be waiting for you, and many clients will accomodate you. But there will still be exceptions. For example, some large organizations have rather rigid procedures and policies and cannot issue a check until an invoice has been processed and someone certifies that the services or goods invoiced have been delivered in satisfactory condition. That makes getting an advance check an exception to the rule in such organizations, and this can be difficult to manage—for them, as well as for you. And even when the organization is willing to take extraordinary measures to get an advance check issued, sometimes it is most difficult for them to do so in less than 30 days, whereas the engagement may be scheduled for only a few days hence. If, however, you happen to be a celebrity speaker, you needn't worry about it because your agent/manager will handle the whole thing, and you won't even known how it was handled. Moreover, if you are a celebrity, it is likely that the client will do whatever you request!

The fact is that if the client engages speakers regularly, he or she may have some some fixed policy or standard practice and expect you to accept that. Remember that in many, if not most, cases the client is in some line of business and is accustomed to handling payables according to some organized procedure, with speakers getting paid the same way others get paid.

Still, many clients will look to you to state your own terms—

that's a time-honored practice in the American business community too. So it is entirely possible that you can arrange to have your check ready and waiting for you when you arrive, or at least when you finish your presentation.

EXPENSES AND ARRANGEMENTS

Since a great many of your speaking engagements are going to be "out of town"—in cities and places at airline distances from where you live and maintain your business base—you have the expense factor—travel and per diem expenses to cope with. The travel, lodging, and meals are necessary and legitimate expenses incurred in the course of carrying out your speaking engagements—providing the services to your clients—and these are normally items for which you are to be reimbursed, in addition to your regular fee.

Travel is generally by air (except for short distances, when it would normally be by automobile and billed on a mileage basis), but there are also the home-to-airport and airport-to-hotel expenses, and there may be some local travel expense, as well. (In many cases the event is a great distance from the only available municipal airport. For example, I was to conduct a seminar at a country club in Sheboygan, Wisconsin, well over an hour's drive from Milwaukee, where I had landed. I had no choice, of course, but to rent an automobile and drive to Sheboygan.)

Lodging is typically at a nearby hotel, often in the same hotel where you will be making your presentation, if the occasion is an event being conducted in a hotel. It is generally for a single night, unless you are making more than one presentation on more than one day. Meals are for the time that you are in transit and at the location.

Properly, you are not entitled to run up a bar bill and charge it to your client, and you are not entitled to bring your wife along, except at your own expense. There are exceptions, and you may even be invited to bring a spouse along, or the client may wish to entertain you at lunch, dinner, or elsewhere. Situations vary widely, and each calls for the exercise of good judgment and your own sense of propriety. A lack of sensitivity or good judgment on your part may result in being scratched off that client's list of speakers to be called on in the future, and might even result in a complaint being lodged with your agent or speakers' bureau, if you were sent out by one. But there are some other considerations, too, about expense money and how you can or should handle it. In fact, it is not totally unrelated to your remuneration in general and how promptly it can be paid, but may have an effect on that matter, too.

If you are laying out all your own expense money, to be billed to the client, it can become an obstacle to getting paid on the spot because you don't know what your full expenses will be until the trip is over. Some clients may pay your fee on the spot and have you bill them for the expenses. Others may give you a flat sum to cover all expenses. And still others will attend to all travel expenses by having a ticket waiting for you at the airline counter and having your hotel accommodations billed to them. Too, some may arrange to have someone meet you at the airport and transport you.

Having the client pay or prepay all your travel and hotel expenses is an excellent idea because it eliminates many problems, not the least of which are your own cash-flow problems: it often takes clients, especially when they are large business organizations, weeks to get a reimbursement check out, by which time you have had to pay the charges, tying up your own operating capital. And if you are busy, traveling about a good bit, this can soon become a tidy amount of capital to have tied up in this manner. Unfortunately, I have known some rather large and prosperous corporations to take two and even three months to pay me what they owed. This is bad enough when what they owe you are your fees, but it is intolerable when it is reimbursement of your own money at actual outlay, which in today's economy means it is actually at a loss. It is therefore good business to either charge some kind of handling fee or overhead surcharge on expenses or ask the client to handle them.

My personal experience has been that I have rarely met with any serious resistance from clients about this, since they tend usually to look to me to state my terms, policy, or required procedure.

And I have found that once I explain that it is my policy to ask the client to make all travel and hotel arrangements because the client is often able to do so at more favorable rates than I can and it simplifies the whole transaction for everyone, there is usually no difficulty about this. (If there are occasional exceptions, as there are, at least they are exceptions.)

SUMMARY OF FEE RANGES

The fees can range, as you have seen, from extreme lows of minuscule honorariums to rather celestial heights of celebrity fees, where perhaps the expenses are even greater than the fees. In more practical terms, ruling out those extremes because they are impractical for most of us, let's consider the practical working range for the able professionals who are not celebrities, except perhaps in the most limited or provincial sense.

In this perspective, you may consider $500 to be the bottom scale for any truly professional speaker for even the briefest address. In fact, as you will see in a later chapter, few agents, if any, are interested in a speaker even at that range. Most lecture bureaus cannot handle a speaker profitably unless the speaker commands $1000 or more per address. And among those who may be considered the hardy perennials, those who are truly expert professionals and working steadily at their professions as speakers, motivators, spellbinders, and whatever else a great speaker may be said to be, few work for less than $2000 minimum to at least $4000 for a full day's work on a platform.

SEMINAR FEES, EXPENSES, AND ARRANGEMENTS

If you choose to conduct your own open-registration seminars, you have an entirely different situation to confront. Here, you are the producer, sponsor, entrepreneur, and speaker, all in one, seeking a profit, rather than a fee. In fact, the fees are those the attendees pay to register and attend, and your own financial reward is whatever profits you can realize from the venture. But we'll discuss this in greater depth in the next chapter.

=== CHAPTER 9 ============================

EXPANDING YOUR INCOME

Many, probably most, professional speakers do not have to depend on speaking fees alone, for speaking meshes nicely with many other professional activities.

NOT ALL PROFESSIONAL SPEAKERS
IDENTIFY AS SUCH

There are speakers who write and consult, consultants who write and speak, and writers who consult and speak. The differences among them? Probably none—no really signficant ones, anyway—except how each conceives his or her own major role: which is his or her main career field and which are the ancillary ones. The fact is that contrary to public opinion or, perhaps, contrary even to your own opinion, by far the majority of professional speakers do not rely upon speaking alone for their subsistence. Nor do all professional speakers necessarily think of themselves as engaged primarily in public speaking careers. Those who do make a full-time practice of public speaking and who are, in fact, exclusively or even primarily public speakers—those who derive their entire or at least main incomes from public speaking and do little else as a career or business activity—are very much in the minority. Like writers, consultants, and numerous other busy (and self-employed, even if as part-time or as ancillary to another career activity) professionals, the majority of public speakers keep many irons heated to incandescence, and speaking professionally—for fees—is only one of those glowing in the fire. As you have already gathered from numerous previous intimations, many public speakers are also entertainers, trainers, instructors, writers, consultants, publishers, and even part- or full-time executives of organizations, frequently their own organizations.

RELATED PROFESSIONS

Frequently these several career or professional activities are connected with each other by cause-and-effect interrelationships; one, that is, has given rise to the other, and the individual conceives of himself or herself as a speaker who writes, or perhaps as a consultant who writes and lectures. And in many cases, the individual would be hard put to decide what his or her main career activity is. That is especially true where the individual is simply one of those enterprising and versatile people, as so many are in these professions, who would simply be totally unhappy at being confined to one field, who has an actual *need* to be busy, even to have an overfull schedule at all times. Nor is it necessarily economic necessity that compels speakers to also be involved in other activities, although that may be an important consideration. But quite often it is deliberate choice by individuals for whom participation and involvement in all the several professions and activities is simply a labor of love or impelled by an unconscious drive.

Jack Anderson is a well-known journalist and book author, who produces a widely syndicated daily newspaper column, and is a busy speaker as well. (He keeps a busy speaking schedule, reportedly, and is reputed to generate a major portion of his overall income—reportedly about $250,000 annually—therefrom.) Many other writers and journalists—Kitty Kelley, James Kilpatrick, Edwin Newman, Shana Alexander, and George Plimpton, to name just a few well-known scribes—are invited often to the platform, and probably also derive significant income from this. But there are many other well-known figures from other fields to be found on the platform: John Denver, the singer, actor, and song writer, is also a public speaker, as is Jeane Dixon, real estate broker and psychic, and Henry Heimlich, physician and inventor of the now-famous "Heimlich maneuver," which has saved so many people from choking on unexpected obstructions in the air passages. Malcolm Forbes, the millionaire publisher of *Forbes* magazine, J. Willard Marriott, Jr., the equally successful restaurateur and innkeeper, and Doug Henning, that popular young stage and TV magician/entertainer (all of whom are obviously among those not motivated primarily by the speaker's fees they receive) also speak publicly, as do a great many other highly successful people. But many physicians, judges, lawyers, musicians, composers, engineers, scientists, consultants, politicians, hypnotists, poets, and sundry others speak publicly often enough to qualify as professional speakers.

THE COMMON THREAD

Quite possibly a major attraction that draws many individuals to all these professions and career activities is the simple fact that all these professional activities are essentially creative and enable practitioners to *express* themselves to clients and audiences. Writing, consulting, entertaining, and the other activities named relate well to each other, in this respect, and afford their practitioners much the same kind of satisfactions, as well as a diversified income base, which for many, if not for others, is a matter of some importance.

WHY DIVERSIFY?

In the case of self-employed individuals, as in the case of many companies, one activity may be "carried" by another, more profitable one, simply because the individual believes that some motive other than immediate profit makes it desirable to carry on that activity which makes less than a full contribution to income overall, or even represents a loss on the books. The reason may be simply satisfaction in being involved in the other activity—even hard-headed pragmatists heading up major corporations sometimes develop a social conscience or some other reason than financial gain for doing something—but it may be long-term income prospects, too, with the activity carried as a kind of continuing investment, with the hope of eventual reward.

THE DIVERSIFICATION IS NOT ALWAYS INTENTIONAL

On the other hand, frequently the individual had no original intention of being in more than one of these fields, but seems naturally drawn into several adjacent fields, once entered seriously into any one. The diversification is a progressive one, and the lines distinguishing one from the other become more and more indistinct, as the individual devotes more and more time to those things which were originally ancillary—"sidelines," in effect.

The movement is analogous to that of companies, which quite often wind up in businesses quite different from those in which they set out to establish their presence. For example, an organization named Federal Publications in Washington, D.C. began life as an organization dedicated to publishing information about the federal government—principally information tending to the legalistic aspects of procurement, labor relations, and other issues in which there is much government regulation and activity generally. (The founder of Federal Publications is a lawyer.) Before long, however, seminars sponsored and produced by the organization began to assume major proportions, as a share of the revenue producers of the company, and are undoubtedly dominant today in company operations, although publishing that special information is still very much a major element in the company's operations.

Consider the busy Dottie Walters, a well-known figure in the world of paid public speaking, and publisher of the popular periodical, *Sharing Ideas! Among Professional Speakers and Their Friends*, as one example. Dottie started out, by her own account, as a self-employed entrepreneur and businesswoman, busily making her own sales calls and building a business. She started to speak publicly as a marketing measure for her business, but soon found herself widely accepted and paid as a professional speaker. However, today she is not only a speaker, but she is a writer; the publisher of her popular speakers' newsletter-magazine, books, and audiotape programs; a lecture agent; a seminar producer; and in general serving the interests of both speakers and clients in a variety of ways.

The most obvious reason for diversification of activity is to diversify and multiply income sources and income opportunities, and those are, indeed, true potential benefits of diversification generally. However, the relationship among these fields is such that many individuals find themselves *propelled* into adjacent fields almost automatically and almost involuntarily. For example, it is all but impossible to be a practicing consultant without doing at least some writing and speaking, even if it is only writing reports and making oral presentations to your clients. And it is almost impossible to become successful in any professional or even paraprofessional field without being eventually invited to speak, write, and/or consult on relevant subjects. In short, frequently diversification is sometimes all but forced on you by the natural evolution of your activities, or grows spontaneously, even almost invisibly by minute degrees, out of those activities. You suddenly find yourself in an adjacent field with both feet planted there solidly, hardly aware of how the change took place. (In my own case, for example, being fortunate enough to write a number of successful proposals for government contracts led to friends and acquaintances insisting on becoming my clients—paying me to act as a consultant and help them with their proposals. And becoming a proposal consultant led, in turn, to my being asked to appear as a speaker on the subject, launching me into those two added activities, consulting and speaking, whereas I had begun as a writer of proposals and other such "paper.")

DIVERSIFICATION BY INTENT

The fact that a great many people drift or are maneuvered by circumstance into other fields does not mean that everyone diversifies in this manner. Quite the contrary, a great many entrepreneurs consciously and deliberately set out to diversify. (And yet it is impossible to predict where an ancillary activity may eventually lead, or whether it will become the dominant activity, as witness the story of Federal Publications, already presented, or that of Adam Osborne, to be presented in a moment.)

You can start with or from any of the activities listed and diversify into any or all of the others, with products, services, or both. However, one highly significant factor about those several fields already listed—speaking, writing, consulting, teaching, publishing, entertaining, and perhaps even a few others—is that they are to a large extent mutually supporting: Each activity helps make the others more successful and rewarding, usually, whether by intent or by the nature of the activities. For example, many an entrepreneur launches a complimentary newsletter as a device to promote some other enterprise, and ultimately discovers that the newsletter can be itself a good income producer. And the newsletter publishing often develops into the publishing of reports, books, and other material. For example, Adam Osborne wrote a book, *An Introduction to Microcomputers*, with the intention of using it principally as a giveaway to promote the new consulting practice he planned to launch, but found the book (the first book published about microcomputers) rapidly developing into a best seller, which changed his entire course: It led to his abandonment of the consulting idea, and the launching of a publishing enterprise, which he sold to McGraw-Hill, and which latter transaction led eventually to establishing his computer-manufacturing venture and the world's first portable computer.

Writing and publishing can help you become more successful as a public speaker, but it has also helped many who began as writers to become speakers, entertainers, and even actors. Mel Brooks, the actor/comedian, is one example of a writer who became a performer (he was a writer on the TV "Show of Shows," writing for comedian Sid Caesar, years ago) but he is by no means the only one. Woody Allen, Dick Cavett, and Bob Orben, among others, progressed from writing to performing or speaking, although they continued to write.

Writing helps you gain a greater, and perhaps even a more prestigious, public "image," and so helps your speaking career by giving you one, greater prominence generally, and two, greater credentials as a communicator and presenter of ideas and information. In fact, if you are successful enough in your writing— produce a best-selling book or a highly controversial article of some sort, for example—you may even achieve a celebrity status of some degree and become a desirable speaker on that account alone.

But "writing," like "speaking," "publishing," and many other broad generic terms, is so general as to be almost meaningless. It must be discussed in the more specific terms of its many applications, manifestations, and implementations to be useful for our purposes here. Moreover, we will address marketing, including the use of writing for that purpose, in a later chapter. In this chapter we are concerned with writing and other ancillary activities as methods for expanding the income, although still based on a speaking career.

THE MANY FACES OF "WRITING"

Writing is, of course, an activity with almost infinite possible applications. You may write magazine articles, professional papers, books, monographs, newsletters, reports, comedy material, or many other kinds of material, as you may write for direct income or for other purposes. And there are three ways, in general, to put writing to work in expanding your income base:

1. Write articles, books, and other material relevant to your special field, for publication by others, to be paid on whatever is the regular basis in that field.
2. Write speeches, humor, other material for other speakers or entertainers.
3. Publish your own writings.

Each of these alternatives merit—require—independent discussion.

WRITING FOR PUBLICATION BY OTHERS

The publishing business produces both periodicals, such as newspapers, newsletters, magazines, and annual or semiannual tomes, such as directories; and single pieces: books, reports, monographs, training manuals, audiovisual scripts, and other such stand-alone publications. Although some publishers, particularly those of periodicals and specialities, maintain staffs and often have at least some of their work staff written, by far the more widespread practice is to solicit contributions from freelance writers, for which most publications pay (although rates of pay vary widely, from very low to very high, along with a few who "pay" authors only in free copies and perhaps in satisfaction in appearing in print). The main markets for freelance contributions lie in books and magazines, and we'll discuss these primarily, although without completely neglecting the other markets.

WRITING FOR PERIODICALS

The chief periodicals of interest here are magazines. Newspapers are not a very good freelance market and newsletters rarely pay very much, even when they buy contributions. For that matter, many magazines do not pay very well, either. However, what are referred to here as "magazines" fall into at least three classes:

1. The general circulation magazines which appear on news-stands because they have a broad enough appeal to the general public to be worth retailing in that manner. (Some of these address specialized subjects, such as computers or weight lifting, but the population of interested readers is large enough to merit this kind of distribution.)
2. The special interest magazines which are narrow enough in appeal to bar selling on newsstands, and which are there-fore sold by mail-order subscription and in special estab-lishments, patronized by potential readers.
3. Trade journals—may be slick-paper magazines or tabloids on newsprint—usually circulated free of charge as "con-trolled circulation" periodicals to qualified individuals within the periodical's range of interest. Most professions and industries have such trade journals.

The Several Magazine Markets

Ordinarily—but not always—the rates of pay offered by these pe-riodicals are approximately in the order in which they are pre-sented here, with general interest magazines usually the highest paying ones, and trade journals the lowest paying ones. (But there are exceptions, and sometimes the reverse is true.)

There are full-time freelance writers who derive their entire or near-entire incomes by writing for periodicals, and if they happen to specialize in writing for trade journals, they ordinarily must be quite prolific to earn an adequate income because of the unusual low rates, and they thus generally employ many special measures to increase their productivity. In any case, this is rarely a very prof-itable market for speakers and consultants.

Special and general interest magazines are another matter, es-pecially since many are in highly specialized fields, which usually require rather specialized and often technical knowledge to write for, making writing for this field a rather impracticable prospect for the general freelance writer, while offering opportunity to qualified writers. Computer magazines, for example, popular although they are and appealing to the lay public, usually require a fairly large degree of technical knowledge to write for. Much the same thing can be said for many other kinds of periodicals addressed to investments, aviation, telephones, banking, two-way radio, and numerous other specialized fields and industries. This makes these kinds of magazines probably the best targets for the writings of consultants and speakers who specialize in relevant fields.

Magazines come and go with a fair degree of frequency. The microcomputer field alone has been responsible for the creation of over 200 new periodicals, of which a fair number are to be found on well-stocked newsstands. And even these have been subdividing rapidly into different classes, such as hardware, software, home computers, game computers, computer graphics, computer communications, business computers, and others. But there are many other magazines springing up, to match other developments. For example, the introduction of videocassette recorders into millions of homes has spawned several new magazines devoted to that industry, covering both hardware and software—videocassettes. The growing interest of average individuals in the stock market as an investment (where once only the relatively affluent played the market) has encouraged the growth of periodicals in that field. Relatively new, too, are such special branches of older fields as lasers, fiber optics, and microprocessor chips, all of which have spawned many new products, and even entire new industries and new professions, as well as new publications. And in recent years the enormous proliferation of automobiles, foreign and domestic and in such a variety of types and sizes, has brought about an equal proliferation in magazines devoted to the interests of automobile enthusiasts and hobbyists, including those who have a direct interest in or fascination with automobile racing and its related activities.

More and more, new periodicals are specialized in their appeals, in some cases to a widespread portion of the lay public, and in others to a given industry or profession newly created, or at least of relatively recent origin. And, of course, new magazines are often the best targets because their editors have not yet built a backlog of materials (most editors try to have enough material in reserve to cover an issue or two, and generally try to gather materials to plan several issues ahead.) And so many of the newer magazines are still rather hungry for material and are relatively easy to break into.

How to Approach Magazines

Once it was the usual practice to bundle up one's manuscript and send it off, with return postage, to the editor of the magazine chosen, and wait hopefully, while writing other articles and sending them off to other magazines. Typically, many weeks passed in waiting, before getting the manuscript back with a form declining the offering. (The form was and is known far and wide as a "rejection slip.") Occasionally, a check or an offer for the manuscript arrived, or an offer may have even come by telephone.

The Query Letter

Today few editors want to see unsolicited manuscripts. Most want a "query," a letter explaining what the writer proposes to write, with enough information to enable the editor to judge his probable interest (that, the readers' probable interest or lack of it!), and some information about the credentials of the author, both as a subject-matter authority and as a writer. Tell the editor what the proposed article is to be about—a reasonably complete outline would be a great help to the editor—and approximately how long it will be; information about illustrations, if there are to be any; and how long it will take you to write it and submit it. Clippings of your previously published work and some bio data help the editor judge your qualifications to write the piece. But don't go on and on; be businesslike and get straight to the point. Editors are busy people.

If interested, the editor will write or call with an acceptance and a dollar figure, but usually "on spec" (speculation), which means that the editor does not guarantee acceptance of the finished article, but will probably buy it, if it is done well. (The experienced professional writer, with an established reputation, especially if well-known to the editor as a former contributor, may get a firm assignment, with a "kill fee," which is an agreed-upon payment in case the editor changes his or her mind and does not, ultimately, buy the piece.)

Of course, you should not select magazines at random as your targets, but must study them and choose the right ones. The idea is to determine what the magazine's style and specific interests are. For example, if you write about computers and you write highly technical pieces, you need to send your queries to magazines addressed to those who want highly technical information, not to those who buy "home computers," with which to play games. By reading writer's magazines and books such as the annual *Writer's Market* (published by *Writer's Digest* magazine), you can get a good idea of which periodicals are the best targets for you, but nothing is quite as helpful as reading the periodicals personally.

Simultaneous Submissions

Once it was considered a cardinal sin—totally unethical and dishonorable—for a writer to submit either a manuscript or a query to more than one editor at a time, no matter how long the editor might take to respond. Fortunately, those days are behind us, and most editors today accept the necessity for and justice of writers submitting queries simultaneously to several editors, although many stipulate that the writer must advise the editor that the submission is a simultaneous one. In fact, it is simply good sense to make simultaneous submissions, if there is more than one periodical which is suitable for whatever article you propose to write. In fact, it is in your interest to do this, for often an editor will advise you as to how to make the article most suitable to his or her own publication. For example, one editor's response to one of my own recent queries was along the lines, "Can you hold this to 1500 words? I 'll pay $____." (And to give you an idea of how busy most editors are, this was scrawled on the bottom margin of my own query letter, the fastest way this editor could respond, and a not-unusual way for busy executives to handle brief correspondence.)

WRITING FOR BOOK PUBLISHERS

Far more relevant and appropriate to writing as one of several professional activities is the writing of books for publication by any of the established commercial book publishers. In fact, in many ways it is even easier to get a book published than it is to get an article published in a magazine. (It is even possible that more authors find publication in books than in magazines every year.)

The Book Publishing Industry

Today there are 40,000 or more books published each year by several hundred established commercial publishers of books. The largest of these publishers bring hundreds of new titles to print every year, and there are many "small presses," who publish a handful of titles—even as few as one or two—every year, while the majority of commercial publishers fall somewhere between these extremes, probably in the range of 50 to 150 new books per year.

Fiction Versus Nonfiction Books

More than one-half these many titles are nonfiction books. Some are exposes, some are memoirs, some are arguments pro or con some prominent issue, some are anthologies or collections of essays and previously published articles, some are professional papers, and many are how-to-do-it, how-it-works, and where-to-find-it books. In this increasingly technological and complex world there is an increasing demand for information of many kinds and on many subjects, and this has affected the book publishing industry to at least the same degree that it has affected the magazine publishing industry. The microcomputer explosion alone has provoked the writing and publishing of hundreds of books, probably the majority of them of the genre known as "trade paperbacks." But the exploding technologies require also the writing and/or rewriting of many professional books and textbooks, to pass on new knowledge and new ideas to students and functioning practitioners in the many fields. (The shelf life of many kinds of books, especially those dealing with modern high technology, seems to grow shorter and shorter, in step with more and more frequent advances and breakthroughs in various technologies.)

BOOK PUBLISHING AS AN INFORMATION INDUSTRY

Economists and other seers and prognosticators speak of this as an "information age" and of our economy as being headed away from the traditional "smokestack industries" and toward leadership in the "information industries." They are referring primarily to computers and software for computers, and their thinking is greatly influenced by and reflective of what have become traditional concepts of the computer as a handler of enormous stores of information at blinding speeds. Of course, there are many other applications of computer automation, especially today, when the ubiquitous microprocessor chip is finding its way into our automobile controls, onto our wrists as the chief functional entity of our digital watches, and ever more pervasively into all corners of our world. But computers are not the only medium of information handling and dissemination. Publishing is very much an information industry in its own right, just as public speaking and consulting are, in most applications.

Some books, both fiction and nonfiction, are purchased primarily for entertainment and diversion generally, while others are purchased primarily as sources of useful information. Of course, that latter class are always nonfiction books—readers do not buy fiction when seriously in pursuit of useful information—although not all nonfiction should be classified generally as part of the book-publishing's contribution to the information industry. Obviously many nonfiction books do not belong to such a classification. Nor is it to say that a speaker who writes may not write fiction or nonfiction designed to amuse, rather than to inform. Some novelists and other authors of books written to entertain become speakers and humorists may very well write books to amuse readers. Anyone, for that matter, may write such books, of course. However, those are the more difficult books to write and sell—

humor, for example, is quite difficult to write and sell, as witness the few humorists who manage to achieve any large success in doing so. The difficulty in getting a novel published, let alone having a significant success with it, is almost legendary. Books offering information for serious purposes are far more viable in the marketplace, even if few ever turn into the blockbusters known in the trade as "big books." (Still, there are exceptions here, as witness such best sellers as *Megatrends, Future Shock, In Search of Excellence, The Word Processing Book, How to Prosper During the Coming Bad Years,* and more than a few other "serious" books. Writing books is something like being in show business, in that outcomes are most difficult to predict: some of the most successful books have been rejected by many large publishers before finding a home, and many books for which great success seemed certain laid an egg.

WHAT ARE THESE INFORMATION BOOKS?

The kinds of books referred to here fall into several specific categories, although admittedly many are difficult to classify and appear to be hybrids or crossbreeds among these classifications. But it is necessary that you have some specific objective or purpose to serve, in conceiving book ideas—you need to know *who* is likely to want such a book and *why* those readers will want it, if you are to persuade a publisher to invest capital in publishing it. Here are the general classes, along with some brief explanation of each which reflects the general objective or purpose of each type:

The How To

How-do-do-it books are among the most popular types today. The personal computer industry has provoked the publishing of a great many how-to books related to computers in the past few years, but there have always been how-to books—how to keep your taxes as small as possible, how to save money with cents-off coupons, how to win contests, how to type, how to do virtually everything that would interest enough probable readers to make the publication of the book worthwhile. (This is itself a how-to book, of course.)

The Where To

Where-to-find-it books are closely related to how-to books, and some publishers may not even distinguish between where to find it and how to find it. In fact, some are simply directories, while others include both how-to and where-to information between a single set of covers. One writer, Matthew Lesko, of the Washington, D.C. area, wrote a successful book called *Information USA*, which is a how-to/where-to on the subject of finding information, and two executives, Andrew P. Garvin and Hubert Bermont collaborated to produce *How to Win With Information or Lose Without It*, another hybrid how-to/where-to.

Variations of Where-to/How-to

There are many variants on these where-to/how-to ideas. Specialized dictionaries are one example. There are today a number of dictionaries of computer terms. A dictionary of CB-radio jargon was a great success. A great many directories of colleges and universities are published every year, and one writer, Dr. John Bear, has been successful in writing about the many ways individuals can earn college degrees without spending four or more years attending classes. Roger von Oech wrote a book on how to be creative, called *A Whack on the Side of the Head*, and two writers, H. G. Jerrard and D. B. McNeill, collaborated to produce *A Dictionary of Scientific Units*.

Self-Help

There is a category of books known as "self-help" books. These are generally of the "inspirational" type, such as Norman Vincent Peale's *The Power of Positive Thinking*, Zig Ziglar's *See You at the Top*, Og Mandino's *The World's Greatest Salesman*, Mark Haroldsen's *How to Wake Up the Financial Genius Inside You,* Napoleon Hill's *Think and Grow Rich,* and sundry other books intended to inspire the reader to a form of autosuggestion or self-hypnosis known as "positive" thinking, or otherwise instructing the reader in how to solve his or her problems (especially emotional ones and family problems) and achieve both greater success and greater happiness in life. These are most often written by psychologists, clergymen, and sales executives, who often attribute their own success to the methods recommended.

Of course, there is often the thinnest of dividing lines between inspirational or self-help books and how-to books. Many books have elements of both. These classifications are with reference to the main thrust of the books, for few of them are "pure" in the sense of the classifications.

Training and Education

Some books are intended as more or less training manuals in the formal sense of being structured as training manuals, with end-of-lesson summaries and review examinations, and recommended other reading. Of course, these are inevitably and unavoidably specialized variants of how-to books, and even where-to books. The chief difference is that instead of the somewhat informal style of how-to/where-to books written for the public, these are formally organized especially for training and education, and make no pretense of being anything else.

The Barnes & Noble *College Outline Series* are books intended for students, serving them as reviews in preparation for examinations of various kinds—college entrance, finals, term, or other. They have been highly successful, and have had their own imitators.

The different versions of "made simple" books are educational in their intent, although less formal than many training manuals, but still more formal than popular paperback how-to books. They purport to make learning easier than it ordinarily is. The success of the original series has inspired imitators, as successes always do, and today there is more than one such series, and each covers many academic and general subjects.

Memoirs and Biographies

Many prominent people write their memoirs and autobiographies (although many also have them ghosted by professional writers). Virtually all surviving former Presidents of the United States have done so in recent decades, for example, as have other surviving public figures—entertainers, government officials, well-known executives, politicians, and almost everyone whose personal and professional life and whose thoughts and ideas are likely to appeal to enough readers to make the venture worthwhile. (It is generally a major investment for the publisher.) Among some recent ones have been Jimmy Carter's *Keeping Faith*, Rosalyn Carter's *Lady From Plains*, and Alexander Haig's *Caveat*. Of course, the infamous, as well as the famous, sometimes offer their memoirs, too, or sometimes another party offers an account of the life of someone well known to the public: frequently writers have written "authorized" and "unauthorized" biographies of others—that is, with and without the consent and cooperation of the subject of the biography.

Miscellaneous

Most of these books fit one or more of the foregoing descriptions, and are quite often hybrids of several categories. But there are also a few that tend to defy even the relatively loose and flexible classifications offered here, and are thus best classified as "miscellaneous." *Free to Choose* by Milton and Rose Friedman, a discourse on the economics of our current system and government policies, with predictions, is one such example. So is *Rejection*, by John White, a somewhat humorous account of history's recorded turndowns that proved eventually to be totally wrongheaded and lacking in vision. (E.g., Kodak turned away Chester Carlson and thereby missed the opportunity to acquire the machine that made tiny, faltering Haloid Corporation into the towering Xerox Corporation of today.) And there is *Positioning: The Battle for Your Mind*, by Al Ries and Jack Trout, which is an explanation and philosophical discussion of the advertising concept known as "positioning," a subject which is deemed to be of great importance to everyone concerned with marketing.

Many politicians write small books intended to serve as their credos and philosophies, in which they discourse on government and related subjects, and so contribute to their general public image. And some write such books on what appear to be unrelated or only indirectly related subjects, such as John F. Kennedy's *Profiles in Courage*, which was a well-received collection of biographical sketches of famous American figures in history. (It has been rumored that Kennedy did not write this himself, although his name appears as author.)

There are also books which are pure exercises in polemics—books arguing some point of view, often a self-serving one. Sometimes these are offered—perhaps even disguised—as memoirs, sometimes are openly political appeals or economic arguments. But note, again, that a great many kinds of books fit this description, even if they are nominally another kind of book, again illustrating the difficulty in classifying these books.

Getting Ideas

The classifications offered here should have suggested at least one avenue for generating ideas for books—or for articles, for that matter, since the general classifications and purposes described here can be applied to articles, as well as to books. Articles, too, are writen as how-to, where-to, self-help, personality sketches, interviews, and for other purposes, similar to those of books, for the most part. Studying the classifications and categories described in the foregoing pages, therefore, may very well trigger ideas in your own head for books and articles. Moreover, you can cross-pollinate ideas, developing articles into books, and spinning off book material as articles.

This is not to say that a book is only a lengthy article. Far from it, an article generally deals with one facet of a topic, where the book deals with the entire subject. And reading an article (or writing one) may give you a book idea in itself, by suggesting that the subject merits an entire book. For example, after writing articles and a newsletter about proposal writing, I included a fat chapter on the subject in a book on government marketing. But I followed that with an entire book on proposal writing, for the subject merited the treatment. One reason I perceived the need was that I found myself compelled to omit many important details on the subject, when I wrote the chapter. Obviously, there was a great deal more to be said on the subject, enough to fill the pages of a substantial book.

On the other hand, not every article is "big" enough to support a book. After solving a troublesome problem by buying a computer program called a "spooler," I decided that the solution should be of interest to others with the same problem, which is a common one. I decided, in short, to offer readers a magazine article on the subject, and had no trouble selling the idea and the subsequent article to *List*™ magazine. That subject, however, would not support even a small book, on its own, although it could be made a useful part of a book on computer software, or one on some other related subject.

If a subject is sometimes not big enough to support an entire book, the reverse is also true: some subjects are so big that a single book will not do them full justice. Just as an article might suggest the need for an entire book, a book might suggest the need for an entire series of books.

Again, using my own case as an example, I found that marketing to the government offered opportunities for several books: a general book on how the system works overall—the forms, the procedures, and other general data; a book on proposal writing; and a directory—principally a where-to, with how-to elements— on where/how to find federal purchasing offices and determine what each buys. And there is room for still more, other specialized books about government marketing, because the subject is such a huge one.

Computers are another subject that offers the opportunity to do entire series of books around some central subject or theme. But so do many subjects and fields. You need only use imagination, and think in terms of the reader: what kinds of problems do people have? What is available to help solve them? What kind of information or advice do they need? What is new that you know about and which has not yet had very much coverage? Or what is covered only in highly technical language that only specialists can appreciate, but which is of interest to the general public?

Developing Your Idea

Once you get a basic idea for a book or article, you need to develop it into a specific plan. You need to decide to whom it will be addressed and for what purpose. And, once you have set the main objective, you need to outline the approach to match those first decisions.

Obviously, it will not pay you to spend a great deal of time and energy doing this for a brief article, since at best the article is not going to earn a great deal of money for you. (You usually get a single payment for all rights, and even when you retain secondary rights or get them returned to you, they are rarely worth a great deal, with one exception, to be explained later.)

THE ECONOMIC REALITIES OF ARTICLES VERSUS BOOKS

For the most part, magazine articles produce enough income to make their writing economically worthwhile only if you can produce them at an efficient rate, which means that you can't devote a great deal of time to research and planning. What this means is that your best prospect for earning a significant part of your income from commercial writing is in authoring books. Whereas that single payment is likely to be all you ever get from an article (with that single exception, promised for later discussion) a successful book can continue to return income for a long, long time—sometimes for many years. (Lancelot Hogben's *Mathematics for the Million* has been in print continuously since 1937, through many hardcover editions, and in recent years through paperback editions. The late Frank Bettger's *How I Raised Myself From Failure to Success in Selling* has had a similar history over many years, and is still in print in at least three editions—hardcover, trade paperback, and mass market paperback.)

Typically, when you sell a book manuscript to a commercial

publisher, you get an advance, which is usually on the order of from $1000 to $5000 (although some publishers do not offer advances or pay advances only rarely), depending on circumstances, against a royalty schedule. Royalties vary somewhat, but are today usually paid as a percentage of the publisher's actual dollar receipts, rather than of cover price, and the typical schedule is along the line of 10 percent on the first 5000 copies sold, 12.5 percent on the next 5000, and 15 percent thereafter. And mail order sales—which are usually against cover price because the publisher sells directly to the consumer—are generally on the royalty schedule of five percent through the life of the book. Consequently, a successful book can pay quite well, although a distressingly large percentage of all books published never earn back the royalty advance.

QUERYING BOOK PUBLISHERS: THE PROPOSAL

The editors in book publishing houses, like those on magazines, do not want unsolicited manuscripts, and many will return them promptly (unless you have failed to provide return postage, in which case your manuscript may never be heard of again). Book publishers also want queries, although those must be a bit more elaborate than the ones submitted for articles. In fact, it is probably a misnomer to call them queries at all; they are or should be proposals. And this does not refer to their form and format alone; it refers to the very philosophy of the query. Here's why:

The very idea of a query is against all "positive thinking" philosophy—against all marketing philosophy, in fact. And you should recognize that when you approach a publisher with an idea for a book you are definitely trying to market your idea. The query idea is a defensive and negative one, suggesting that it should ask an editor for a yes/no answer to the question, "Would you be interested in publishing a book about . . . ?" That is almost begging for "no." It's a hat-in-hand approach that makes it so easy to say "no."

The proposal is in a different philosophy. It doesn't *ask* anything; it *proposes*. That means that it *sells*. It describes an idea, explains the market, argues the case, works at giving the editor reasons to buy.

To do this, you should explain the proposed book in two or three—or even more—pages, with an analysis of the market, competitive books, reasons for predicting success in the marketplace, explanations of what you, the author, can do to help promote and sell the book, what your credentials are, in both terms of subject-matter expertise and writing ability, and anything else that appears to be of interest and helpful in explaining and selling the idea. The proposal must also include a reasonably detailed outline of coverage, explanation of illustrations, tables, worksheets, or other special material to be included, and perhaps even a few samples of material to be included, especially if the samples are unusual or otherwise will command attention and illustrate what you are trying to do with your book. (In a proposal for a book on contracting with the government, I explained that in one case the government had paid me some $6000 to answer their mail, and I so titled the first chapter of the book.)

When you are proposing, you submit a working title for your book. The chances are that the book will wind up with an entirely different title, finally, but that's immaterial for the proposal. The final title is intended to help sell the book to the customer. The title in the proposal is intended to help sell the book idea to the publisher. Don't use cryptic titles and, above all, don't try to be clever or "arty" in that title. Use a title that *explains* the idea, and even use a subtitle to help with that task. Don't strive for short titles; *How I Raised Myself From Failure to Success in Selling* is not a short title, but it has been a remarkably successful book. And Ted Nicholas sold several hundred thousand copies of *How to Form Your Own Corporation Without a Lawyer for Under $50*, which is itself hardly a short title (and which book is still in print today). A title can be, and often should be long, especially in the proposal stage of things, where the title is perhaps the first thing the editor will study.

SOME BASIC PUBLISHING LORE

Book publishing is a relatively simple business, from the product development and manufacturing viewpoint, but complex from the "distributing"—that is, marketing—viewpoint. There are so many factors that affect marketing and dictate both manufacturing and marketing decisions, that it is almost inevitable that virtually every book published is a gamble. So what probably appears to the outsider to be a rather simple and straightforward business is deceptive in that appearance.

One feature of book publishing that distinguishes it from most ventures that are based on manufacturing and marketing a unique product is that in publishing the manufacturer (i.e., the publisher) rarely conceives and designs the product. Instead, the publisher reviews a great many candidate offerings and selects just a relative few for investment in manufacturing and marketing. There are some exceptions to this, of course, such as when a publisher spots a distinct trend or an opportunity to bring something to market, but those are, indeed, exceptions. (There are also book "packagers," individuals who assemble "packages" of author, manuscript, publisher, and contracts, very much along the lines of a producer assembling a stage, TV, or movie package.)

SOME BOOK PUBLISHING ECONOMICS

Front-end Costs (Investment)

The amount of money a publisher must invest to bring a book to market varies, of course, according to size and nature of the book, advances paid, promotional budgets, and many other factors, but probably few books bound in cloth (hardcover, that is) get to market for an investment of much less than $20,000. Even paperbacks approach that because the differences between the two, as far as costs are concerned, are primarily in paper and binding, and these differences are relatively insignificant in costs overall. (Typically, a book may cost from $2 to $3 each to manufacture, although that is a rough, middle-road figure, which can vary widely, according to many factors, and is furnished here merely to furnish some ballpark idea of book-manufacturing costs.)

Advances and Royalties

Dealers—booksellers—generally work at approximately a 40 percent discount from the publisher's list price (again, this can vary widely) and the author's royalty advance often approximates the royalty payments that would accrue from a sellout of the initial printing, which may be as little as 1000 to as much as 4000 copies for a book of unknown or uncertain potential. (But a book by a former president or movie star may well run to many times this initial print order.) The fact that a great many published books fail to earn back the initial advance, much less pay additional royalties, furnishes some idea of the uncertainties of book publishing. Moreover, selling out the first printing, in probably a large majority of the cases, will probably only enable the publisher to reach a breakeven, at best, which means there is little or no profit in the book until and unless the demand requires a second printing.

Shelf Life

One important variable in book marketing is its shelf life. Certain kinds of books have a short shelf life inherently. A sensational news story often inspires the almost-instantaneous writing (often not much more than reprints of news stories because there isn't time to do much new writing and still be timely with the book) and printing of a mass-market paperback. In such a case, it is predictable that the shelf life of the book will be short, as little as a few weeks. In fact, it is unlikely that many will buy the book when the story has vanished from the newspapers and other news media. And that probability dictates that the book must be a mass market paperback, which is the least expensive book to manufacture and the lowest priced book.

Some subjects are, by their nature, likely to be of interest indefinitely. Basic books on various academic subjects, for example, and books that serve well as texts, are likely to be viable products on the shelf for a large number of years.

And there are others that fall between the two extremes, and are likely to be viable inventory for at least several years.

Inevitably, some books surprise everyone and do the unexpected, so that the book which was expected to be a front-list book—one that would sell well for a number of months (maybe even a best seller) and then go into a rapid decline and possibly early demise becomes a staple for some years, whereas the book expected to be back- or mid-list—sell unspectacularly but steadily for a long time—does something else. However, it is necessary to start with an assumption that a given book will fall into one of those classes.

Paper, Binding, and Cover Prices

Several factors, including expected shelf life and total number of sales anticipated, dictate how a book is to be printed and bound. There are three basic classes of books:

Clothbound, the traditional hardcover book
Trade paperbacks, the expensive paperback book
Mass market paperback, the pocket-size, cheapest type

Typically, clothcound books are books in which pages are collected in "signatures" of 32 pages and sewn together. The several signatures are then assembled, with cloth-covered stiff cardboards serving as covers. Quality varies widely, both in the paper (from expensive, glossy stock to less expensive "book paper") and in the covers.

Trade paperbacks are of much higher quality than mass market paperbacks, and may be manufactured very much as clothbound books are, except for the covers, even to the extent of sewn signatures, in some cases (but are more likely to be "perfect" bound, separate pages glued together).

Mass market paperbacks are the least costly, are printed on cheap pulp paper stock usually, in a small (pocket-size) format, typeset with very small margins, and sold at a price that requires quite a large sale to turn a profit on the book.

Many books are first printed in hard covers, then, if successful, in trade or mass market paperback when hard cover sales have begun to decline, and some books achieve such success that they become available in all three kinds of editions. Frequently, a publisher will produce a book in a trade paperback, as the main vehicle, but will print a limited quantity in hard covers as a "library edition."

All of these are matters of judgment, based on estimates of the book's appeal, the probable markets in which it will sell best, the price it will bring, the anticipated shelf life, the value of the author's name, and other factors.

Costs and Marketing Considerations

All of the costs and related considerations—those hidden costs and many risks—add up to a need for a rather substantial markup. For example, a selling price of approximately $20 on a book that costs perhaps $3 in actual manufacturing costs enables the publisher to allow substantial discounts, pay royalties, and recover initial investment. However, not all books are sold through dealers. Many books are sold primarily via other means, such as by mail or other "direct response" methods, in which the publisher sells directly to the consumer at the full cover price. Of course, the cost of doing so is relatively high, so the publisher may realize a greater *gross* profit, but no greater a *net* profit than by discounting to and selling via dealers. But there are other considerations, many of which are the principal decisive factors in how the book will be brought to market.

DIRECT-RESPONSE MARKETING

The chief reason for direct-response marketing is simply that some books, by their nature, do not sell well in bookstores: they are not books that are suitable candidates for "impulse buying"—that bookstore browsers are likely to pick off the shelves. It is difficult, for example, to sell textbooks, technical and professional books, and even many business books via typical bookstores. There are, however, campus bookstores and specialty book dealers who are exceptions to this and who do sell significant numbers of such books. For the most part, these kinds of books are sold most effectively by mail or other direct-response means. (Mail order is the chief direct-response medium for selling such books.) And there are several ways this is accomplished:

☐ The publisher often has a mail order department, and mails out appeals—usually offering a list of books, even an entire catalog—to a list of candidates. (Often, the mailing is of a "card deck," postage-paid 3 × 5-inch cards, one for each book, which can be returned as an order.)

☐ The publisher lists one or more books with marketing service firms who send out card decks and/or other direct-mail literature, under any of several possible arrangements.

☐ The publisher places advertisements in suitable publications, or allows bookstores an advertising allowance to do so and, usually, furnishes advertising copy.

☐ All book dealers will accept mail orders, and some have a regular trade in mail order. But there are some book dealers (e.g., B. Dalton) who make a concerted effort to sell by mail, and do a large portion of their business in that manner. And there are newsletter publishers and others who will handle certain books that appear to be suitable for their markets. They, too, may mail card decks, catalogs, or other literature.

☐ Publishers make deals with book clubs, some of whom specialize in technical or business books, and who sell by mail.

☐ Certain specialty books are sold through retail outlets other than bookstores or book dealers. Computer books, for example, are found in stores selling computers and related equipment and supplies.

Most publishers employ more than one means to sell or "distribute" books, and may very well sell books via all the promotions mentioned here, and perhaps even others.

CREATING AND SELLING YOUR OWN PRODUCTS

A great many speakers publish their own books, tape cassette albums, and other such products. Publishing, however, means something more than editing manuscripts and manufacturing books; it means, also, distribution—marketing the books. The self-publisher must have some means for doing that effectively, if the whole proposition is to be worth the trouble of writing and manufacturing the book to begin with. And there are at least three general ways of doing this:

☐ Having the books printed and bound (and/or other products manufactured), and making a deal with an established publisher and/or wholesaler-distributor (there are several such organizations) to handle "distribution."

☐ Any of the mail order methods described.

☐ Selling them in "back of the room" sales activity, following their talks or presentations to audiences. (This requires a sales presentation, of course, and requires that your client agrees to such a sale, if you are being paid by a client to appear, but there is rarely any difficulty here, if you handle the request discreetly.)

This latter is a favored approach by a great many speakers, and many of those state flatly that the sales ought to be at least equal to the speaking fee, to make the whole event worthwhile for them.

Art Fettig, an experienced and well-known professional speaker whom we have met earlier in these pages, is also president of his own firm, Growth Unlimited Inc., which publishes his books, including the one cited earlier, *How to Hold an Audience in the Hollow of Your Hand*, originally published by Frederick Fell, a New York publisher. Fettig is also the author of other books, booklets, albums, cassette tapes, and other such items.

Nido Qubein, that extraordinarily resourceful and successful speaker/consultant/entrepreneur offers a good bit of advice on the subject, and has a special twist, in which he cleverly combines the best of both worlds, getting his books published commercially by established publishers, while still gaining the profits of selling his own books at the end of his speaking engagements. Instead of getting the typical advance—perhaps $3000, in many cases— Nido has managed to persuade his publishers to give him the equivalent value—*at cost*—in printed copies of his books, so that he has, at the *cover price*, several times the value of the advance in the form of over a thousand copies of his book to sell at his presentations.

Dave Johnson, writing in Dottie Walter's *Sharing Ideas* periodical, says that he manages to sell an average of $35 worth of products (i.e., books and cassette tape albums) to each attendee at his seminars. He admits that he would never have thought it possible, but that more experienced professionals—his mentors—taught him how to do it.

Nido Qubein, however, in his peerless newsletter, *The NIDO QUBEIN LETTER, A Confidential Report for Speakers, Trainers, & Consultants,* has several other bits of sound advice and inside information to offer: For one thing, he offers advice on getting started by first preparing tape cassette albums—using your own presentations as material—and offering them. (They bring higher prices than do books.) Later, he says, you can use these tapes as the basis for books.

Of course, the same thing can be done with articles, as Hubert Bermont, publisher of *The Consultant's Library*, points out. Once you have had a sufficient number of articles published, you can assemble a related group and make a book of them, even if you have to do some slight rewriting or add a few words (such as a preface and a few transitions).

THE COOPERATIVE BOOK

Dottie Walters offers speakers an exceptional opportunity to acquire books of their own without writing more than a portion of the book. She publishes anthologies, which include chapters written by perhaps 15 different speakers. You can write a chapter of your own, agree to buy a certain minimum number of copies to sell as your own book, and get those copies with an individual dust jacket, featuring your own name and photo, thus having a book of your own to sell at your presentations. (See Figure 1.) Dottie has produced many of these books—does one each year, in fact.

Among the many anthologies Dottie has thus produced are *The Sunshiners, Star Spangled Speakers, Success Secrets, Positive Power People, The Great Persuaders, The Magnificent Motivators, The Man-*

FIGURE 1 Plan to become "author" of anthology.

agement Team, The Pearl of Potentiality, Here is Genius, and *Those Marvelous-Mentors.*

ON CREATING CASSETTE TAPES AND ALBUMS

There are two ways for speakers to produce cassette tapes: One is to record your presentations live, and the other is to record your presentations in a studio, under studio conditions. Obviously, the latter produces a much smoother and more professional tape. Unfortunately, the studio-recorded tape tends to lack the spontaneity of a live presentation, and sounds somewhat mechanical and dull. On the other hand, live recording comes off as somewhat amateurish, if not "cleaned up" by editing.

Again, Nido Qubein comes to the rescue with an original idea: He recommends that you do the studio recording, but insert segments recorded live—introducing each such segment as an example of something and advising the listener that you are dubbing in a live segment—and thus get the best of both worlds, the polished perfection of studio recording and the spontaneity of live presentation and audience reaction. Nido says that he has thus created over 100 tape cassettes.

Dottie Walters has also created tape cassette albums to sell to interested prospects, as have Dave Yoho, Earl Nightingale, and many other speakers. For many customers, tape albums appear to have more appeal than books do.

OTHER SELF-PUBLISHING

Books and cassettes are not the only items you can self-publish. There are many others. One that comes to mind immediately and is a popular item is the newsletter.

Newsletter Publishing

There are an estimated 30,000 or more newsletters published in the United States, by large publishing companies, by individual entrepreneurs, by associations, by public agencies, and by others. They are published for a variety of purposes, and in a variety of formats. Some are simple and inexpensive, others are quite "flossy" and costly.

The newsletter is relatively easy to publish, and is quite a versatile product. You can use a newsletter as a promotional giveaway, you can sell subscriptions, and you can use a newsletter to help sell many other things—books, cassettes, consulting services, training programs, speaking services, seminars, and whatever else you have to offer.

To publish a newsletter, as to publish anything else, you have to decide just what you want to accomplish and for whom (who are the readers to be and why they will find it worthwhile to subscribe). You have to decide where you will get your information. And you have to decide how you will market the newsletter.

Research Methods and Sources of Material

Even a small monthly newsletter requires a great deal of raw input material—information. You may only use from 3000 to 4000 words in each issue, but you will sort and sift through many thousands of words to select out that smaller quantity of information that is useful to you. And the ratio is even greater when you are writing an article or a book (unless you are basing your book on previous articles and presentations you have written and used). In typical cases, you are likely to use only 20 percent, at best, of the source material you research and review. That is, for every thousand words that appear in your final article or book, you will have probably gathered and studied some 5000 or more words of source material.

There are several ways to conduct research and gather source material. Here are the most common ones available for your use:

□ The public library

□ Other libraries and files to which you can gain access (such as those of government, university, associations and newspapers)

☐   The bookstores (Many writers, if not most, acquire the major portion of our libraries in the process of researching what has—and has not—been written on the subject before.)

☐   The well-stocked newsstand, and all the periodicals displayed there

☐   Interviews of suitable people, in person and by telephone

☐   Press releases and other such material, freely circulated by companies, associations, government offices, others

☐   Your own files and records

☐   *Guest articles.* Many individuals will be happy to write pieces for you, without payment, for the prestige of being published or for whatever reasons impel so many people to write articles free of charge.

☐   *Paid contributions.* Some newsletter publishers find it worthwhile to pay for contributed articles, and announce their solicitation of material in suitable writers' journals, such as the *Writer's Digest* and *The Writer*. (But there are a few others.) When you pay for contributions, you have the luxury of a great many more offerings from which to choose those you like best.

It's easy enough to get yourself on distribution for press releases and other material of interest; you need only to ask. A form letter, mailed out to government offices, companies, and other organizations likely to have information of interest, will soon bring you a flood of material. (See Figure 2 for a sample letter.)

You need also to read fairly widely, too, to keep abreast of what's happening in your field of interest, for many kinds of newsletters. You need to read your mail and respond to your readers; inquiries from readers will guide you to certain kinds of coverage required, and often readers' letters themselves furnish useful material. And you probably need to write some material "off the top of your head"—pass on your own knowledge, ideas, tips, and so forth, out of your own personal experience.

The quality of what you write depends heavily on the quantity and quality of the research you have done. In general, the greater the amount of useful and interesting detail you provide in whatever you write, the more useful and valuable the product is to the

HRH COMMUNICATIONS, INC.
P.O. Box 6067
Silver Spring, MD 20906
(301) 460-1506

NEWSLETTER PUBLISHER SEEKS HEALTH INDUSTRY INFORMATION

We are the publishers of HEALTH INDUSTRY NOTES, a monthly newsletter with a
substantial circulation among health professionals at all levels and in all
specialties. In producing the newsletter every month, we seek to bring our
readers accurate, complete, and up-to-date information about all happenings
in the health industry, including the activities of your own organization.

To help us advise our readers about your own activities, as well as those
generally in the industry, we request that you place us on distribution for
your press releases, special reports, brochures, photographs, and any other
other material which you wish to release for dissemination in the industry.

Thank you for your cooperation.

                                        Cordially,

                                        Herman Holtz
                                        Publisher

hrh:sg

FIGURE 2   A typical request for information.

reader, and that is a measure of its quality—not literary quality,
for that is of no concern here, but *value*, for that is the standard
by which it will be judged.

Special Reports

Once you have launched a newsletter, you have a vehicle for making other sales. Subscribers to newsletters are good prospects for

whatever else you have to offer, especially for special reports. Some newsletter publishers make little or no profit from their newsletters but find them the key to profits sold via the newsletter, such as reports written especially for subscribers. One key to the need—and opportunity—for a special report is your reader reaction to articles in your newsletter. If, for example, an article offering some ideas arouses a great deal of interest—lots of mail and inquiries from readers—there is a good chance that a special report, expanding coverage of that subject, will sell well.

One gentleman in Washington, D.C. (where a great many newsletters are produced every day) publishes a newsletter devoted to the public health field, and makes little or no profit on that newsletter. However, once a year he publishes a hardcover book written by his newsletter editor, and sells copies to virtually his entire list of newsletter subscribers, thereby generating enough income and turning enough profit to make the newsletter venture worthwhile, whether it produces much income and profit on its own or not.

These publications are reasonable enough extensions of your main service, inasmuch as they are simply additional ways of reaching your audiences, even of reaching people who are interested in what you have to say but are not able to be directly in attendance when you speak. But there is yet another way to reach audiences.

SEMINARS

Seminars have become both a popular way of learning certain, specialized skills and knowledge, and a steadily growing industry in the United States. That is not really surprising, in light of the many highly specialized, esoteric, and technological developments of modern times. It is increasingly difficult for anyone to gain a complete education via the classical routes today, as a result of the enormous—exponential—increase in knowledge. And the situation will not become easier, but will continue in the same pattern as far into the future as we can see, despite the development of more efficient ways of managing information and knowledge.

There has been a steady decline in the generalist in business and industry for a number of years; it is becoming increasingly difficult to find employment in any true career capacity unless you are a specialist of some sort. And that goes beyond being merely a lawyer, accountant, engineer, or other such professional: specialization requires being a specialist within the field. There are, for example, no general electronic engineers any more; one is a computer engineer, a communications engineer, or some other specialty within one's field, and even that is only the beginning. Before too long, each of those engineers is further narrowing the field of his or her specialization. Consequently, the vast increase in the popularity of seminars as a means of gaining special knowledge not ordinarily acquired in the normal channels of education.

Seminars are a means for passing highly specialized information and skills along to people who already are generally qualified in the field. Rene Gnam, for example, is a specialist in direct-mail methods, especially in preparing direct-mail copy, and he gives seminars to marketers in which he imparts to them his special knowledge, ideas, tips, hints, methods, and other valuable information. Nido Qubein conducts seminars in sales techniques and related subjects. Federal Publications offers seminars in federal contracting. Fred Pryor stages seminars in office practices. Howard Shenson produces seminars in the art of becoming a consultant. There are hundreds and hundreds of subjects and fields in which seminars are offered every year; these are only a few representative samples.

Most seminars are for one, two, or three days, although a few run for an entire business week (five days), and there are some that run for one-half day. Probably one day is the most popular because executives and professionals are not usually eager to be away from their offices for more than a day at a time, nor are employers who send employees to seminars especially eager to have them absent for several days. (Still, there are many two- and three-day seminars conducted successfully.)

There are two ways in which seminars are staged:

1. Open registration, which means that anyone is free to pay the registration fee and attend.

2. Custom or in-house, in which the seminar is conducted for a "captive" audience, such as employees.

Open Registration Seminars

To conduct an open-registration seminar, the producer must design the program, rent the meeting room, advertise, handle all the administrative detail, and conduct the session. There is some risk, the amount of dollar risk depending primarily on how much you invest in advertising, for the other expenses are not great— rental of the room and printing, primarily. And there are three ways to advertise the event and seek registrants:

1. Media advertising—newspaper and radio, primarily.
2. Direct mail—mailing a literature package out to mailing lists you have rented or acquired in some manner.
3. PR—public relations or publicity, which means sending out press releases to newspapers, newsletters, radio and TV stations, and other avenues of free advertising.

Which method will work best for you—and you should always try to get some free advertising, of course—depends primarily on who is to be your audience. If the seminar is one that helps employees become better employees—teaches job skills or other information/skills that benefit employers—employers will often send employees at company expense. In that case, a good approach to marketing the seminar is to get a mailing list of suitable companies in the area and mail literature and registration forms to them. Very much the same consideration applies to the case where the seminar is such that it offers useful business or professional skills to self-employed individuals (who actually constitute small businesses of course). However, if the session is such that it is likely to attract only people who must pay for their own registration, as individuals, media advertising is probably necessary because it is usually difficult to get mailing lists of individuals who would be good prospects for seminar registration.

The chief difference between these cases is, in fact, that difficulty of getting mailing lists. It is usually possible to rent mailing lists of large and small businesses (and, therefore, of self-employed individuals), but difficult to get good mailing lists of people who are private citizens and are being asked to attend a self-help seminar of some sort, such as one to help attendees lose weight, learn speed reading, or some other special training that is helpful to the individual but not to the employer.

Custom or In-house Seminars

Where the employer is in such a situation that there are a fairly large number of employees to be trained—perhaps 20 or more—it is often possible to sell the seminar to the employer as a package, to be conducted in-house (for the employees only) and even to be customized, in some cases. The organization may be a for-profit company, of course, and often is, but associations and other organizations also hire speakers to deliver seminars to employees and/or members (especially for such events as conventions). And in the case where you are customizing the material to suit the individual organization, your fees should reflect that work of customizing the material, as well as the presentation itself.

Seminar Materials

Seminar attendees should not leave the seminar empty-handed. Having spent an entire day—or even more time—in the session, they should have something to carry away, other than the notes they have made. And here are some of the kinds of handout materials you may consider:

☐ Individual sheets of paper, issued periodically during the session, containing exercises, answers to exercises, case histories, printed copies of slides or transparencies used during the session, photos, and other such material.

☐ A binder in which to assemble those many handouts

☐ A complete manual, which may be a summary of the session and/or include the same kinds of materials as described for individual handouts.

☐   A hardcover book you have written

☐   Copies of your newsletter

☐   Materials you have gotten from other sources, such as government brochures.

Materials you may use, other than the handout material, may include any of these:

☐   Slides, transparencies, filmstrips, or other audiovisuals

☐   Models

☐   Posters

Whether you charge separately for handout materials or include them in your price overall is a matter for your own decision; speakers have many different opinions about this. Of course, you do need to be compensated for these materials, one way or another. (And you should, as Nido Qubein would probably remind you, be sure to have your own identity and other offers plainly identified in some of those materials for the spin-off work you are likely to win.)

PRODUCING PRINTED MATERIALS

All the materials we have been discussing—books, newsletters, reports, manuals, handouts, and perhaps even other written and printed products must be produced in some manner, of course. Newsletters and special reports—even books—do not have to be formally typeset. They can be composed on a good electric typewriter or, even better, on a word processor, which gives you many added capabilities, such as right-justification of copy, boldface characters, and other refinements not normally available on a typewriter. Moreover, word processors make it far easier to make up copy—organize and reorganize material, fit copy to the space available, and otherwise do all the cut-and-paste operations electronically. If you are going to get seriously into these other income-producing activities, it would be wise to consider acquiring an inexpensive word processor.

WORD PROCESSORS

There is such as thing as a "dedicated" word processor, a piece of equipment that is truly dedicated to word processing—it does word processing well, but can do nothing else. However, most users today buy small, general purpose computers—commonly referred to as microcomputers, personal computers, and/or desktop computers—which are equipped with word-processing software (programs), and which can do all the other things that computers can do. (Except for those few truly dedicated word processors, the term *word processor* really refers to the word-processing software program, and not to the machine.) In fact, this is almost certainly a more effective approach for the small enterprise, especially one that will not use the system for word processing all day every day. In this approach, you can employ other programs in the system to do accounting, handle mailings, generate reports, and help with the marketing, too, as well as doing many other useful jobs to help you administer and manage your enterprises.

PART 4

MARKETING

Economic or entrepreneurial success in public speaking and its related enterprises, like success in most ventures, depends more on successful marketing than on any other single factor except, perhaps, persistence. (But persistence is an element of marketing properly.) Marketing is more important, even, and has more to do with being successful than does talent and other virtues. Marketing properly and persistently all but guarantees your success.

CHAPTER 10

MARKETING YOUR SPEAKING SERVICES

The *methods* of marketing yourself as a speaker must be special—different than marketing soap and automobiles. But the basic *principles* of marketing and selling are the same. The first step in successful marketing is to understand them. The second step is to apply them.

WHAT IS MARKETING?

A great many people believe that marketing and selling are the same thing—that the two words are synonymous. But although they are closely related in many ways, there are distinct and important differences. In practice, selling follows marketing and may even be considered to be the final act of marketing, although for purposes of explanation it is helpful to discriminate carefully between the two and consider them to be completely separate functions. In any case, marketing is everything that goes before that act of getting the order, and prepares the way for making the sale. Marketing is what makes it possible to get the order. In fact, the difficulty or ease with which you get orders—speaking engagements, that is—is tied directly to how effectively you carried out the marketing functions.

Perhaps even more important, marketing is deciding what orders you should pursue and win, as well as how to do so and how to prepare to do so.

SOME BASIC PRINCIPLES OF SELLING

The Promise

The most basic principle of selling lies in the promise. And the promise is your claim as to what the item you are selling, whether product or service, will *do* for the customer. In the final analysis, the customer does not really care about anything else except the all-too-human "what's in it for me?" question. No one is ever overjoyed to part with money, which is the symbol of security in our world, and the entire art of selling is the art of persuading the prospect that what you offer is worth more than the money— more desirable to have than the money. But the only effective way to do that, ordinarily, is to promise the customer something the customer wishes very much to believe, and somehow persuade the customer to accept and believe the promise.

That means that the promise must be one that provides an

emotional appeal. Whether we like to admit it to ourselves or not, all our buying decisions are emotionally motivated. You may buy an automobile because you need an automobile, but the model you select is almost surely one that appeals to you emotionally. For example, if you buy the big luxury model, it is probably an act of ego gratification, doing something to impress others (or perhaps even yourself), perhaps by "proving" that you can do anything that your brother-in-law can do, and you may be "proving" it to yourself, even more than to others. And if you buy the least expensive model, it may well be fear that you cannot afford anything more costly, and perhaps trepidation about ability to keep up the payments, unless they are the smallest possible ones, or even a great reluctance to spend more than the minimum necessary. (Even well-to-do people often buy the least costly automobile.)

Good salespeople probe gently until they are able to judge what your most basic concerns or desires are, and then they steer the sales appeal to those concerns and desires. Consider how Madison Avenue (the advertising experts, that is) structure the appeals in the well-known TV commercials:

☐ Selling beer: Almost invariably the commercial sells, not beer, but the promise (by clear implication) of fun, good times on the beach and at the neighborhood tavern. A few sell the macho image, which is another promise, but still an emotional appeal. And some sell "light beer" as acceptable to those trying to lose weight, still another emotional appeal. "Good beer" is strictly a secondary argument, lightly stressed, not because it is difficult to prove, but because it won't sell beer.

☐ "Ring around the collar": This hardy perennial is obviously most effective—its long life proves that. The basic appeal is fear—fear of embarrassment—and the promise is that the product will prevent that embarrassment.

☐ Insurance: Fear is the most often used motivator in selling insurance, for the obvious reason that most insurance is conceived as a hedge against disasters. The promise is to take the major pain—financial ruin or, at least, financial hardship—out of such disasters. A variant is the more general promise of security, as symbolized by the Rock of Gibraltar, a more general but still

highly emotional and effective appeal, since we all have some in-
securities about something or other.

☐ Greeting cards: That most famous manufacturer of greeting cards appeals to your vanity—"when you care enough to send
the very best"—and the affection you have for those to whom
you normally send cards. Highly emotional, with the promise that
you are sending "the very best," with its broad implication that you
should feel guilt if you send anything less than that alleged very
best. Again, a fear/worry item (of guilt) introduced.

There are two basic emotions that underlie most effective selling and advertising: greed and fear. Not greed in the usual sense
of avarice, but in the sense of ardent desire for benefits. (Advertising experts and sales trainers use that term "benefits" to
identify those splendid results that must be promised in a sales
appeal.) Those much-to-be-desired results, however, are at least
equaled as a motivating force by fear—by appeals which are
promises to avoid or overcome that which is to be feared. In fact,
there is a great deal of evidence that fear is an even more effective
motivator than greed.

Worry Items

Expert writers of proposals are well aware of the fear motivation
and its effectiveness. In writing proposals, marketing specialists
often search for something called the "worry item"—that which
appears to be the major concern or worry the customer has. If
you can determine what that worry item is, you can structure your
entire sales appeal to it, to an argument that you hope will convince your prospect that your proposal is the one most likely to
cope successfully with that feared event or condition.

On the other hand, if you cannot find such an item—perhaps
because the customer has not thought things out and is not aware
of the hazards or possibilities for disaster—you may wish to employ the sales strategy of creating a worry item, of giving the customer a worry item by searching out that which, you believe, *ought*
to concern and worry the customer, and then offering the solution
in your proposal. This has been a successful sales strategy for

many organizations, and is the basis for many sales presentations in use today. Consider, for example, how many insurance companies dramatize the possibilities of disasters to give prospects worry items preparatory to selling policies.

Proof

Most people in today's society are not naive. Modern schooling, newspapers and magazines, radio, movies, and TV—especially TV—have made even those in the most rural areas relatively sophisticated. Most people today are sophisticated enough to question and doubt unsupported claims. If you claim that your detergent cleans more effectively than any other, a certain number of prospects will give it a try because it doesn't cost much to verify or disprove your claim. But not many people will buy an automobile to test your claim; that's too expensive an item to buy casually. Few, if any, will accept that much risk without lengthy and thorough investigation. They want some proof that your claim is valid—that you can and will make good on your promise, that is. Even in the case of that inexpensive detergent, a great many more people will buy some to put it to the test, if you help them believe your claim by furnishing some proof. For that is what "proof" is, in this case: that which will help the customer believe your promise. The promise is something the customer wants to believe, but you have to help with some kind of reassurance that the claims are true and the promise a valid one that you will deliver on.

In this case, proof is not what a court of law would require under the rules of evidence, of course. It's not even what a grand jury would require as enough evidence to indict. It is whatever the customer will accept as proof or persuasive evidence. Bear that in mind: we are concerned, in marketing, with the customer's perceptions, nothing else.

With that qualification, let's look at what kinds of evidence are offered for some of those TV commercials used earlier as examples:

☐ *Selling beer* Most commonly, the evidence consists of dramatizations of people—actors—drinking the product and having a good time. Occasionally, a well-known public figure, such as an entertainer or sports figure, offers a testimonial. Not very good evidence, you say? Perhaps not, but it's what viewers will accept, and so it's effective, especially if and when the testimonial is offered by someone the viewers like or admire, and *want* to believe.

☐ *Ring around the collar* The evidence here is also dramatization, with many of the scenes showing embarrassment in public—the worry item—followed by the "white knight" galloping to the rescue with the product that cures the trouble. It has conflict, suspense, a villain, a victim, and a hero or heroine: all the elements of drama. Here, the proof is cumulative, inasmuch as the characters—actors—change frequently, which is another good tactic for an extended campaign. Repetition and the cumulative effect it inspires is itself accepted by many as evidence.

☐ *Insurance* The evidence here is, again, dramatization, often of real cases, in which the burned-down home is exhibited, along with the story of the help. Again, drama—villain, victim, conflict, suspense, hero, and rescue. And this is a more valid proof, when actual cases are used, even though actors reenact the scenes.

Fortunately for most marketers, prospects do not require a great deal of proof or evidence, nor do they ponder much over how valid the evidence is. The real key to this is desire: the customer wants to believe the promise, and is thus eager to accept as sound evidence just about anything that appears even plausible.

HOW THIS RELATES TO MARKETING

It is not possible to create a single sales appeal that will work effectively with everyone. The sales presentations and arguments that sell Volkswagens will not sell Continentals. There are Volkswagen-type customers, and there are Continental-type customers, and if you sell Volkswagens you have to attract Volkswagen-type customers to your sales presentations. That's marketing, or a part of marketing, at least. You have to decide who Volkswagen-type buyers are, where and how to find them, where and how to get them into your showroom so that you can make your sales presentations. That's part of marketing too, a large part of it.

But marketing started even earlier. It started when you decided to go into the automobile retailing business and open a showroom. You had to decide then what kind of automobiles you would handle—if not what specific make, at least what general type (e.g., price level). You should have also decided on general marketing strategies, too, such as how you would address the problem of giving prospects a reason for favoring you over competitors. Price is, of course, perhaps the most commonly used sales argument and appeal in the automobile business: virtually every dealer promises best trade-in allowances and lowest prices, so there is not much appeal in those promises, unless you can find some special way to be more believable than your competitors. One way might be to stress service, especially fast service, free loaners for jobs that take more than a few hours, and other appeals. (Here, again, think out the typical worry items of people who buy automobiles, and try to find ways to counter them.) Successful marketing is based on successful strategies.

Marketing, then, includes deciding what you will sell, to whom you will sell it, and how you will reach your prospects so that you could do your selling, as well as deciding on general marketing/sales strategies, and otherwise preparing to begin making sales.

HOW THIS RELATES TO SELLING YOUR SPEAKING SERVICES

Before you get to the last page of this book, you will perceive that all of this applies to you, too, as the chief marketer of your own services and, if you choose to do back-of-the-room and other sales, marketer of those items which are the byproducts of your speaking. The methods by which you will sell your services and products will be different than those by which you would sell automobiles, beer, or greeting cards, but the principles will be the same: You will have to do your marketing effectively, and then do the selling effectively. If you master the principles and apply them properly to your own situation, you will find success, inevitably.

Such is the power of marketing and selling, when they are done well.

MARKETING AND SALES METHODS

Entrepreneurs go to market in many ways: directly to consumers, via retail establishments; indirectly, via wholesalers and distributors; by mail and other direct-response methods; through agents and brokers of various kinds; and even by sundry other means. Let's consider a few of these ways, especially the use of agents and brokers, because they are so visible in the speaking profession.

AGENTS AND BROKERS

The role of middlemen—agents and brokers—has long been an honorable one in world trade and commerce generally. They are known by a variety of names, some of which reflect what they deal in: author's agent, manufacturers' representative, stockbroker, real estate agent, finder, talent agent, printing broker, and lecture bureau, to name a few. Their role is to be the go-between, point of contact, and/or finder of buyers and/or sellers. The finder, for example, is an individual who may be retained by a buyer to find property, scarce goods, a source of financing, or something else, and is paid a fee—usually some small percentage—if and when successful in the mission. However, the finder may be retained by a seller to find a buyer for any of those or other commodities, again for a commission of some sort.

The chief difference between a finder and broker or agent is simply that finding is usually a onetime function for someone who happens to have something to sell or wants to buy something as a unique situation, not to be repeated, in all probability. An agent, broker, or representative, on the other hand, usually represents buyers or sellers on a regular basis or, at least, with some consistency.

Such agents generally represent either the buyers or the sellers. A real estate agent usually represents the sellers—the seller pays the commission out of the sale price—rather than the buyers, as does the manufacturers' representative. The talent agent may be retained by an actor or other entertainer, and will represent the entertainer, usually—again representing the seller. Stockbrokers, however, are agents of the buyers: the buyers pay commissions for the service.

There is one other factor in the relationship among the three parties represented by the brokerage function: In many such relationships there is no service beyond that of arranging the exchange—bringing buyer and seller together (in theory, at least, since in many cases the two never actually meet), whereas in others there is a close, ongoing relationship. A stockbroker, for example, is often expected by clients to provide the additional service of advice on what and when to buy and sell. And a real estate agent is expected to be helpful to buyers and prospective buyers, even though commissions are paid by the sellers.

LECTURE BUREAUS AND THEIR ROLE

It is fairly well known that an author's agent represents the author and is usually the exclusive agent of that author, representing the author in all marketing and other business affairs dealing with that authorship. And a great many writers who are not thoroughly experienced labor under the delusion that all it takes to get their books accepted by publishers is to persuade a first-class agent to represent them.

Probably most of those who are unfamiliar with the public speaking field are under a somewhat similar impression that a speaker signs an exclusive agreement with a lecture bureau, and that the chief key to finding early success as a speaker—getting all the speaking engagements one wants, that is—is to be the client of a first-class speaker's bureau or lecture agent. But unfortunately, that is virtually a reversal of the facts on all counts: Celebrity speakers may negotiate exclusive agreements—and they are generally "in the driver's seat" when they do so because they are in demand—but they are the typical exception to the rule. Other than for that sole exception, the lecture bureau and the speaker do not have an exclusive agreement between them; the lecture bureau, in fact, usually does not represent the speaker at all, and the chief key to becoming the client of the biggest and best speaker's bureaus is to be a success already—to be in demand as a speaker. (That does not mean that you must be a celebrity speaker; you may be very much in demand as a professional public speaker, and yet be almost completely unknown to the public at large and to anyone not directly interested in public speaking as a participant or customer. In fact, the true professionals in the business, both the speakers and the booking agents, do not consider many of the celebrity speakers to be professional speakers at all, if they do not make public speaking an important and permanent part of what they do professionally.)

Sometimes the question of distinguishing between the speaker's agent and the Speaker's Bureau arises, and when someone wrote to Dottie Walters and asked her what she thought the difference was, she replied in her *Sharing Ideas!* periodical that speaker/agent Mike Frank, had provided an answer to that, using the new Code of Ethics adopted by the National Speakers Association Special Interest Group in Las Vegas. According to Dottie's reply, Mike Frank defined agents as those who work for one, two, or at least a limited group of speakers (represent the speakers, that is, on some kind of exclusive basis), whereas bureaus work for buyers (represent the buyers, as noted earlier) and supply anyone they can. (For our purposes here, we are generally referring to the definition given for a speaker's bureau, no matter what designations are used to identify the bureau in these pages, as the next paragraph will make clear.)

The speaker's bureau is not [normally] the agent of the speaker, but is usually the agent of the customer—the organization who wishes to engage a speaker and who will pay the speaking fees out of which the bureau will collect a commission. It is that customer, not the speaker, who is the client of the lecture bureau—whom the lecture bureau represents and must please. Typically, where an author's agent represents the interests of the author, a lecture bureau represents the interests of the buyer. The buyer ap-

proaches the lecture bureau with either a specific kind of speaker
or specific individual speaker in mind, and asks the lecture bureau to find and engage that individual speaker. Customers send
lecture bureaus in quest of such well-known platform luminaries
as Art Linkletter and Norman Vincent Peale, and such in-demand
speakers often have personal managers or agents who work with
the lecture bureaus and attend to all the details of their engagements.

On the other hand, if the customer does not have a specific
individual in mind, the lecture bureau will usually make recommendations, according to the kind of speaker the customer wants,
what the customer is prepared to spend, and other considerations.

For this reason, few speakers and lecture bureaus have exclusive agreements between them; they have either general, nonexclusive agreements or they sign agreements individually for each
booking. And, in fact, even then the agreements are quite informal and stipulate little beyond the bare essentials of the engagement. In fact, quite a number state flatly that while they do take
the trouble to list themselves with a number of lecture bureaus,
they get most of their speaking engagements through their own
marketing efforts.

It's interesting to note that in a number of cases of small lecture
bureaus the owner-operator of the lecture bureau is the chief
client of the bureau also. This is one method of self-marketing
that many speakers employ.

COSTS OF BEING REPRESENTED: FEES AND COMMISSIONS

Lecture bureaus, like other kinds of brokers and agents, work on
a commission basis, which is often a percentage of the fee paid the
speaker, but may be a figure added to the speaker's normal fee,
depending on surrounding circumstances. Not surprisingly, since
the fee structure is so flexible and ranges so widely, the rates upon
which commissions are based also vary widely, according to several factors. Most commission rates start at approximately 25 per-

cent of the fee, range to 35 percent, according to Bob Montgomery's estimates, in which a great many others concur generally. Dan T. Moore, of the venerable International Platform Association, points out, however, that in the case of celebrities who are very much in demand (and who command extraordinarily high rates, as a result), commissions may run as little as 10 or 15 percent. That's because those speakers can dictate their terms, and because even 10 percent of a very large speaking fee is a goodly sum. Others make the same point about commissions on booking celebrities. And one agency reports that their commissions are 25 percent on speaking fees to $5000, but drop to 20 percent on fees ranging above that. So there is only a rather rough uniformity in fees and commissions, but there are some approximate standards.

SHOULD YOU SIGN WITH A BUREAU?

You can apply to lecture bureaus for listing as a speaker, if you wish to. If you have some experience and can command at least $500 minimum for a speech—and if you provide such bona fides and marketing materials as are usually considered necessary— you will probably be accepted, especially by those who charge a registration fee. (Registering new speaker does involve some costs.) Whether this will bring you bookings is another matter: By now you should be aware that by far the majority of professional speakers who are not national celebrities do the bulk of their own marketing and find their own bookings, although there are exceptions. (E.g., if you have some unusual qualification, and it is in a field or subject that has great appeal, you may become such an exception.) In the typical case, you will—ultimately—get some of your bookings through bureaus, but like most of the others, if you can manage to stay busy as a speaker it will be largely through your own marketing efforts.

The answer to the question, then, is yes, you should sign with several bureaus, and supply them with suitable marketing materials (which we will consider in detail in the next chapter) then go on to market yourself just as vigorously as you can.

SOME BEGINNING TACTICS IN SELF-MARKETING

As in the case of consulting and consulting services, marketing success depends largely on image and reputation. Media advertising and typical promotional materials are needed, but will rarely do the job alone; they are most effective when they are combined with image- and reputation-building marketing activities. Of course, you can do all the media advertising and get some results from it. Will Jordan, who is at least as much a professional entertainer as he is a public speaker, advertises his services in business magazines as a mimic/impressionist of General George S. Patton, and since he continues to run those advertisements, we must conclude that they produce bookings for him. (However, he has been a professional entertainer for many years, and probably has many credentials to support and reinforce his advertisement, when he gets inquiries, so his example probably does not have application to most others.)

The way a beginner gets started, usually, is by being seen and heard by those who hire speakers, and there are at least two ways to accomplish this feat:

1. Speak as often as possible in as many places as possible, for whatever is offered, even if you must speak only for the practice and exposure—without payment, that is. Even professionals who are earning good fees for speaking still do some free speeches.

2. Enroll for as many showcases as possible. (More on this presently.)

FINDING OPPORTUNITIES TO SPEAK

To further facilitate getting experience and to help uncover speaking opportunities join associations. Most of those professionals I questioned are members of NSA (the National Speakers Association) and all are emphatic in urging beginners to join a local chapter of NSA. (In fact, that and the advice to speak as often as possible, to get practice, were the most common urgings of all the professionals.) But there are other speakers associations, too, and there are many other kinds of associations—professional societies and trade associations, for example—and belonging to any association provides opportunities to speak—to *volunteer* to speak, at meetings, at conventions, at seminars, at symposia, and at just about all such gatherings.

On the other hand, you do not have to be a member of an association to be invited to speak before the membership. In my own case, I have been invited to speak before a great many association events, some of them meetings of a small, local association, meeting in a private home, after business hours. On other occasions, I have been invited to address a large assemblage in a large hall during the business day, and often without fee in both cases.

Every community has some local groups, some business associations, some social or community groups, and other organizations that represent opportunities to speak, sometimes with small fees, sometimes without fee, but always with the opportunity to gain valuable experience and exposure, two absolutely vital ingredients of your investment in a successful career in public speaking. However, before you can make even the first moves, you must do some preliminary work.

FIRST STEPS IN PREPARATION

The first thing you must do is a market analysis, but even before that you must first make some preliminary decisions—to decide for yourself what general class of speaker you are or are to be. There are, in fact, at least two factors to consider here: content and style. You might, for example, teach or speak about quite serious subjects, and yet have a humorous or light style. But let's look first at the kinds of content you might opt for. Here is a starter list, and one that is only general:

Entertainment
Inspiration

Self-help
Skills training
Sales training

There is also the matter of style, and your style might be one of the following:

Humorous
Comic
Laid back
Wildly enthusiastic
Didactic

Let's consider what these mean by discussing each a bit.

CONTENT

Entertainment

You may, of course, be a stage magician, a musician, a dancer, or some other type of entertainer, but we'll restrict the use of the term here to that of humor, since we are concerned primarily with verbal or oratorical delivery. And if humor is your field, you may be any of three general types: humorist, comedian, or comic. Let's define each one briefly:

A comic is someone who strives for loud and sustained laughter by a combination of humorous patter, characterizations, and/or "sight gags," including as laughter-provoking "props" funny hats, baggy pants, exploding cigars, and other such things.

A comedian also wants loud and sustained laughter, but depends on verbal devices—funny stories primarily, sometimes accompanied by facial gestures and accents, to create characterizations—including mimicry or "impressions." (The well-known professional mimic/impressionist Will Jordan was cited earlier as one such example.)

A humorist amuses the audience, although not necessarily provoking true "belly laughter," and often speaking on some serious subject, but finding at least occasional humor in the subject.

Inspiration

There are many inspirational speakers, speakers whose appeal is designed to inspire listeners to greater achievements, perhaps in personal matters or in business affairs. Such speakers are always sincere, enthusiastic, and quite often charismatic. (In fact, charisma is almost a necessity to succeed as an inspirational speaker.)

Self-help

Self-help is closely related to inspirational speaking, in many cases. Basically, it includes such things as developing positive mental attitudes, learning how to cope with personal problems, and coping with the complex and frustrating world generally.

Skills Training

Skills training is a broad field, generally includes more or less formal sessions—classrooms and/or seminars—to develop specific abilities that will be useful on the job or in personal life, such as typing, "computer literacy," shorthand, speed reading, and dozens of other such subjects, academic, vocational, and avocational.

Sales Training

Sales training is quite a large and opportunity-filled field for the speaker who is good at training others in sales techniques. Sales training generally includes inspirational elements, skills training elements, and perhaps even self-help and humorous elements, but because it is so popular a subject, it merits its own special classification.

STYLE

As you may have guessed, by now, it is not always easy to separate style from content. "Humor," for example, describes a style as well as a content, as does "inspiration." It is necessary, however, to decide what your style is and what your content is to be, if you are to decide what your logical market is. A light and humorous approach may be a great help—appealing to the clients—in some cases, but a complete turn-off in others.

CHOOSING STYLE AND CONTENT

The choice of what you will offer, in both style and content, should not be arbitrary. It should be dictated by what you are expert in, as far as content is concerned. Or, if you choose a topic that you ardently prefer to speak on but do not believe yourself to be a true authority, get busy and make yourself an authority. Research, read, study whatever you can find on the subject. Buy books or borrow them from the library. Subscribe to appropriate newsletters and magazines. Study the subject until you *feel confident* that you are totally knowledgeable—a master in the subject. Only then are you ready to speak publicly about it, because your audience expects you to be totally knowledgeable in the subject you elect to speak on.

You cannot be arbitrary in choosing a style, either; it must be one that is natural to you and that you are comfortable with. It is most assuredly not necessary to be a comedian or even a humorist, for example, contrary to naive opinion. Humorists—good humorists—are always in demand, but that's because good humorists are rare, and the effort to force yourself to be a humorist, when the style is not a "natural" one with you, is almost surely destined to result in disaster.

The same thing may be said for all other styles of delivery. There are many successful and in-demand speakers who rarely provide laughter, but are prized because they are interesting, either in their style or in their content, and often in both.

CONTENT VERSUS DELIVERY

It's interesting to read opinions about which is more important, style or content, and the consensus appears to be that style is more critical to success than content is. It's probably true that a speaker with a good enough style—delivery, that is—can liven up even dull material, while a dull speaker will not become much more interesting, even with excellent material. I suspect, however, that this is not an invariable truth, but depends frequently on the kinds of audiences and kinds of occasions. Obviously, you should strive to have both good material and good delivery, but make it material that you are truly authoritative about and a style that is naturally yours and that you are entirely comfortable with.

MAKING THE MARKET MATCHES

Once you have made your basic decisions about style and content, you can next analyze your market—decide what kinds of prospects are most likely to want to hear what you have to say. And that is not an easy task, for again, there are no easy answers, nor can you make arbitrary decisions here, either. What you have developed in the preliminary analyses of your proper content and style dictate the market segments which are suitable for you. For example, if you are a sales trainer, you may conduct seminars at sales meetings or conventions. This is serious business delivering some serious training content, which should be delivered with great enthusiasm—what would unenthusiastic presentation of sales training be? But you must have some credentials as an expert in that field and as a trainer; if you are a mime or a comedian, sales training is not a market for you. On the other hand, if you have been invited to be the luncheon speaker at such a conclave, your client may well want something entirely humorous, as a complete break in the more serious business of the day.

It is necessary, then, to study the many kinds of speaking occasion and determine which ones are a fit for you, and which ones are not.

MARKET ANALYSIS WORKSHEET

Figure 3 is a worksheet, designed to help you analyze what you have to offer and what your proper market targets are or should

CONTENT		CONTENT (Cont'd)	
ENTERTAINMENT		SALES TRAINING	[ ]
Comic	[ ]	_____	[ ]
Comedian	[ ]	_____	[ ]
Humorist	[ ]	_____	[ ]
_____	[ ]		
_____	[ ]	**DELIVERY STYLE**	
INSPIRATION		HUMOROUS	[ ]
Positive thinking	[ ]	COMIC	[ ]
_____	[ ]	LAID BACK	[ ]
_____	[ ]	ENTHUSIASTIC	[ ]
_____	[ ]	DIDACTIC	[ ]
SELF-HELP		_____	[ ]
Auto-suggestion	[ ]	**MARKETS**	
Sensitivity trng	[ ]	LUNCHEONS/DINNERS	[ ]
_____	[ ]	SALES MEETINGS	[ ]
_____	[ ]	TRAINING SEMINARS	[ ]
		COLLEGES	[ ]
SKILLS TRAINING		CRUISE SHIPS	[ ]
Personal	[ ]	CONVENTIONS	[ ]
Office skills	[ ]	ASSOCIATION MEETINGS	[ ]
Computer literacy	[ ]	_____	[ ]
_____	[ ]	_____	[ ]
_____	[ ]	_____	[ ]

NOTES: _____

FIGURE 3 Marketing analysis worksheet.

be. There are three broad categories—the kind of content you have to offer, your delivery style, and the potential markets the combination of content and style best fits.

It is, of course, not possible to list all possible categories and nuances here, but some suggested ones are offered as starters, and blanks are provided in each case for your own additions.

CREATING SPEAKING OPPORTUNITIES

You can, of course, wait for opportunities to speak to happen along, and one will happen along occasionally. However, there are serious drawbacks to waiting for chance to favor you. It is possible to mount a campaign that will create opportunities to speak often, so that you will gain some experience and even get paid a fee now and then—or at least an honorarium. Here is one way to assemble a program and put it to work.

First make up a letter (see Figure 4 for example), preferably on a business letterhead, if you have one, explaining your offer. List some credentials, including books, articles, references, and whatever else you can summon up to add to your credibility.

Make up a mailing list, including local associations and local branches of national associations (you can find them listed in your local telephone directory), local colleges and universities, local government agencies, and local offices of federal and state government agencies. Address your letter to the chief executive (e.g., the president, manager, or director) of the organization. (That individual will see that your letter gets into the right hands.)

There are some small associations that are not listed in the telephone directory because they are strictly neighborhood groups, are often made up of members who have daytime jobs and who meet in a member's home, and have virtually no treasury. Here are some of the types of associations that meet this description:

Computer clubs	Writers' groups
Toughlove groups	Parent peer groups
Recreational groups	Neighborhood big-brother type clubs

Herman Holtz
Proposal Consultant

P.O. Box 6067
Silver Spring, MD 20906
(301) 460-1506

In the course of pursuing my profession as a consultant in marketing to government agencies, and especially in the art of developing winning proposals for government contracts, I make many addresses to interested organizations, large and small. And despite the fact that I am customarily a paid speaker, when the occasion appears to warrant it and my schedule permits, I often address organizations as a public service.

My presentation is primarily a "how-to," for those who want to learn something of how to succeed in this special field (a market counted in hundreds of billions of dollars), although there are a number of rather amusing stories I tell, too, since the bureaucracy does do some ironic and humorous things.

My credentials include a great many years experience in this field, as a proposal specialist, as a Director of Marketing, and as a General Manager, winning and performing on government contracts in both technological and other fields. I am also the author of several books on marketing subjects generally and on government marketing especially.

I have spoken before the members of numerous national associations, to groups of government executives, and to the staffs of many companies, on these subjects. (Names on request.)

At the present, there is some time available in my schedule, and I would be entirely willing to consider addressing your group in the near future as a public service. Please feel free to write or call to discuss and make suitable arrangements.

                                        Cordially,

                                        Herman Holtz

hh:sg

FIGURE 4   Suggested format for form letter.

To find these groups, you should watch the bulletin boards in supermarkets, town halls, public libraries, and other such places, as well as local newspaper columns that provide free listings of meetings of such groups. (Most newspapers do.) And you can use some of these "media"—especially bulletin boards—to post your own notices of your availability.

You should get some inquiries. There are always organizations who want speakers, and many of them cannot afford to do more than buy the speaker's meal; some cannot even afford a small honorarium.

STILL, YOU DO NOT NECESSARILY HAVE TO WORK FOR NOTHING

Despite all of this, and despite all admonitions to accept—even to solicit and seek out—all speaking dates for the tiniest of fees and even no fees at all, you need not necessarily work for nothing. For one thing, you should be charging the work off to gaining experience and marketing, and it is probably among the most economical marketing you will ever get. But if you have developed books, newsletters, cassettes, and/or other items for which you can charge dollars, you can still earn a good day's pay by selling these things at your free speaking engagements. Even experienced pros who can get full speaking fees admit that they sometimes speak without fee because they can sell a great many of their products to their listeners.

GUESTING AT SEMINARS

Many seminars use panels of speakers, and producers of seminars which are relevant to your own field (if your material fits into seminar presentations) may be interested in having you make presentations, and will probably even pay you an honorarium. Get yourself on mailing lists—it's quite easy; just send in some of those coupons in *Training* magazine and other trade journals which are relevant to your field—and you'll soon be getting seminar announcements in your daily mail. But let your friends and acquaintances know of your interest, too, and they'll send you the seminar announcements and brochures they receive. (It was, in fact, my own free guesting on a seminar panel that started me in public speaking for fees.)

A FEW CASE HISTORIES

Dottie Walters' *Sharing Ideas!* is a treasure chest of case histories on the subject of getting started in speaking. Here are a few typical tales from a few of Dottie's many readers:

Will Robertson was inspired to want to become a speaker after hearing Mark Victor Hansen speak. He joined the NSA and for a solid year Robertson spoke without asking for money, attended NSA's winter workshop. Then he finally summoned up enough confidence and courage to ask for the princely sum of $35! And he claims to have learned that a speaker's fees are based on (1) the value of what the speaker has to say, and (2) how easily the program chairperson can replace the speaker for someone else for less money.

William T. Brooks also urges all who would succeed in this field to speak at the drop of a hat, even if you have to drop the hat yourself. Speak anywhere, anytime, for any fee (even a thank-you), but always on your own subject. Never compromise with quality of presentation, that means, as you will if you venture to talk on a subject in which you are not totally qualified. And, also, counsels Brooks, be sure that you learn how to sell. (If you believe that selling is "beneath" you, he says, choose another profession.) And he has more, much more, to say in the same vein. Significantly, he reports that learning these things are what brought him from doing only 20 part-time speaking dates in 1980 to 150 annual engagements for full fees only two years later.

San Jose TV star "Tish" Morgan says it her own way. No one will book you for paid speeches, she says, until you become well known, and no agent really wants to handle you until clients begin asking for you. So speak free of charge, sell your books and tapes, do your own publicity, and keep slogging away at it.

Note the emphasis on learning to sell and selling at your presentations, whether free or not. It's an important element of the business, and all the professionals are agreed on that.

But even these are not all of the many ways you can prepare for the big day when you find yourself a true professional and ready to stake out and claim your own position in the profession, nor is it the only way to market yourself. You should learn about showcases too, one of the ways many speakers who have served their apprenticeships and mastered their craft—have become reasonably proficient and professional in their presentations—find their best opportunities to propel themselves into the mainstream of the profession by attracting the attention of the leading meeting and program planners. For as in show business, the competition is so great that even an absolutely superb performer can be undetected—not "discovered"—by the "big league" meeting planners for a long time. Don't believe that old adage about building a better mousetrap: it is highly unlikely that the world will ever beat a path to your door, no matter how good your mousetrap is, if you do not seize the initiative and show them the way. You have to go out and do something about *marketing* your better mousetrap, and showcases are one excellent way of doing so, once you are ready to climb the steps and stand alongside the true professionals of the platform.

SHOWCASES

A showcase is a conclave where meeting planners can observe speakers, trainers, and related talent in action, and the performers can show their wares and do some of their most productive marketing. There are a number of showcases available each year. These are organized occasions when, if you get yourself on the program, you will be heard by people who hire speakers. A successful appearance on a good showcase can be your launching pad, as it has for many speakers who are today great successes in their field. One such event, for example, is the annual Professional Speakers Showcase, produced by the Success Leaders Speakers Service, a division of Jordan Enterprises, of Atlanta,

Georgia. It is advertised as an event held principally for the benefit of meeting planners, inasmuch as it gives those planners a week-long opportunity to preview a large number of speakers and other talent used in meetings and related programs.

The speakers who appear run the gamut, in terms of experience, status, and reputation, with many of them well known to the public, others well known only within the circle of those connected directly with the profession, and some relative newcomers and relatively unknown. For example, among those who Jordan Enterprises offer as available talent of their lecture bureau (and many of whom have also appeared on the platform at one or more of their annual showcases) have been Mel Blanc, the well-known voice of many Hollywood cartoon characters (e.g., Porky Pig and Donald Duck), former President Gerald Ford, newsman Irving R. Levine, and entertainer/wit Mark Russell. Zig Ziglar, Buster Crabbe, Nido Qubein, Cavett Robert, Ira Hayes, Will Jordan, Dave Yoho, Marguerite Piazza, and Jeanne Robertson are also among those who have made presentations at this annual showcase event in Atlanta.

The event usually is surmounted by special meetings and seminars conducted by such experts as Nido Qubein outside the showcase hours (the weekend before or after the showcase or during the evenings, after hours). These special events offer both newcomers and seasoned professionals the opportunity to learn additional secrets of success from the unusually bright and successful talents who conceive and run these special programs.

Another major annual showcase is that of the International Platform Association, which is one of the oldest organizations in the United States, and the oldest speakers association. A major feature of IPA, the acronym for the Association, is the huge number of celebrity speakers who appear at the event each year and whose names are to be found listed among the officials and directors of the IPA. Typical of these well-known speakers are Jack Anderson, Senator Robert Dole, Kitty Kelley, James Kilpatrick, Edwin Newman, Congressman Claude Pepper, Jack Valenti, Richard Valeriani, Glenn Seaborg, Victor Borge, Art Linkletter, Hal Holbrook, Ann Landers, Bob Hope, and Isaac Asimov.

The National Management Association (NMA) has taken to

holding such showcases each year at its annual convention by making the Ron Fellows Professional Speakers Showcase an integral part of their national convention program. As in the Jordan Enterprises case, the program targets meeting planners, but the speakers who register and attend the event get numerous opportunities to meet with meeting planners and make valuable contacts, as well as learn many useful things, so that like other showcases, the real significance is that these two parties with a mutual interest get the opportunity to meet each other, talk to each other, observe each other, and learn about each other. NMA's interest in this is its own need for platform talent, since the Association engages the services of thousands of speakers and seminar leaders each year.

The National Speakers Association (NSA) has its own showcases. First of all, there is the Annual Winter Workshops program, held in various cities, with the local chapters acting as hosts, a practice of many national associations. Then there are local showcases and similar events, conducted by local chapters of NSA, such as those of the Washington-area chapter: The Washington-area chapter, National Capital Speakers Association, has held its own "minishowcase" programs, and also, together with the Greater Washington Society of Association Executives, has cosponsored a full-day showcase.

OTHER EVENTS AND OPPORTUNITIES

Other Conclaves and Gatherings

There are several special seminars held each year by and for speakers, especially by those who have had special successes and for those who most need to learn how to be successful or more successful in the profession. Dottie Walters and Nido Qubein are among those who organize and produce such events, but there are many others also. NSA's annual convention and other seminars, symposia, conferences, and conventions offer opportunities to meet "the right people," too.

Promotions in Print

Participating in Dottie Walters' anthology publishing program offers an opportunity for profits earned by selling your own copies
of the resulting book. But there is another aspect to this: because
all the authors who have contributed to this cooperative publishing effort sell copies of the book and the chapter you yourself
wrote is in each copy sold by each other, your name and material
reach a great many more people than only those you have personally sold copies to. That in itself increases your exposure to opportunity, and can lead to speaking dates.

There are directories of speakers, such as that prepared and
published by the National Speakers Association, which is circulated to meeting planners and other executives and lists NSA's
1600 members.

There are such special publications as the annual *Corporate
Guide to Effective Programming, A Directory of Speakers, Consultants,
and Performers,* published by Lecture Consultants, Inc., which is
headed by Fran Slotkin, who calls herself a "lecture consultant."
This is also a directory, listing many speakers and other talents, as
the title promises, and accepting advertising. The monthly publication of NSA, *Speak Out,* and the quarterly publication of IPA,
Talent, also accept paid advertising, and many speakers and consultants advertise in all these publications, as do some others in
the speaking profession.

Of course, no single marketing or promotional activity is going
to guarantee overnight success, or any success at all. It is quite
likely, in fact, that some of these activities will not pay off for you
at all, which is only one of the reasons that you would do well to
engage in as many of these activities as you possibly can: one or
more will almost surely be the "open sesame" for you, but there is
really no way to know which will work best for you. You must work
at all; it requires time to become an overnight success.

CHAPTER 11

THE MARKETING TOOLS
YOU NEED

Marketing is something of a craft, and like all crafts, it has its own special tools. They are tools you can buy, in some cases, although most of the time it is better and even necessary to create your own marketing tools.

THE PRODUCT

You can start your marketing analysis from either of two vantage points: by deciding what you will sell or by deciding to whom you will sell. Whichever way you decide to go, you will arrive at the same point: you will have to match the two questions up. Let's discuss product first: what will you sell?

As a speaker, you can sell either of two things—yourself or your information. Many speakers are, in fact, performers—entertainers or something very close to entertainers. The audience wants to see and hear the speaker because the speaker is witty, funny, interesting, charismatic, or otherwise entertaining to the degree that the content of the presentation is less important or appealing than the style or manner of the presentation.

There are other cases, where it is what the speaker has to offer in the way of information and ideas that matters most—the content of the presentation that is the product being sold.

Perhaps there are cases where the product is both—where the content is valuable, but the speaker is also entertaining, interesting, diverting, and otherwise is as much the product as the content is. But whatever the case, it is necessary for you to know what the product is, if you are to market it effectively.

THE BUYER

What you will sell is one matter. But you must also know to whom you can and will sell—deciding who are the best or most logical customers—if you are to have any hope of marketing the product effectively. That latter point—who are to be your customers—is what you must ponder and decide on when you begin your marketing analysis by deciding first what you want to sell (as contrasted with first choosing the customers and then deciding what they are likely to buy). But before you go any further, you must determine how you will *reach* those prospects you plan to sell to—how you will manage to make your offer or present your sales presentation to them. This is critical, especially if what you want to sell appeals to only a certain, highly specialized group of prospects and you are unable to reach those prospects. In that case, it won't matter how valuable your offering is or how good a speaker you are; you won't make the sale.

PACKAGING

Everything, especially in this century, must be packaged for the market, and frequently it is the package, rather than the content, which is being sold. (In some cases, such as in the case of some cosmetics, the package actually costs more than the contents.) Packaging is a modern art, and the very term has more than one meaning, as do many of our terms today. In some situations, it has a literal meaning, referring to the physical package in which the goods are encased. In other applications, the term is more abstract in meaning, and refers more to the sales promotion and adverising presentation—what the product is made to *appear* to be—than to any physical packaging.

Packaging is, then, more than an art, although it is that, too: it is itself sometimes the product that is sold, and it is of critical importance in selling a speaker or other performer. Packaging is both a marketing art and an advertising art, and the successful speaker must learn how to package himself or herself today, if he or she is the product, or to package the content of the presentations, if that is the product.

A CASE HISTORY

In my own case, for example, I began with the decision to package and market information on how to sell to government agencies and, especially, on how to write winning proposals, proposals that win contracts from government agencies. And I decided that the way I would package this information for sale would be as one-day seminars.

Now obviously, not everyone in the world is interested in this subject, and my success in this enterprise depended on something more than my knowledge of the subject, and even my ability to present that knowledge. It depended, even, on more than my ability to convince them that I could help them learn how to succeed at this highly specialized activity, and that it was worth their time and money to sit and listen to me all day. It depended on my success in finding people who wanted to know more about this subject. It is something like that famous recipe for making rabbit stew: first you must catch your rabbit. And for a while that proved to be the most difficult part of the job.

But I had still another lesson coming: I soon learned that there were lots of small businesses and even individual entrepreneurs who wanted to learn more about selling to the government, but that the real want many had was to learn how to write more effective proposals, which is only one facet of marketing to the government, although an important one. A seminar in proposal writing brought a more enthusiastic response than a seminar in government marketing generally.

I permitted the market to dictate to me what I would sell, as I should have. (No matter how thoroughly you have done your early research or how knowledgeable you think you are, actual experience often turns up surprises and demonstrates that at least some of what you "know" are really only assumptions and are not accurate.) I modified my original decision to sell general how-to information on government marketing, and designed a program in how to develop winning proposals for that type of government contract that is won only by writing the winning proposal. I knew, of course, that certain types of procurement are made only by soliciting proposals and selecting the proposal that appears to be the best one. That's how bidders are judged in that situation. I knew that certain kinds of companies proposed regularly to the government, and that it was a major activity—often the principal marketing activity—in many companies.

ONE MAJOR MARKETING TOOL: GOOD MAILING LISTS

I soon learned that the only effective way to reach these companies with appeals to attend seminars was via direct mail, although some coverage could be gotten via free publicity. But the real trick was to get suitable mailing lists, and that soon turned out to be a rather difficult job. While there are many major list brokers, and they have literally millions of names and addresses stored in their computer files, they have no reliable way of determining which are of companies writing proposals or how to separate such companies' names from their main files.

I found my solution by doing what is generally considered by mail order experts to be a poor method of acquiring mailing lists: I compiled them. I compiled them from a variety of sources, using my own knowledge and judgment to select those which I thought suitable. Here are some of the sources from which I selected and compiled my lists:

☐ The *Commerce Business Daily*, a federal government publication listing contract opportunities and awards made. I copied the names of companies winning awards, many of which names I recognized, of course.

☐ *Help-wanted advertising.* Most of the companies in which I was interested advertise for help eventually, and I was able to easily recognize most of the kinds of companies I wanted from their names, the businesses they were in, and/or the kinds of help they wanted and the descriptions of the jobs offered. (Among the best sources for these names are the business pages of the Sunday edition of the *New York Times* and the Tuesday and Wednesday editions of the *Wall Street Journal*, although the classified sections of many newspapers are also good sources.)

☐ *Membership rolls of several associations.* Frequently you can get these free or buy them for a small sum as small booklets. Some associations will not surrender such membership lists, but many will.

☐ Lists of contractors and subcontractors released by certain government agencies for various purposes, such as aiding small companies in pursuing subcontracts.

☐ Other advertising of many companies, sometimes in trade magazines, sometimes in other types of periodicals.

☐ Swapping lists with others in businesses that were not directly competitive, but appealed to the same kind of prospects.

☐ Buying the subscription list to the *Commerce Buisness Daily* from the government. (It was then possible to do so.)

☐ From sundry other sources, such as the news columns of many periodicals which list relevant information.

☐ From inquiries coming in to my own office, as a result of word of mouth, my own publicity releases picked up in newsletters and other periodicals, and my own small advertisements.

Ultimately I had many thousands of names, more even than I could use comfortably.

THE DIRECT-MAIL PACKAGE

The typical direct-mail package is likely to include the following items:

A one- or two-page sales letter
A brochure or "broadside" (perhaps both)
An order form
A postage-free response envelope

There is another type of direct-mail piece that contains only a brochure or a broadside (a large flat that is folded down to manageable size, but is on the order of 17 × 23 inches or larger, when unfolded). This is usually what the trade calls a "self-mailer," which means that it does not need an envelope, but is mailed as a "flat" (so called by the Postal Service), with a label on the outside somewhere.

A great many seminar producers favor the 11 × 17-inch self-mailer brochure—four 8½ × 11-inch pages—as a mailing piece, and this is probably the most popular way of promoting seminars. (See Figure 5.) The piece is mailed in great quantity—often as many as 50,000 pieces—usually announcing an entire series of seminars in several cities, so that the cost of the mailing is prorated among a half-dozen or more sessions. This is one advan-

→ **Sell <u>more</u> NEW SUBSCRIPTIONS, RENEWALS, BOOKS and TAPES**

with the tested, payoff techniques you'll learn
at the direct mail course
you've been waiting for...

YOU CAN create more effective mailings...

by using savvy, proven Rene Gnam methods...

for your magazine, newsletter, books or tapes.

René Gnam's
SUBSCRIPTION SUMMER SCHOOL

in Your choice of locations:
WASHINGTON...August 14-15-16
CHICAGO...August 20-21-22

where You'll learn:

1 How to evaluate and select MAILING LISTS,
2 How to devise attractive, effective OFFERS,
3 How to write persuasive, compelling COPY,
4 How to design powerful, action LAYOUTS,
5 How to increase direct mail READABILITY,
6 How to ANALYZE results for more profits,
7 How to use all the PRIME MOTIVATORS,
   PLUS:
8 How to turn a small budget into a powerhouse!...
9 How to increase your paid order percentage!...

"Rene Gnam is the dean of direct mail." — **LARRY DOBBS**, publisher, MUSTANG MONTHLY MAGAZINE

"Thank you. Thank you. Thank YOU. You've done an unbelievable job on our behalf. The ratings I've reviewed put you on the very top of our speaker list. You've helped make our entire program a success."
JOSEPH J. HANSON, publisher, FOLIO MAGAZINE

"When Rene describes a concept or technique, he tells you who used it, just how, and what the results were! Rene has worked for and with publishers of literally hundreds of newsletters, magazines and a myriad of other types of direct marketers. He has always received far and away the most outstanding participant evaluations at any NA meeting, ever!"
FRED GOSS, executive director, NEWSLETTER ASSOCIATION

RESERVE YOUR SEATS RIGHT NOW...

"The nation's top lecturer on direct mail." — **LESLIE NORINS**, publisher, AMERICAN HEALTH NEWSLETTERS

FIGURE 5 Front page of a typical seminar mailer.

tage, but this also offers the additional advantage that it allows many respondents some flexibility in their scheduling, since they have several dates available, as well as several locations. Too, because of the sheer size of the mailing, there are two savings: one, the unit cost of printing the brochure falls sharply at the larger quantities, and two, it, now becomes practicable to turn to bulk mailing and reduce postage costs sharply.

SPECIAL ALTERNATIVES

Some speakers prefer to make small mailings, at first-class rates, using a more conventional direct-mail package—sales letter, brochure, order form, and return envelope. This, in fact, is how I did my own seminar solicitations. I preferred the first-class mailing and the conventional direct-mail package. But I had another, special reason for wanting to do my mailings this way. I did something else, something analogous to the practice of many speakers who sell books and tapes at their presentations: I made up mailing pieces for my own books, newsletters, and other materials and enclosed them in the seminar mailings. And the response I got to these was quite good. Many who could not make it to the seminar instead ordered books and newsletters, and some did both. So I made the mailing do double duty, which brought in more income, while it also reduced the cost of the seminar mailing, and made the seminar that much more profitable.

But I also did something else, which may be a useful idea for anyone who wants to offer seminars. The sales letter ended with a message along the lines of Figure 6.

Of course, I did place the names of these special respondents on a special mailing list, and used these inputs also to provide some guidance on where seminars should be held. And I also made up special lists of those who responded to mailings by buying books and newsletters. That was, of course, a customer list, and no mailing list you can buy, beg, borrow, or steal is quite as good as a customer list.

```
    If you are unable to attend this seminar but wish to be placed

    on our SPECIAL MAILING LIST for announcements of future seminars,

    please complete the form below and return it to us:


    Yes, please keep me posted on future seminars.  In fact, my

    preference would be for a session on or about _____(date)

    and in the area _____(approximate location).

    Name & Title: _____

    Company: _____

    Address: _____

    Telephone: _____
```

FIGURE 6   Special marketing feature in seminar sales letter.

HOW TO WRITE A SALES LETTER

The principles of writing a sales letter are those already enunciated as the principles of sales and marketing generally—reason out those highly motivating benefits you can promise the reader, find and present the proofs that will help the client believe your promise, and ask for action or plan the next step. But do find the *specific benefit* to promise, something that is entirely concrete, and not abstract. For example, I made an entire series of mistakes, in this regard, before I began to understand the difference between the two when I first launched my own enterprise. Here is how I floundered around at first, and how I gradually evolved my approach until I finally mastered the art of being entirely specific and concrete:

1.   I started by coining a term, "proposalmanship," to distinguish what I taught from ordinary "proposal writing." It met with

a lukewarm reception. A few people loved it, a few despised the term, most didn't care too much one way or the other. Net gain of my creativity: virtually zero. Few people were especially enthused by the prospect of learning proposalmanship.

2.   I characterized my seminar as the "postgraduate course" in proposal writing—definitely not for beginners or amateurs at the game, but for the experienced proposal writers who wanted to pick up the most advanced knowledge of the art. This was somewhat better received, and aroused some enthusiasm and a good bit of interest. But it did not deter beginners from signing up for the course, and I had to teach fundamentals, despite the billing as a postgrad course.

3.   I offered "inside information" on proposal writing. No change in response.

4.   I offered to teach more than merely "writing" proposals; I would teach attendees how to write *winning* proposals. No change in response.

5.   Finally, I began to realize that even what I thought was highly specific—"winning proposals"—was still somewhat abstract for this reason: what the customer wanted, *as an end result*, was not a winning proposal per se, but a *contract*! I began to promise that I would help or enable my attendees to win contracts. That did it! I had finally found the right promise, one that did not require my prospect to *translate* my promise into what he or she really wanted as a final result.

An abstraction is something one must translate into a concrete equivalent. Abstractions do not sell well at all. Don't promise abstractions; promise concrete results—final, end results . . . what the client wants to see happen.

WHAT IS AN ABSTRACTION?

The very idea of abstraction is somewhat difficult to explain because it is a relative idea: what is highly concrete to one individual is abstract to another. As a marketer, then—and you are a marketer, even if you, yourself, are the only property you are marketing—you must decide what will be abstract and what will be concrete to your prospective client. And to help you decide on that, be aware that *you can never be too concrete*; if you must err, err on the side of being more concrete than necessary, for you will never go wrong that way.

This is not to say that abstractions have no place in your sales literature; they do. But they belong in that material which is part of the "proof," not part of the promise. And that is the difference: The proof can be somewhat abstract, and it may even be advantageous to be somewhat abstract there. But the promise must be entirely concrete.

Take the example of Figure 5, as an illustration. Note the concrete nature of the *promise*: "SELL <u>MORE</u> NEW SUBSCRIPTIONS, RENEWALS, BOOKS AND TAPES." Then look at the proof: It promises such items as "How to evaluate and select MAILING LISTS," and "How to devise attractive, effective OFFERS," among other things. These are more abstract, but that's okay because the basic promise was concrete enough: it explained the specific benefit as an end result—selling more new subscriptions, and so on—a truly virtuoso performance by a master in preparing copy.

Put that into your sales letters, your brochures, your presentations. *Explain* the benefit by painting the prospect a picture—in words—so the prospect can all but feel, hear, smell, taste those benefits. That's how you sell benefits, and that's how to present the promise. (Never forget that the basic buying motivation is always an emotional one.) But don't expect the customer to translate from abstract language so as to visualize the benefit. It won't happen. Translating your abstract language into concrete images is selling, but the customer won't do your selling for you. You have to do it.

MOTIVATORS: WHAT ARE THEY?

Psychologists advise us that humans have deep emotional needs for a sense of security, for loving and being loved, for recognition, and for ego gratification in general. Perhaps it all adds up to the need for security, in both the emotional and material sense, the need to feel that one has a secure place in society, in career, in family, and in all other respects. Whatever the case, for purposes of selling it is important to recognize these drives as the motivating factors that underlie our decision-making and note too the verification that our motivators are all emotional factors.

SELF-INTEREST IS THE PRIME MOTIVATOR

Whatever names and characterizations we assign to the human motivations we recognize, all motivations fit into a single general characterization: self-interest. Everyone acts out of self-interest. Most of us are reluctant to acknowledge this, since we prefer to believe in the basic goodness of humankind and we find something cynical about the idea that all acts of humans are inspired by self-interest. But it is naivete to believe otherwise, and it is simple objectivity, not cynicism, to recognize the truth of this. Even acts of charity, while ostensibly and nominally selfless, still reward the giver with some sense of satisfaction and comfort, perhaps assuage the ego or help reinforce a favorable self-image. (This does not make the good deeds or the doers of good deeds less noble, for these are, indeed, noble ways of serving our human need to feel good about ourselves, to do things which bear out and verify our fondest images of ourselves.)

The importance of this is not to explain why most of us give to charities and otherwise lend a helping hand to others but, rather, to make the point that in every exchange, each party must gain something, or the exchange will not be made. Ergo, don't make sales; make exchanges. Exchange what you have to offer for money, and regard what you are doing as a bilateral agreement, in which both of you benefit equally in the exchange.

FEAR AND GREED

The two prime sales motivators, some cynics assure us—and perhaps they are realists more than they are cynics—are fear and greed. (Note that both have a profound connection with security.) "Greed" is, of course, a highly charged word, and is used for dramatic effect; the more accurate word which should be used here is "gain," rather than greed. Everything we buy, we buy in either the hope of gaining something more satisfying and rewarding than the money or in the perceived necessity of avoiding some distasteful result, perhaps even disaster. And there is some evidence that this motivator, fear, is by far the more powerful motivator.

Take note of national advertising to see these principles at work. Holiday Inns has lately been pledging "no surprises" (meaning you won't arrive and find that you don't have the room reservation you thought you had) in their advertising, with the clear appeal to a sense of security. In *Meetings & Conventions*, a trade magazine, virtually all the hotel advertising stresses the recreational pleasures available, rather than the business-meeting facilities and related amenities. (And most of these advertisements feature expensive full-color illustrations of the pleasurable activities and facilities, including one of hotelier J. Willard Marriott, Jr. in casual clothes, driving a golf cart on the grounds of one of his resort hotels.)

The assumption on which such advertising is based is that the customer will take the acceptable meeting facilities for granted, in any case, and will choose a site and hotel on the basis of other factors than their suitability for a business meeting or conference. (Or, at least, that the latter considerations can be discussed later in the advertising and sales presentation, after the customer has first been lured and had interest aroused by the blandishments of pleasure.)

In the event that some of the customers may not be so motivated on their own initiative—may not be deliberately seeking the most pleasurable place for a meeting—the advertising copes with that, too, by directing the customer's attention to an implication that good meeting facilities can be taken for granted, but other amenities cannot, and that the other amenities offered will contribute heavily to making the business meeting a success. The stress is on gain, but is made as emotional as possible.

A car rental firm features gifts offered to renters, rather than more relevant aspects of its car renting service. These are also gain motivators, and in terms that are clearly emotional appeals, as well.

On the other hand, consider how insurance, fire and burglar alarms, and many other products are sold—through fear, of course. Fear is an almost unavoidable basis for sales appeal here because these are services and products which are designed specifically for coping with unexpected disasters. They are "tailormade" for fear selling.

THE WORRY ITEM

In proposal writing, we refer to the customer's fears as the customer's "worry items." Find the customer's worry item—that which the customer fears most or is most concerned about—and you have a good basis for the sales strategy. And if you are unable to determine what the customer's chief worry item is, do what the "ring around the collar" TV commercial does: *give* the customer a worry item, and see if you can't make fear your star salesperson. (It evidently works well for that detergent manufacturer, for the commercial has been on the air for a long time, a sure sign that it is producing sales.)

These, then, are the chief basic sales strategies: Base the appeal on what the customer has to gain (wants or can be made to want) and/or on what the customer wants to avoid or solve (fears or can be made to fear).

APPLYING THIS TO YOUR OWN MARKETING

The nature of whatever you sell dictates the kinds of prospects you sell to, obviously. If you are a humorist and engaged entirely to lend a light note and the pleasure of laughter to an occasion, you are obviously wasting your time and money trying to sell yourself to companies who want to organize training seminars in-house. You must somehow seek out those who are legitimate prospects for your kind of presentation, those who have a "felt need" for what you offer.

THE MEANING OF NEED

One piece of business advice given so often that it has become an almost meaningless platitude is, "Find a need and fill it." But there are a few things wrong with that advice. For one thing, you need not search to "find a need." Needs are all around us, and have been since the beginning of humankind. Basic needs don't change; only the ways of satisfying them change. We have always had needs for warmth, food, clothing, recreation, love, and a few other physical and emotional items of interest. The platitude ought to be changed, if it is to survive at all, to say, "Find a better way to satisfy a need and offer it."

Marketing people sometimes speak of "felt" needs and "creating" needs or wants. The implication is that there are needs people already feel, consciously, and there are needs they do not feel consciously, but can be made to feel. There is, of course, some justification for the idea, but it still reflects an inexact and shallow understanding of marketing and sales motivation. These are better understood by understanding *basic* needs, which never change, and ever-changing, ever-improving ways of satisfying those needs.

Take the need for entertainment or diversion, for example. It is a real enough need, and it is a felt need. But the ways of satisfying this have changed enormously, even in our own lifetimes. Just in this century types of entertainment have progressed from such things as picnicking, band concerts, and vaudeville to such modern amenities as worldwide TV, videocassette recording, and walkaround stereo radios with audio cassettes. There was, of course, no felt need for these modern devices before they were invented and offered to the public, but they were accepted immediately because they were obviously huge improvements on that for which there was a felt need—entertainment, especially home entertainment.

Note the powerful influence of convenience as a gain motivator.

The so-called convenience stores find ready acceptance of their higher prices because they are open at all hours, parking is at the door, and little marching around and searching is required to find what you want. But note, too, the steady march to entertainment in the home, rather than outside. Movie attendance fell steadily after TV arrived on the scene, and videocassette players have made further inroads into movie attendance. It's so much more convenient to watch movies of your own choice in your own home.

WHAT YOU NEED

All of this is, of course, entirely relevant to your own situation in marketing yourself. While sending out letters and brochures will not, of themselves, bring you speaking engagements ordinarily, you will not be able to market yourself effectively without these and other tools. In fact, you need to have at least the following, to do any kind of reasonably effective marketing of yourself:

An introductory letter
A brochure
A photograph of yourself
An audio cassette

Questioned on the subject of what specific marketing tools the speaker needs, Dave Yoho spells out a "strong brochure (one that sells benefits)" and shows "what he/she can do for the meeting planner." Yoho also urges the speaker to have an audition cassette and, if possible, a video tape. He himself, as a major figure in the field and one commanding major fees, has such materials, including a quite elaborate and obviously costly presentation folder. It is far too impressive and superbly professional to be disminished by the epithet "brochure," which is printed in color on heavy, smooth stock—card stock, rather than paper, that is—and folds out to four 8½ × 11-inch panels printed on both sides. The presentation includes a full-color head-and-shoulders photo of Yoho in action at the microphone and another photo of him on the cover, has nine black-and-white photos of satisfied clients, with their testimonials to the excellence of his presentations, and includes a smaller card, notched to fit a card file, bearing his photo and advertising message. So complete is this presentation that it requires little else, if anything, in printed matter to accompany it.

The text of Yoho's presentation folder explains what and how he works at his profession, with explanations of his background and other credentials, lists many of his clients and occasions on which he spoke, and lists five different keynote and after-dinner speeches, and eight different seminars and workshops he offers. It is a model to emulate, although most speakers, even seasoned professionals, might be hard put to compete with this model.

Robert L. Montgomery suggests that a speaker ought to have photos, audio cassettes, video tape (preferably), testimonials, biography, and a good brochure. Michael Podolinsky, of Key Seminars in Minneapolis, recommends that speakers have a brochure, audio cassettes, and, if possible, a video tape. One professional mentioned a "full press kit," but that would be covered, essentially, by the other materials mentioned.

In general, this is the consensus. Most of those interviewed agreed that marketing tools must include some kind of brochure, photos, testimonials, bio data, audition tapes (audio) and, if at all possible, a video tape. Several included client references (but testimonials would serve that purpose, as long as the source is identified clearly). No one mentioned press releases, except indirectly, by reference to press kits. But let's look more closely at each of these items, one by one.

THE LETTER

For your promotional package which you use to market yourself as a speaker, you must employ a style and type of literature that suits your image as a professional. That is, you must avoid "huckstering" in your presentation. No garish scrawls, exclamation marks, crude writing, or other devices used commonly to sell merchandise by mail. That does not mean that you should not sell, however, but only that you make sales presentations that are strong, but in good taste.

The Dave Yoho presentation described here could probably be used without an accompanying letter, simply because it is so complete and does almost everything that a letter could do. Still, even with a powerful package such as that described, a letter serves a useful purpose, especially if it is addressed to the meeting planner specifically. (It is well worth your time to discover that individual's name, whenever possible, and address your package accordingly.)

The letter is usually the central element of the entire package. It can be a single page, or it can be several pages. To some degree, that depends on what else is in your package: if you have a small and simple brochure, you will have to rely on the letter to present much of your sales argument and presentation, and the letter may then be several pages—both sides of two sheets, for example. But if your brochure is large enough to present most of your information and sales arguments, you can keep the letter short. (In general, the more material and information you offer in a package, the more powerful the package is and the greater the results it produces. My own personal experience bears this idea out quite firmly.)

Use a good quality paper for the letterhead on which your letter is printed, preferably one that has your name, address, and other information tastefully presented in raised type. If you have a word processor or can manage to retain the services of a local service for the purpose, you will gain even more impact by using a mail-merge program to address and type all those letters individually.

THE BROCHURE

The very word "brochure" can be and is applied to a wide variety of printed literature, ranging from leaflets or pamphlets that would fit comfortably into a number 10 business envelope to such elaborate presentation folders as that of Dave Yoho, described a few paragraphs ago.

Public speakers, like consultants and other kinds of professionals, cannot afford to send out brochures that are obviously "done on the cheap"—composed on a typewriter, poorly written, printed on cheap paper, and otherwise done with concern only for the least expensive way to get things done and no concern for quality or professional appearance. Unfortunately, there are some speakers who do offer prospective clients and agents such brochures. But as a speaker, you must create and maintain a highly professional image. No sensible meeting planner is going to risk his or her own reputation for good judgment and expert execution of job responsibilities by hiring someone who has been working at creating the wrong kind of image—an image for shoddiness. Sending a prospective client such a piece of literature is almost insulting. Such a product can do only harm by convincing a prospective client that you are not a serious professional. If you must economize in creating your brochure, do so by making the brochure small, not cheap. For example, you do not have to have eight, six, or even four panels; you can make do with a single sheet, printed on both sides (two panels). But be sure that it is well written, properly typeset, and printed on a decent grade of paper. (Actually, it costs little more to do it right than to do it wrong, if you practice reasonable self-restraint.) And, as the paragraph discussing the letter observed, you can compensate for a small brochure by a longer letter. (A letter is usually far less expensive than a brochure.)

You do not have to use color. Color is expensive, and while color may help, the lack of color—printing in black and white, that is—will not hurt you. Better a well-done simple brochure than a cheap and *cheap-looking* product that attempts to be elaborate and sophisticated.

PHOTOGRAPHS

You can get a photograph in any good studio, but you do not have to go to that much expense. Despite all humor to the contrary, it is possible to get good photos made by a passport photographer, and they are usually quite inexpensive. You can buy the negative—you usually have to pay a bit extra for it (and I never understood why you should not automatically own the negative when you pay for the sitting)—and get as many copies made as you wish. However, if you are going to send out a great many pieces of literature, it might pay you far better to have your photo printed on your brochure and dispense with the more expensive prints from the photolab.

AUDITION TAPES

Speakers do not audition in person, as entertainers do. Speakers audition for prospective clients via audio cassette tapes or, preferably and when possible, via video cassette tapes. I say "when possible" because there are two potential problems in this situation:

Video cassette tapes are relatively expensive to make—it's almost inescapable that you will have to have a professional expert in the field make the master cassette for you—and even copies are rather expensive to produce, so you may have to defer making one of those for a while, until you are in a position to afford such tools. Moreover, you would need to have both the Beta and the VHS versions, since you have no way of knowing which type of machine the meeting planner has (both are in popular use) and the two are not interchangeable.

Moreover, not every meeting planner has a video cassette player conveniently at hand, and so may not be able to use a video tape, even if you have one to offer. Or even if the meeting planner does have a player available, you can't know in advance which type it is, and so will not know which type of cassette to send.

Audio cassette tapes are another matter. They are easy to make, inexpensive to duplicate, and fit virtually all audio cassette players. You can easily make a master tape yourself, although it may not turn out well to do so, inasmuch as you do not have the kind of recording equipment an audio expert would use. It is better to have such an expert make your tapes for you, and is not especially expensive to do so. In fact, what you might do, as a compromise, is record all your live presentations and have an audio service review your "home made" tapes and see what might be salvageable.

If the background noise is not prohibitive and the general sound quality is acceptable, the audio experts might be able to salvage enough to patch together an acceptably good tape.

PRESS RELEASES

The press release is a powerful tool, when used well. For one thing, it brings you publicity, which is free advertising. In fact, it is even better than free advertising, for it is at least nominally objective, whereas paid advertising is obviously biased in the favor of the advertiser.

By far the vast majority of press releases wind up unused in wastebaskets everywhere. That's not because press releases are worthless of themselves, but because a great many press releases are badly done and merit the fate they meet. Even those that are badly done sometimes manage to do their creators some good, simply because competing press releases are not any better.

The base idea of a press release is to provide information to newspapers, magazines, radio, TV stations, wire services, and anyone else who gathers and disseminates news and related kinds of information. Congressional committees, for example, issue frequent press releases, some of them on an almost daily basis, announcing the results of their deliberations. Because what Congressional committees do is inevitably news, those news gathering and disseminating organizations use the information, even though the press releases are usually badly written.

On the other hand, the majority of press releases written by the PR (public relations) offices (some of whom are PR firms, but many of whom are departments in companies) are blatant attempts to get free advertising for their organizations and/or products and services, and are readily recognizable as such. This does not mean that news organizations will not use the information and provide some publicity, even though they are well aware that the originators of the releases are simply trying to use the news organizations. They will use some of these releases, if they are worth using—if they have something in them that is newsworthy.

And what is "newsworthy" requires some separate discussion here:

Newsworthiness

The term "newsworthy" has more than one level of meaning. There are events and information that merit page one coverage and headlines because they are, indeed, news. There are items that are news, but not page one news—obituaries, for example, and stock market reports. And there are items that are not exactly news, but get treated as news—special features, interviews, movie reviews, and other such material.

All of these are newsworthy, even if not literally news—they merit being printed and reported to readers, for one reason or another, but principally because all fit into a single category of being items that, the editors believe, readers will want. After all, what the readers want is the final criterion of what is and what is not newsworthy.

Editors want everything that is newsworthy. They want everything that they think their readers will want, and they do not want to be "beaten"—to have rival organizations get news they don't get, or print news they had but failed to print. So they try to use as many press releases as possible.

In short, getting an editor to use your press release is a trade, like a sale: the editor gets some usable material free of charge, and you get some publicity free of charge.

That means that you cannot be totally selfish in developing a release, and you cannot be unrealistic and expect to get your release used. Your date to speak before the Rotary Club of Fallen Arches, Texas is not front-page news, although it might fit on the business page or perhaps in a special events column. And it may depend on how "dull" a day the editor is having. If there is little news, that improves the chances of your release being used. But you can improve its chances yourself by making it as newsworthy as possible. Do something to make it more newsworthy.

Figure 7 is an example of a press release. Note the elements:

1. It identifies itself clearly as a release.
2. It says "For immediate release." (It might have given a fu-

**News Release**

FOR IMMEDIATE RELEASE
July 10, 1984

Contact: Robert Milko
703/237-7200

PHILIP STEFFEN TO ADDRESS GENERAL SESSION
OF 1985 ICIA CONVENTION

NAVA, the International Communications Industries Association is pleased to
announce that Philip D. Steffen, CSP, will be the keynote speaker at the First
General Session of the 1985 ICIA Convention to be held January 18, 1985 from 9:20 -
11:30 A.M. in the Anaheim Convention Center, Anaheim, CA.

Mr. Steffen's presentation will be both inspirational and motivational, with
special emphasis for the communications industry. One past attendee at a presentation by Mr. Steffen described him as "electrifying."

Mr. Steffen has an international reputation as a speaker and is a holder of
the coveted Certified Speaking Professional (CSP) designation conferred by the
National Speakers Association. He has traveled world-wide giving motivational presentations to a wide variety of corporations, associations and professional organizations.

Mark your calendar now and plan to attend the 1985 ICIA Convention January 16-
21 and Commtex International, "The Showplace of the Communications and Information
Technology Industry," January 18-21, 1985.

For further information contact ICIA, 3150 Spring St., Fairfax, VA 22031 or
call 703/273-7200.

NAVA, the International Communications Industries Association is the trade
organization of the communications industry, representing audio-visual/computer/
video dealers, commissioned agents, manufacturers, producers, non-theatrical entertainment and religious film distributors, and education and trade publications. It
is headquartered in Fairfax, VA, a suburb of Washington, DC.

1201-784   # # #

NAVA, the International Communications Industries Association ▪ 3150 Spring St., Fairfax, VA 22031-2399 ▪ (703)273-7200

FIGURE 7   A typical press release.

ture release date—been "embargoed" until that date—under other circumstances.)

3. It bears the date on which it was sent out.

4. It lists a "contact"—someone to call for more information, if the editor wants to follow up and get a more complete story.

5. It bears a headline, to summarize what it is all about. (Most editors prefer to write their own headlines and captions, but this helps the busy editor grasp the story at a glance.)

6. The copy is double-spaced, so that the editor can mark it up easily for use, with deletions, changes, or other editorial marks.

7. It has an identification number (lower left) so that anyone calling to discuss it can identify the release. (The organization has issued many other releases.)

8. It says "end of story" by the symbol # # # at the bottom. (It might have said "END" or "-30-." If there were a second page, it would say "more" at the bottom.)

Unfortunately, this is an example of a release done without imagination and without effective effort to make it more newsworthy than it is inherently. It is not what I would consider to be a model to emulate, except for general format. It does adhere to the general "rules" or principles, in a mechanical sense, but at least two things could have been done (and at least one of them should have been done) to increase the probability of its being used as the basis for news coverage in the press—to give the editor a reason for using it:

1. Put some pizzazz—sales appeal—into the headline.
2. Put some pizzazz into the body copy.

WHY THE NEED FOR "SALES APPEAL"

The typical reaction to the headline of this release is ho-hum; what makes this worth the trouble of reading? Who is Philip Steffen? What makes this worth more than a listing in "events to come" or the "meetings" column? (If it's even worth mention there?)

The writer of this release should have searched for something that would have made this release more attention-getting, as he did with one other release he wrote. That one was headlined, "ICIA '85 IS TOUCHING TOMORROW TODAY," and the release made it clear that the convention is looking to and dealing with tomorrow's communications industry, using the theme "Touching Tomorrow Today." That is a bit more exciting—at least, it appeals to the imagination—than the headline of the release shown in Figure 7. Somehow, the two could have been tied together. Even the headline, "CSP PHILIP STEFFEN TO KEY-NOTE 'TOUCHING TOMORROW TODAY'," would have been some improvement. The editor might have wondered, "What's a CSP?" and read on to find out, and while "Touching Tomorrow Today" is not the most dramatic way to present that idea, it is certainly better than the headline used.

HOW TO GET RELEASES PUBLISHED

A release must be sold to editors just as anything else must be sold. The payment is not in dollars per se, of course but it is real payment nevertheless—payment in publicity, often publicity that no amount of money could buy you. An editor wants to "buy" good material—skims through releases swiftly and skeptically, hoping to find something useful, but not really expecting to because so many releases are not worth the trouble of reading them, unfortunately. So it's hardly worth your own time to write a release if you do not do it well. And that does not mean only grammatically correct and punctuated properly. "Well done" means containing some information or idea worthy of adoption for publication in someone else's medium. But there is more than one kind of material that fits this description of being worthy of publication elsewhere, and can be made to be appropriate to some of your own activities:

News

There are many kinds of "industry news" that fit into various columns and departments of a publication. If you have other business interests (e.g., own another enterprise or are on the staff of some organization) be sure to send out releases when there is some change in your status—perhaps a promotion or change to another function—as a "personnel changes" kind of industry news. But be sure that the release makes prominent mention of your speaking activities. For example: "Jason Smythe, often found on the platform speaking to civic and business groups, has been elevated to Branch Manager of the AlumoPlastic Corporation. Mr. Smythe is a member of the National Speakers Association. . . ."

Of course, there are many other categories of such "back of the book" news items. Whenever you are scheduled to speak somewhere, make up a little release announcing the speaking engagement and get it out to the media, especially the media in your own home town and in the town where you are to speak. And in such case, be sure to identify both, to wit: "Jason Smythe, a longtime resident of Frostbite, North Dakota and an executive in local industry, specifically Mining Tools, Inc., will address the Aurora, Montana Industrial Society Annual Banquet as the after-dinner speaker. Mr. Smythe is well known on the lecture circuit. . . ."

Many news releases, especially those that deal in true "hard news," bear a dateline, as the first words of the text, following the headline (if a headline is used) in this manner: "Washington, D.C., January 20, 1985:—The White House announced today. . . ." This is a very useful device when you want to point out that the item is of local interest, which always increases the probability of its being picked up and used. In such a case as that just cited, it might be advisable to issue two versions of the press release, with datelines for each city.

Once, when I managed one of two Washington-area offices of a New York-based company, I received fairly frequent releases from the home office, which I was asked to send on to the local newspapers. The other local office simply forwarded the items to the local press, and rarely got one published. I had the releases retyped, used a local dateline, reworked the lead to make it clear that the release emanated from a local office and worked in some angle to give it local interest (such as mentioning a major local business activity of the branch), although it was a New York company, and was able to get most of the releases published, as a result. The local angle is always a compelling one for editors.

Features

The media publish many items that are not news, even by the widest stretching of the word. They are features, and they range from crossword puzzles and household hints to man-bites-dog tales and character studies done as interviews. Editors love this kind of material, if it is well done, largely because it is not time-critical. It can be run any time, which means it can be saved to be used on a dull day. If you can tie your speaking activities to some other item—perhaps you are a local inventor and have just been issued a patent for something or other. Or perhaps one of your ancestors founded the town you live in or had something to do with its founding. Or perhaps your speaking specialty is a novel one, in subject, in the kinds of audiences you address, or in some intriguing novelty you use when speaking. Johnny Cash probably has gotten more publicity for performing in penitentiaries for prisoners than for anything else he has done, for example. (Do you talk to some special audiences, such as handicapped persons, immigrants learning English, parents' groups, or other such special kinds of listeners?)

You can write a release around some novel item you present in your talk or in a book you have written. When I used releases to gain publicity for one of my books about marketing to the government, I used headlines and leads about such things as being paid thousands of dollars to answer the government's mail and the government's contracts hiring mules and handlers, among other procurements that raise both chuckles and hackles when taxpayers learn of them. Search your speeches and books for items that make attention-getting headlines and strong leads, such as "SPEAKER JASON SMYTHE DEBUNKS VITAMINS."

WHERE TO SEND RELEASES

Newspapers are the obvious targets of releases, but magazines are good targets too. There are also newsletters, trade journals, and other specialty publications. Many of these have limited circulation, but in the aggregate they represent a large and varied readership.

Don't overlook radio and TV stations. They all have newsrooms of their own, and they have specialties, too, just as newspapers do. They have general newscasters—anchor men, anchor women, and other news readers—but they also have their specialists for sports, business and financial news, and other stories.

Include the wire services and syndicates in your mailing of releases—United Press, Associated Press, Field Enterprises, King Features, and others. If you catch the attention of one of these with a release, you will get a great proliferation of your story.

It's not exactly easy to write a good release (one that is newsworthy, for that is the only standard of what is "good" in a release), as you have undoubtedly gathered, but it is not worth writing one if it is not good.

Letters to the Editor

One rather easy way to get some publicity is to write letters to the editor. The results of such letters can be quite surprising. In one case, one of my own business acquaintances had his letter published in *Nation's Business*, and was surprised to receive a letter from a major publisher shortly thereafter, inquiring into the letter writer's possible interest in writing a book for that publisher.

Articles

Writing brief articles for newsletters and magazines, especially those which are trade publications and circulated to specialized audiences, can bring you good results, especially as your name and reputation grow, over a long period. The occasional article, however, is not nearly so effective as is the series of articles, over a long time period.

GET YOURSELF WRITTEN ABOUT

Even better than getting your releases, letters, and articles published—and sometimes the result of getting all the publicity resulting from such publication—is persuading the media to write about you, usually via personal interviews. These things do not come about by accident; you engineer them. When I wanted some publicity for my consulting services, I learned the name of one of the business-page reporters on the Washington Star (now defunct, along with many other evening newspapers) and wrote him a letter. I explained that I was in a rather novel enterprise, helping others win government contracts through a variety of educational and support services. I had earlier written to the editors along this line, without success. But when I put this reporter onto a lead for a good story, he persuaded his editor to let him cover it: Getting the story meant more to him than it did to his editor, and so he fought for it and came to my office with a photographer and his tape recorder. The result was a good news story, with photo, in the newspaper. And that inspired another writer to interview me for a magazine article on the same subject, which in turn led to a number of lecture dates and consulting assignments, and later still another newspaper story with photos. Such events have a tendency to proliferate of themselves, once you get the ball rolling, and they have three payoffs: First, you get the immediate publicity; second, you often get a spinoff from that publicity, with secondary follow-up coverage; and third, you have those lovely newspaper clips, which you reprint in quantity (it's easy to get permission to do so, usually) and use as part of your general publicity and promotional package.

RADIO AND TV INTERVIEWS

Most of what is true for newspapers, even for getting yourself interviewed, is equally true for radio and TV stations. They interview many people, usually on talk shows. Again, this rarely happens spontaneously; you usually have to engineer it yourself.

The individual who arranges for guests and interviews on a talk show is the show's producer, not the star or host. If you write to the host of the show, your request will always be bumped along to the producer, so it is best to write the producer directly, with a copy to the host. And, as in the case of the newspaper, always try to find exciting reasons for the interview—something that will interest the viewers and listeners. Send your clips of other material along, to demonstrate that you are indeed newsworthy, either as a personality or because of something you offer.

As in all cases of selling—and getting yourself onto a radio or TV show is excellent publicity, but it does require selling in a very real sense—you must provide the reason for "buying" what you want to sell. And the larger and more important the station, the more persuasive you must be—the stronger must be your reason, that is. It is easier, for example, to get yourself interviewed by the host of a talk show on a low-power local radio station than to be interviewed on a major TV program. But with enough of the right kind of effort, you can accomplish both.

As in the case of virtually all accomplishment, this requires both intelligent effort and great persistence. Writing a letter, even a great letter, is not usually enough. You need also to follow-up with telephone calls, and even personal visits, if possible. In some cases, the producer and/or host will want to interview you first on a preliminary basis, as a kind of audition, to see how you come across and how you handle yourself spontaneously. (Some fine speakers and even top performers do not do at all well in an unrehearsed, spontaneous situation.)

If you can be available on very short notice, be sure to make that known, and be sure to keep in touch with the producers through regular telephone calls, cards, and letters, so they do not get the opportunity to forget you. Especially, if you can be available on short notice, keep reminding them of this asset, which represents an emergency resource for them. Sometimes, there is a crisis situation, where a scheduled guest becomes unable, at the last moment, to appear. This can give you a sudden opportunity which might not have come your way otherwise, as it gave me an opportunity to appear on Washington's "Panorama," a few years ago, with quite pleasing results.

Be aware that you do not necessarily have to be on "live"—in the studio, actually broadcasting at the time—or even interviewed in person. Many guest shots and interviews are on tape or on both tape and live, and many radio interviews are done via telephone, again both live and on tape.

Not all guests are booked by producers, nor all newspaper stories authorized by editors. (Everything has exceptions!) In some cases, the host has the privilege of choosing whom to interview, and I have been interviewed to discuss some of my books in such situations. And, in the case of newspaper stories, syndicated columnists have a great deal of freedom, and on several occasions I managed to persuade columnists to interview me, with resulting publicity.

THE SALES CLOSE

All of this tends to produce prospects and sales leads, rather than sales per se. Making a sale involves getting prospects and sales leads, making sales presentations, and closing. "Closing," to the sales professional, does not mean getting the order, although others think that that is what the term means. To the sales professional, closing is *asking* for the order. Usually, it's asking for the order indirectly, however, trying to use methods that make it as difficult as possible for the prospect to refuse the order, and as easy as possible to place the order. It's asking the prospect such questions as, "What color would you prefer?" or "What is the best day of the week for delivery?" If the prospect answers "red" or "Wednesday," the salesperson immediately *assumes* that the order has been placed and proceeds to write it up. If the prospect demurs and makes it clear that the answer is not an order, the salesperson accepts that as a signal that more selling presentation is necessary. And the experienced sales professional knows that while talking too long—talking on after the prospect has become convinced—can kill a sale, it is also a mistake to ask for the order too soon—before the prospect is truly convinced, and thereby polarizing the prospect's viewpoint prematurely. Closing is therefore a means for helping the experienced salesperson judge when it is time to write the order and when it is time to do some more selling.

That works well in selling commodities and even commodity services, but it is not appropriate to selling speaking, consulting, and other professional services. This requires a great deal more sophistication in marketing. The basic steps, however, are the same: there is the prospecting—determining who/what organizations are suitable prospects for you. There is the sales presentation—whatever it takes to get some attention and help you determine which are serious sales leads. And there is, then, closing. And in the marketing of professional services, closing is probably done most effectively by proposals. In fact, in these times, more and more organizations demand proposals. But in light of the increasing popularity and the many advantages proposals offer marketers, it is wise not to wait to be asked; volunteer a proposal whenever you have a prospect who appears to be even slightly interested. This offers you more than one advantage, which we'll discuss shortly.

PROPOSALS AND PROPOSAL WRITING

There was a time when a proposal was little more than a set of specifications, a price quotation, a set of contract terms, and perhaps a brochure or two. That is how someone proposed to build your garage, equip your soda fountain, organize your office, or provide other goods and services beyond the simple off-the-shelf purchase.

Perhaps there are still some businesses submitting such proposals today, but if so they are few in number, for the idea of a proposal has grown considerably over the years, influenced by the vast increase in and proliferation of government procurement, as well as other factors, such as the enormous increase in service industries in the United States.

As a result, today a proposal is a custom document, tailored to the specific requirement of a specific client, offering a specific, custom solution, described in detail, and presenting the proposer's qualifications. Today, the specifications and contract terms are relatively minor elements of the proposal; the major elements are the textual descriptions and the sales presentations.

The basic elements of a proposal are these:

Introduction

Identify the proposer and proposer's basic qualifications briefly, define the basic requirement as succinctly and clearly as possible. Keep the introduction short, to the point, define things clearly.

Discussion

Follow up the definition of the requirement by exploring it, make your sales presentations and arguments, explaining why the client should buy what you offer (e.g., explain the benefits by making the promise and offering the evidence).

Specific Proposal

Come to the point here by listing or describing precisely what you propose to do—description or outline of your talk or seminar, schedule, terms—your specific *commitment*, that is. You may include fees here, or you may want to submit them on a separate sheet, as many do.

Credentials

Here you present your qualifications and credentials in greater detail (you may have advised the reader in your introduction that you would provide more details later). You can include here your other services, talks, seminars, books, and so on. List other clients, describe your triumphs, special awards, citations. Include copies of newspaper stories about you, letters of commendation, other items to support your credentials and qualifications.

This does not mean that you must write up a unique proposal for each quotation. Quite the contrary, a good bit of the proposal, especially the credentials section, can be standard boilerplate, and portions of the other sections can be also, although you should update it, from time to time, to include later information.

The proposal need not be printed. Typewriter composition is quite acceptable, and even desirable, to bear out the idea of a custom proposal written especially for the client, rather than suggesting that it is a standard brochure, which refutes the very idea of a proposal.

You can have a standard, printed cover, on whcih you type the information that is specific to this proposal, or you can use any of the off-the-shelf report binders you can buy in any good office-supplies emporium. Even if your proposal is only a few pages and the engagement would be a small one, it is wise to use a report binder. It lends the proposal much more dignity, makes its importance to you and to the customer apparent, shows clearly that you truly *care* and are eager to serve, lends a highly professional tone to your marketing, and—as a most practical consideration— makes it much more difficult for a client to mislay it among a lot of letter correspondence. It is less likely to get overlooked, therefore.

Many clients need only a single copy of your proposal, but others need more than one copy: sometimes there are several people who want to study your proposal and make a decision. Inquire about this, and submit enough copies for their need.

THE COVER LETTER

A proposal should always be accompanied by a cover letter, advising the reader of the proposal submittal, affirming the offer, pledging best efforts, and otherwise documenting and reinforcing the proposal submittal. The cover letter is a usual courtesy, should always accompany a proposal and draw the reader's attention to it, but should never contain information vital to the proposal that is not also in the proposal. It may, however, summarize the major messages in the proposal, so that the reader need not necessarily read the entire proposal, especially if the reader is top management in a large organization and does not want to read all the details personally, but wants to pass the proposal on to a subordinate to study.

Be sure that your cover letter concludes with an invitation to the reader to call on you unhesitatingly for any additional information required, and express your willingness to provide additional information and/or answer questions by mail, by telephone, or in person (if the latter is practicable). In fact, do everything you can to encourage the prospective client to follow up and give you the opportunity to follow up. A follow-up of any kind improves the probability of making the sale because it enables you to sell some more.

THE LETTER PROPOSAL

There is such a thing as a "letter proposal." This is simply a proposal presented as part of a letter (which is the letter, of course) usually only a page or two. It makes for a simple method of offering a proposal, but it also tends to trivialize the proposal. For that reason alone, I would advise against the letter proposal. And bind the proposal somehow, even if it is only a few pages long.

DON'T WAIT TO BE ASKED

If you wait to be asked, you'll get a few requests for proposals. But you will probably write a great many fewer proposals, and that is not a blessing because it means you will almost surely make fewer sales. In fact, a good proposal is such a powerful selling tool that you should seize every opportunity to submit a proposal.

Too, the proposal approach to marketing handles that problem of trying for the close too soon, at a time when the prospect has not yet heard enough nor had enough time to consider your offer. If you press for an answer immediately, you polarize the situation, and compel the prospect to back off. And once "no" has passed the prospect's lips, it has become fixed in the prospect's mind as well, making your situation far more difficult.

The fact is that a great many people require time to reach a decision. Even if it were used only as a delaying tactic to give the prospect ample time to study your offer and think about it, the proposal would serve a most useful purpose. But it has more utility than that: It gives you the opportunity to "speak" without interruption, to think out all your sales arguments, and it enables the prospect to read and re-read your presentation and to discuss it with others. Too, in many organizations, where your prospect is not the top decision-maker, the proposal helps your prospect sell it to his own superiors or committees.

Never forget the importance of this latter consideration. Sometimes you have a champion in the organization, someone who wants to help you make the sale, but needs your help to do so. In that situation, a proposal is a must, but always discuss the matter with your champion and ask for suggestions of what ought to be in the proposal—even review a draft proposal with that individual before preparing the final version.

In my own work as a consultant and speaker, I don't wait to be asked for a proposal. The moment I come to the belief that I am talking to a serious prospect for consulting, a seminar, or other such service, I *tell* the prospect that I will submit a proposal, and immediately probe for information I will use. Here are some of the things I ask for, if I do not already have them (as I do, in some cases):

Library Research

If the client is large and well known, there may be public information available about the organization. Visit your local library and ask the librarian for help. The librarian will guide you to directories and other sources of information. Always—and make this a cardinal rule—take the time and trouble to learn as much as possible about a prospective client before writing a proposal.

Client Publications

The client may have brochures describing what the organization does, how it is structured, its history, and other data. I try to get as much of this as possible. If it is a public (stock) corporation, I try to get a copy of the latest annual report, which is another useful publication.

Internal Reports

In some cases, the client has some internal reports and/or memoranda on file, which can be helpful. If I can get these, I will use these also as source material.

Verbal Information

I get as much as I can via telephone, too, and in some cases I travel to the company for advance interview. (In some cases, where a great deal of time and travel is required, the client pays for the time and travel expense; in other cases, where the client is local and the time required is not great, I charge the cost to my marketing budget.)

Of course, in all these situations, the matter of confidentiality is involved, since you often become privy to confidential company information. You must be absolutely circumspect in respecting the need to be totally ethical in this.

DON'T MAKE SALES;
MAKE CUSTOMERS

Some marketers concentrate on making sales. Other, wiser marketers, focus their efforts on making customers. It is, of course, far easier to sell a satisfied client than to sell a total stranger. Look at it this way, too: It costs money, usually a considerable sum of money, to acquire a client. That cost represents an investment—or should. And you should protect that investment in every way you can. Consider this, for example:

Suppose you have spent $5000 out of your pocket and $10,000 worth of your time to prepare some marketing tools and get some marketing accomplished. And suppose that all of this effort has produced for you 10 speaking engagements. It has cost you, then, $1500 for each client, which is quite a cost, and it is nothing but cost, if you never do business with or through those clients again. And unless each of those 10 speaking engagements have paid you very well—at least well over that $1500—you have not even made very much money out of the whole thing.

That failure to make a decent profit from all your effort is not because you didn't get ample speaking fees, but because you made sales, not clients. You had to "expense" the entire marketing cost over a single engagement with each client. But if you do more business with or through those clients, you can *amortize* that cost as an *investment*, as you should. If, for example, you can get 10 more engagements with or through each of those clients you acquired, your marketing cost per engagement falls sharply to $150 per engagement.

The fact is that in most cases you cannot afford to spend marketing money merely to make sales; you *must* make clients, clients who like what you have done enough to ask you back for return engagements and who recommend you elsewhere.

HOW TO FOLLOW UP ENGAGEMENTS

Having acquird a client, you will of course do the very best job you can. That's the first requirement for pleasing a client. But there are other considerations affecting how clients regard you, with respect to repeat engagements and recommendations. Here, for example, are some recommended do's and don'ts:

Do follow up each engagement by chatting with your host before leaving, preferably over a cup of coffee or in some similarly relaxed situation, and tactfully exploring the prospects for other engagements and/or recommendations. Do take the initiative here, explaining other talks, seminars, and/or workshops you have to offer, inquiring as to other business and/or association connections your host has (your host may be active in more than one association, may be on the board of several companies, may have friends in many other organizations). Make it clear that you are interested in following up other possibilities. Try to get specific names, and ask tactfully also for help in winning those other engagements. You will be surprised at how eager others are to help you, if you handle the situation well. Example (condensed, of course, to eliminate all the pleasantries and small talk with which this would be interleaved):

You: In case you didn't get a chance to really read through all the material I sent you originally, you may not be aware that I do several different kinds of talks and seminars, and even a few workshops. For example . . .[you explain them quickly].

Host: I wasn't aware that you did all those things. [Some relevant discussion of these matters, pursuing whatever the host shows some interest in.]

You: I suppose you must be quite active in other organizations.

Host: Oh, yes. I am on the committee . . .[names several].

You: I'd like very much to send those organizations some of my literature. I wonder if you would mind guiding me on to the proper persons to address in each of them? [You take out your notebook and a pen, expectantly.]

Host: Sure, glad to help. [With a bit of luck, you can make up your list there and then. Otherwise, you may have to follow up later by telephone and/or mail.]

At this point press gently for introductions or other help in reaching and selling these other people and organizations. Ask for help tactfully, and you will usually get it. But you may be surprised, too: often your host will volunteer more help than you would dare have asked for, if you don't press too rapidly and give your host time to think and react to the trend of your conversation.

Also offer to help your host and/or other clients with custom presentations. Probe to find out what the problems, goals, and aspirations of the people and organizations are, and suggest the ways in which you can help. Never end an engagement without trying to set up another sale—engagement—with the client-organization and with other clients and/or organizations you can get leads on. Not only is this client possibly connected with other organizations, but many people in the audience belong to other organizations and may be able to help you make follow-up sales.

Don't hurry away after you have left the platform. Many listeners approach you to ask questions and chat, after you have left the platform, if you make yourself readily available, and frequently these little chats turn into your next sales, if you handle them well. Certainly, you want to talk to friendly people, get their cards, and plan specific follow-ups—a must, if you are going to benefit from these contacts.

Even if you cannot set up another sale on the spot—and it is not likely that you can get a firm commitment spontaneously—do always plan your next move by probing to find out who is a prospect and planning the follow-up with that prospect. For example, make a definite luncheon appointment with anyone who appears to be a good prospect. Or, if that is not possible, find out when would be a good time to call in the next few days. Or offer to send some information, a package of literature, or even a proposal. But do not leave things up in the air by such inconclusive "arrangements" as "Let's have lunch." Such a lunch "date" will never come off. Try to get a specific next step planned and agreed to.

CHAPTER 12

SPEAKERS, CONSULTANTS, AND COMPUTERS

The ubiquitous desktop computer can support and aid every entrepreneur, even the self-employed consultant and speaker. It can even be an important contributor to your success.

COMPUTER FEVER AND COMPUTER PHOBIA

The desktop computer—known also as the personal computer and microcomputer—is rapidly becoming as standard and as obligatory an office fixture as are the telephone and typewriter. Almost invariably, anyone who begins to use a computer in everyday business life and becomes reasonably proficient in using it soon finds it impossible to imagine business life without this latest boon to capability and efficiency.

Pay careful attention to both those terms—*capability and efficiency*. The desktop computer adds efficiency to a great many office operations, but it also provides the user with new capabilities. It enables you to do things you could not do before, things that you either would have to pay someone else to do or would not do at all because the cost was prohibitive.

Unfortunately, although millions of people have caught computer fever—are ardent enthusiasts—many more millions suffer what the industry regards as computer phobia. But in reality that fear is not of computers per se, but of the awesome and unjustified mystique that has come to surround computers. The fear is of the unknown and, perhaps, of what many think of as beyond their abilities to understand. Probably that is one reason young people have done so well with computers: they are not afraid to learn new things, whereas many adults shrink from any necessity to learn new things. (A great many of us resist change, probably because of such fears.) But it is enough to grasp the basic functions of computers, which are really only a better way to do the same old things we have always done—recording, writing, filing, reporting, accounting, and other such functions. The functions have not changed; only the ways of carrying them out have changed, have improved vastly. Here are some essentials to demonstrate that:

Recording

Instead of scrawling notes and figures with pen and ink in various logs, diaries, and ledgers, we now record them with magnetic spots on disks and tapes. We can use these to make up all kinds of records—accounts of funds, payrolls, inventory records, notes, and any kind of information we have ever wanted to record in the past.

Filing

Instead of paper files in metal cabinets, we now have files on tapes and disks, and with the help of the computer systems, we can locate a wanted file much, much more quickly than ever before. In fact, a corner of your desk can accommodate more information, in these floppy-disk files, than an entire, metal filing cabinet. (The disk files on my own desk represent over 7000 pages of copy.)

Writing

We can use computer help to write, and be more efficient at it than ever, more efficient, even, than we are when using "electronic" typewriters. This will become more apparent when we discuss the subject in more detail, shortly.

Reading Files

Where we once had to pull out a thick "read" file or other files and sit down to read them at length, often with time lost in searching for specific items of information, today the computer helps us find the files and the items we want almost instantaneously. In fact, with the "global search" function of most word processing programs, the computer will search out a key word or a portion of any file which you can identify by some key word.

Making Up Reports

Once we had to work with dozens of files, ledgers, and other records to assemble a report, and even then had to rough-draft that and revise it several times before we had it all together. Now the computer does much of the work for us, transferring, combining, integrating, summarizing, and modifying information from many files into one.

And even this only brushes the surface of the things the computer can do. But the point is that it is not really doing *new* things; it is doing *old*, traditional things, but doing them far more efficiently and effectively, so that it seems as though the things it can do are new capabilities. And in a sense they are new capabilities because they make it possible for you to do things in your own office that once you would have had to have some vendor or contractor do for you.

A TWO-MINUTE COMPUTER COURSE

It is no more necessary for a computer user to understand computer technology than it is necessary for an automobile owner to understand the internal combustion engine or the owner of a videocassette recorder to understand video technology. Unless you happen to be interested in learning the technology of computers and data processing, shun all literature that tries to make you technically knowledgeable; it's frightfully stultifying, as well as confusing, to anyone not really interested in accompanying the busy electron in all its travels around the circuits. Be satisfied with knowing merely that it is a device that processes information through several specific functions, each of which is simple enough, when expressed in the everyday English we use to talk among ourselves. Such terms are as follows:

1. *MEMORY.* This is a short-term storage of whatever you enter into the machine. Its capacity is measured in *kilobytes*, abbreviated k or kb. A double-spaced page of copy represents approximately 2kb—2000 bytes—which means that a 64k memory can hold approximately 32 double-spaced pages. (Many of the more recent desktop computers have memories of 128 and 256kb.)

2. *STORAGE.* This is long-term or permanent (well, really semipermanent storage), usually on floppy disks, coated with an iron oxide, with the data inscribed on it magnetically, very much

as music is inscribed magnetically on audio cassette tapes and video on video cassette tapes. These disks are operated in and by disk drives, can be erased, removed, stored, and otherwise used as files and file storage devices, very much like traditional paper files and the cabinets used to store paper files. Data can be transferred back and forth between memory and storage, and since typical storage in these small computers is from 200 to 800 kb (with many offering even greater storage), the relatively small storage capacity of the computer memory, even at today's relatively small memory of 64k, is not an unduly inconvenient limiting factor for most uses.

3. *INPUT.* New information is entered into your computer in two ways, generally. One is by putting a disk of information into a disk drive and transferring whatever portion you want to work with to the memory. The other is by using your keyboard like a typewriter to type information in. (A third way is to get information from another computer over the telephone, but this is virtually the same as installing a disk in your disk drive.)

4. *OUTPUT.* Most computers output data in two ways: They display the data on the screen, which is very much like a TV picture tube, and/or they print the data out on a printer, which operates very much like a typewriter. (Again, the third way is by telephone, to another computer.)

5. *INSTRUCTIONS.* The computer is a machine—hardware. It can do nothing without being instructed by its human masters. Humans write long lists of instructions, painfully detailed, as though directing a small child to the corner candy store. Such instruction sets are *programs* and are called, collectively, *software.* There are also special sets of instructions installed permanently in the machine to enable it to understand and translate the instruction programs on the disks that are installed in the disk drives. These are permanently inscribed in small electronic units called roms, for read-only memory, and this type of instruction is often referred to as *firmware,* to identify it as an instruction set permanently inscribed in a hardware component, ergo "firm," rather than "soft."

Each type of computer has its own *operating system,* the fixed instructions that direct all internal operations, especially including operating the disk system. The operating system is usually on disk, although portions of it may be in the firmware. There are a number of different operating systems, although the most popular ones are CP/M, for Control Program for Microcomputers; and PC-DOS, for IBM's Personal Computer Disk Operating System, and MS-DOS, for Microsoft Disk Operating System, a system closely resembling PC-DOS and considered almost its clone. (There are several variants of each of these, designed to work with the more recent generations of microcomputers.)

KINDS OF PROGRAMS

That is really all you need to know about computers for a starter, although with practice in using a computer and reading a computer magazine or two, you'll soon learn a great deal more and become thoroughly confused, unless you remember that the foregoing explains all you really need to know about the machine. The other information you need is about software—programs.

You are probably aware that computer people speak of hardware and software. By hardware they mean the computer itself, including all peripheral devices—printer, monitor (viewing screen), and other devices. By software they mean the instruction programs.

There are a few special purpose or "dedicated" computers which were designed to do a single kind of job and that job only. Most micros, however—micro is a familiar and convenient colloquialism for microcomputers—are *general purpose* computers, which means that they can do whatever they are programmed to do (i.e., word processing, accounting, engineering design, scientific calculations, inventory control, management reporting, drafting, and many other things). The programs are removable, so that what the computer can do depends on what program you choose to install in it, and it is extremely simple—a matter of minutes—to change the program so that the computer can do an entirely different job. That is what makes the computer unique and what makes the computer so valuable: A single machine can be programmed and reprogrammed to do an enormous variety of jobs, whereas it would be absolutely prohibitive in cost to design and use a different machine for each of these functions.

WHAT CAN THE COMPUTER DO FOR YOU?

By now, you may be wondering what all of this has to do with you, since you don't have an organization, but are a self-employed entrepreneur, and your "office" is merely a desk where you send out your few letters, prepare your bills, and sit down to rest between speaking and consulting engagements. What in the world would you want a computer for? Let's explore some of the things a computer can do, consider how people use their computers, and how those things relate or can relate to what you have to do to succeed in your own activities as a consultant and/or speaker.

Word Processing

It has become easily apparent that by far the most popular use of micros has been for word processing, and a great many owners of micros use them for word processing exclusively or nearly so. That's at least partly because those owners are unaware of or at least not giving conscious study to the many other useful things their micros can do for them. Whatever the case, be aware immediately that a word processor is not a machine; it's a program that is installed in a machine. (There are exceptions, known as *dedicated* word processors, but you need not worry about these; they are relatively rare, and you are unlikely to encounter them.)

If word processing were the only thing you were going to use a micro for, you would be amply justified in buying one. A word processor is a powerful aid in both marketing and other activities. For writing proposals alone, a word processor will pay its way. However, it is equally valuable for creating letters, compiling and handling mailing lists, making up handouts for your seminars, preparing reports (for consulting assignments), and for just about all other tasks involving printed copy.

Note that some of these tasks are in support of your marketing functions. And one reason that word processing is so valuable is that it makes it possible for you to turn out a much larger number of proposals than you could turn out by older methods. Here is why:

The nature of most word processors is such that you can store "boilerplate"—standard information that changes only slowly, if at all—in files and retrieve that information at your convenience. You can print it out directly, as it stands, or you can make a copy— in the computer—display that copy on the screen, and make any changes to it that you want within seconds. You can then incorporate that material.

Suppose, for example, that you wanted to list your recent clients in some other order than that in the boilerplate file. Perhaps you have them listed alphabetically, which is an aid to finding the ones you want quickly. But you want to retrieve just a few of them, and you want to list them in order of their relevance to the kind of client you are preparing a proposal for. You could spend a good bit of time doing this by conventional means, but you can do it quickly, with the typical word processor, using any of several methods, choosing the one that appears easiest and fastest, in each case. You could, for example, make a copy of the entire client file, if you wish to use most of it, erase the names you don't want, and then reorganize the rest in the order you want them. Or you can simply select the names you want and copy them in another file, instead of transferring the entire file. And you can do the transfers by any of several different methods, depending on which is most convenient. And in any case, the whole thing will require only a few minutes.

A 20-page proposal, therefore, might require that you write two or three new pages, modify boilerplate material for eight pages, and copy the remainder without change. It thus becomes easy for you to generate proposals, with all the advantages that confers, but it also means that your proposals are going to be more powerful because you don't have to compromise: since the process is so fast and so easy, you can include all the material that will help strengthen your proposal. Quite often, it is the depth of detail that makes the difference because the presentation of detail lends your proposal credibility and plausibility, whereas the lack of it—generalization—destroys credibility.

Using a "mail-merge" type of program, you can combine a mailing list with a form letter, making the letter appear individually composed because the system will *automatically* type each copy of that letter, with the name and addresses from the mailing list. (And you can address the entire list or some selected portion of it.)

Of course, you can turn these many features to advantage to write books and articles, too, as well as many other useful materials. And with a word processor, a large part of the labor of turning out a newsletter is reduced to a mere chore. It may, in fact, make it possible for you to launch a newsletter, where it would have been too much of a task for your busy schedule otherwise.

Once a skeptic myself—I couldn't see how a word processor would speed me up significantly—I am now a wild-eyed word-processor zealot! For one thing, I was wrong; word processing has speeded me up enormously. But for another thing, increased speed is one of the lesser benefits; greater capabilities result too. For example, I use a speller program, although I am quite a good speller. But the speller program is an enormous aid in proofreading my manuscript. I have extremely few typos now, and have saved a lot of time in that chore, too. And for still another—and possibly the greatest—benefit to a professional writer, word processing does incredible things to one's quality of writing because it encourages rewriting, revision, and polishing.

The inexperienced writer naively believes that he or she can create a good manuscript with a first draft. The professional or experienced writer knows better. However, most writers, as far as anyone has been able to find out, hate rewriting for a variety of reasons, of which laziness is only one. (Ernest Hemingway confessed to such laziness and wrote his draft in longhand so he would not be tempted to try to get away without rewriting, but would automatically rewrite as he typed his manuscript up for submittal.) I confess to being typical: I hate to rewrite, not so much out of laziness as out of impatience and eagerness to get on to my next writing task. And in my own case, BWP (before word processing), I used a great deal of whiteout fluid and correction tapes, and did a great deal of cutting and pasting with a scissors and gummed tape. And still I was compelled to discard a mountain of paper. Sometimes, in fact, I had gotten as much as 50 pages written before I decided I was on the wrong track and had to trash it all so I could start over.

No more. I still cut and paste a lot, but I do it electronically. I still flounder around for a lead sometimes, but I doodle on the keyboard until I get going. I still do almost endless juggling of copy to get the right flow and progression, but I do it without snippets of paper and tape all over, and I do it many times faster than ever before. I still find copy that doesn't fit, but I stick it in a computer file somewhere until I find a better place in the manuscript for it. I still write pieces of copy out of sequence—a list that I won't use until the last chapter or until I reach an appendix—but I store it comfortably away in a file that can be summoned up and printed out with two or three button-pushes. And I rewrite, revise, and polish continuously, instead of intermittently: I go back through all my copy at least 3 to 4 times—usually more—before I do my ocular proofreading. I do my final rewriting, revision, polishing in that final proofreading. Then I sic my speller program on it and pick up all the typos I missed or introduced in my final revision and print it out. And even then I sometimes go back and do still one more revision, if I see material printing out that somehow does not satisfy me fully.

Why? Why such an order-of-magnitude increase in the amount of revision and polishing I do? Because word processing has made it so much easier, but also because it does not seem as though I am throwing my offspring away when I wipe out words on the screen, as it does when I throw typed manuscript in the trash basket! (What writer can bear to throw out bundles of pristine manuscript without heart-wrenching agony?)

If, as one old writer's platitude has it, all good writing is rewriting, the word processor removes the writer's last excuse for poor writing: there is rarely validity today in the plaint of not enough time to rewrite, if one writes at a word processor.

Database Management

The word *database* is one heard a great deal in connection with computers. It refers simply to any collection of related information: a mailing list or set of mailing lists, customer files, correspondence files, project records, production logs, or whatever the user wishes to declare to be a database—related data.

Databases are of various sizes. The entire huge set of files on medical data in the MEDLARS system at the National Library of Medicine in Bethesda, Maryland may be deemed to be a single database, or it may be made up of many databases. Again, the user determines what the database is.

Databases need to be managed, if they are to be useful. This is especially so when the database is made up of many different kinds of data. And there are software programs that are designed for this purpose. They enable you to manage the data in the database—sort, merge, combine, edit, generate reports from, and otherwise manipulate it for your own purposes.

Some simple database management (DBM) programs are not even called DBM programs, but are referred to by some users as file managers. However, the principle is the same: they manage the data contained in the files, enabling the user to get maximum utility from the data.

Another feature of DBM programs is that they enable the user to *build* databases, accumulating data into orderly sets of files, forms, records, reports, and other forms necessary for efficient management and use.

For your own purposes, these databases can be used for many purposes—marketing, publications, booking, schedules, appointments, and many other uses.

Accounting Programs

Most people tend to associate computers with accounting primarily. That's the unfortunate consequence of an unfortunate choice of name. The very name, *computer*, suggests that mathematical manipulation is the prime function. That's not true, of course. The prime function of a computer is management, handling, processing of information, and an early experimenter, Charles Babbage, in the previous century, had a clearer idea when he called his invention (a primitive computer) an "analytical engine."

There are literally hordes of accounting programs for your computer, and you can have the little micro take over all book-keeping, posting, issuing invoices, tracking and aging payables, preparing financial reports, calculating taxes, and otherwise managing that part of your enterprise. The program will do the job; you do not need to know a debit from a declining balance to run most accounting programs.

Communications

With a modem—jargon derived from the words *modulator-demodulator*—and communications software you can have your computer talk to other computers over the telephone. There are hundreds of commercial databases and electronic bulletin boards "on line" today, and you can get information from them and even "download"—transfer the information to your own files—from them. Some of the commercial databases charge fees, but there are many that are free, operated by government agencies, large organizations, and hobbyists.

You can often accomplish important research without leaving your desk, use your computer as a telex to send wires and cables to distant points, employ the "electronic mail" facility offered by the bulletin boards. Coauthors use such systems to collaborate on books and papers, companies and individuals correspond with each other via such systems, and you will soon find this a means for corresponding with clients and prospective clients.

Management Programs

There are many management programs, some general and suitable for all enterprises, some specialized and suitable for special industries or special occupations and disciplines. Following are a few listings to exemplify the general idea:

General Business Management Programs

Accounting	Inventory control
Communications	Office administration
File and mailing list management	Product procurement

Finance and planning

Project management
Sales and marketing

Industry-Related Software

Advertising
Architecture
Automotive
Banking and finance
Broadcasting and film
Construction

Consulting services
Contractors
Energy
Insurance
Printing services

Special Trades and Disciplines

Auctioneering
Authors and writers
Mathematics
Market research

Music
Science and research
Social science
Visual arts

SHOPPING FOR A MICROCOMPUTER

For anyone not familiar with computers the market is a bewildering array of makes and models. At the moment, the market appears to be dominated by the IBM PC influence, and the majority of microcomputers being advertised today claim to be "IBM compatible." By that they mean that their machines are based on the MS-DOS operating system, which is close enough to IBM's PC-DOS to be relatively compatible—they will run many programs developed and designed for the IBM PC micro.

These are all 16-bit machines. That is, they have 16-bit microprocessors (also called CPUs, for central processing units), like the IBM PC and unlike the previous generation of micros (produced around 1981) which tended to the earlier 8-bit microprocessor and the CP/M operating system.

Now 32-bit machines, such as the Apple Macintosh, are beginning to appear, and presumably the 16-bit machine will soon be dated. However, that does not have a great deal of significance for the average small business or self-employed entrepreneur; 8-bit and 16-bit micros will serve the needs of most of these for years to come, and do so with complete satisfaction. The 32-bit machines, and even the 16-bit machines are designed for greater needs than those of such small entrepreneurs as these. And there is such an abundance of software already available for CP/M, PC-DOS, and MS-DOS machines, both 8- and 16-bit, that if there were no more programs ever written for these machines, it would still be years and years before the machines would be threatened with obsolescence for lack of software.

A great many of today's machines are billed as being "portable" and as being "transportable," with no standardization of those terms. The transportable micro is generally considered to be one with a nine-inch monitor screen and about the size of a large attaché case or small suitcase. The so-called portable, often called the briefcase portable and lap portable, is small enough to slip into the average attache case, has an LCD (liquid crystal display) screen (a larger version of the LCD digital watch dial), and is intended for carrying aboard an airplane and on the road generally.

Probably you will want one to keep on your desk, where it will serve your needs best. In my own case, I objected to any screen smaller than 12 inches—that's small enough—but many users appear satisfied with a nine-inch screen. That's a decision you'll have to make for yourself.

Most computers are sold "bundled" today. That means that you get some software programs with them. Probably you will get a word processor, a speller, and an accounting or management program, as a minimum, with any micro you buy, and you may very well get considerably more in the way of software. In some cases, you'll get a choice; in others you do not get a choice.

PRINTERS

Strictly speaking, just about everything but the central unit containing the microprocessor, memory, and firmware is peripheral. That includes the keyboard and screen, the disk drives, the printer, and, if you use one, the modem. In practice, you need everything but the printer and the modem for even the minimum usage, but the system would be of very limited use to you if you did not have a printer.

Some micros are sold as a package, including a printer or a choice of printers, but you can always buy a system sans printer and buy the printer separately. Printers are of two general kinds, the dot matrix and the letter quality. Briefly, the dot matrix printers tend to be relatively fast, but the quality of their printing leaves something to be desired, usually, although there are now dot matrix printers which are "near letter quality." However, to be NLQ (near letter quality) they surrender most of that speed which is almost their only advantage, and they go up sharply in price. If you expect to turn out printed material on your system, you should consider a letter quality printer. (Midrange ones print at about 200 words a minute, and the more costly ones can go to more than twice that speed.)

Most printers offer tractor feed, which includes a sprocket on each end of the printer platen, engaging sprocket holes along the edges of the fanfolded paper. After printing, the edges bearing the sprocket holes of the paper can be removed, leaving clean-edged sheets, virtually indistinguishable from ordinary typewriter paper. Printers usually have friction feed—like a typewriter—sometimes with tractor feed an option, sometimes with tractor feed a fixed feature. The friction feed permits you to use single sheets, if you wish to.

Some printers offer automatic single-sheet feeders. These are rather expensive and, from all accounts, tend to be somewhat less reliable than the tractor feed system, although they do offer certain benefits of convenience, especially in changing paper or intermingling different kinds of paper.

MODEMS

A modem is a must for intercomputer communication via telephone lines, and such communication will become more and more important, as more and more micros come into use and more and more online databases (information and research services) become available on the open market. There are several kinds of modems, including these types:

Acoustic

The acoustic modem is one that has a set of cups designed to receive the earpiece and mouthpiece—receive and send—portions of the telephone handset. The electrical pulses that represent computer data are converted by the modem into sound, sent over the telephone lines, and reconverted by another modem at the other end. Information is received in the reverse sequence, of course.

Direct Connect

The direct-connect modem does away with the cups and the conversion, and sends the electrical pulses directly over the telephone lines to the receive-modem. (The modem is actually two modems, send- and receive-modems.) But direct-connect modems are of two types, also:

Internal. Some direct-connect modems can be wired into the computer internally, as a printed circuit board or chip. In fact, some computers can be purchased with the modem already wired in.

External. Other direct-connect modems are housed separately and connected to the computer as external units.

The internal, direct-connect modem is the most convenient one to use, for obvious reasons, although all will operate well enough, and is usually a little less costly than the external modem.

Modems operate at different speeds, called *baud*, in technical language (although that term is from earlier days of telegraphy, and has been adopted by the modern computer-communications industry). In practical terms, baud is the rate at which signals are sent, in pulses per second. The two rates most widely in use today are 300 baud and 1200 baud, and most modems designed for use with micros operate at either 300 baud or 300 and 1200 baud. That is roughly equivalent to about 250 and 1000 words per minute. When you are paying for "connect time," for both the information service and the telephone line, and transferring information to your own files to scan later, the advantage of the higher speed is obvious.

COMPUTER LITERACY AND USER FRIENDLINESS

The term "user friendly" has become well established in computer terminology, especially in the advertising of computers and software. The reason is that the term is intended to mean easy-to-learn and easy-to-use. The fact is that computers are, indeed, becoming easier and easier to learn and to use, partly because of refinements in computer design, and partly because of greater help afforded by features of the software.

One help is that of "menus" and "menu-driven" programs. These are guides presented on the screen to help the user find the right buttons to push for different functions—to delete a word, view a directory, transfer a file, or make other use of the computer's and program's capabilities. In many cases, the on-screen guidance is so complete that it is rarely or even never necessary to refer to the manuals, at least not after the initial reading, to operate the system and run the program.

There are also various kinds of prompts and warnings. Most systems, for example, will warn you when a line of copy is too long to fit the screen or paper, or a disk is too full and you must use a fresh disk or erase files you no longer need, if you want to make room on the disk you are currently using.

Some systems—notably the Apple Macintosh—use "icons," instead of or in addition to verbal menus. These are simple graphic symbols, such as a wastebasket to signify the erase (discard) function, or a filing cabinet to signify a save (file) function. These are generally used with a "mouse," a device that you can roll around the table, moving a cursor or pointer on the screen. When it points to the function you want, you press a button on the mouse to carry out the function. (Some mice have more than one button.)

Ultimately, it will be all but impossible to operate even the tiniest enterprise on a businesslike basis without a micro, and those who read the signs early and took the plunge will be miles ahead of those who have to later run to catch up. This will probably be especially true of those who are in enterprises especially dependent on information, as, we are assured by many forecasters, our economy in general is likely to be. The forecasts have been increasingly in agreement that our former "smokestack industry" economy must inevitably give way to and be succeeded by an information-based economy. There is good reason to believe that that will be particularly true for speakers, consultants, publishers, and others in related professions and enterprises. And there is growing evidence that this is accurate forecasting, as we see an ever-growing computer-communications-database complex developing.

ONLINE DATABASES AND INFORMATION SERVICES

The following are just a few of the many commercial online databases and information services that are available to anyone with a micro, modem, and communications software. Some specialize in certain types of information, such as West Publishing, which specializes in information for lawyers, but most have a variety of databases—kinds of information—to offer.

NEILSEN BUSINESS SERVICES
A.C. NIELSEN CO.
Nielsen Plaza
Northbrook, IL 60062
(312) 498-6300

ADP NETWORK SERVICES, INC.
175 Jackson Plaza
Ann Arbor, MI 48106
(313) 769-6800

BOEING COMPUTER SERVICES, INC.
7990 Gallows Court
Vienna, VA 22180
(703) 827-4603

BUSINESS COMPUTER NETWORK (BCN)
POB 36
Riverton, WY 82501
(800) 446-6255

BRS (BIBLIOGRAPHIC RETRIEVAL SVCS)
BRS/AFTER DARK
1200 Route 7
Latham, NY 12110
(800) 833-4707
(518) 783-1161

BRS/EXECUTIVE INFORMATION
SERVICE
JOHN WILEY & SONS, INC.
One Wiley Drive
Somerset, NJ 08873
(201) 469-4400

CBD ONLINE
UNITED COMMUNICATIONS GROUP
8701 Georgia Avenue, Suite 800
Silver Spring, MD 20910
(301) 589-8875

CHASE ECONOMETRICS/INTERACTIVE
DATA
486 Totten Pond Road
Waltham, MA 02154
(617) 890-1234

CITISHARE
850 Third Avenue
New York, NY 10043
(212) 572-9600

COMPUSERVE
EXECUTIVE INFORMATION SERVICE
5000 Arlington Centre Blvd
Columbus, OH 43220
(800) 848-8990

THE COMPUTER COMPANY
1905 Westmoreland Street
POB 6987
Richmond, VA 23230
(804) 358-2171

COMSHARE
Wolverine Tower
3001 S. State Street, POB 1588
Ann Arbor, MI 48106
(313) 994-4800

CONTROL DATA CORP.
500 W. Putnam Avenue
POB 7100
Greenwich, CT 06836
(203) 622-2000

CORNELL UNIVERSITY
COMPUTER SERVICES
G-02 Uris Hall
Ithaca, NY 14853
(607) 256-4981

DATA RESOURCES, INC.
1750 K Street, NW, 9th floor
Washington, DC 20006
(202) 862-3700

DELPHI
3 Blackstone Street
Cambridge, MA 02139
(800) 544-4005
(617) 491-3393

DIALOG INFORMATION SERVICES
KNOWLEDGE INDEX
3460 Hillview Avenue
Palo Alto, CA 94304
(800) 227-1927/982-5838
(415) 858-3785

DOW JONES NEWS/RETRIEVAL
DOW JONES & CO., INC.
POB 300
Princeton, NJ 08540
(800) 257-5114
(609) 452-1511

DUN & BRADSTREET CORPORATION
299 Park Avenue
New York, NY 10171
(212) 593-6800

EDUNET
POB 364
Princeton, NJ 08540
(609) 734-1878

GENERAL ELECTRIC INFORMATION
  SERVICES CO.
401 N. Washington Street
Rockville, MD 20850
(301) 340-4000

GML INFORMATION SERVICES
594 Marrett Road
Lexington, MA 02173
(617) 861-0515

INFONET
COMPUTER SCIENCES CORPORATION
650 N. Sepulveda Blvd
El Segundo, CA 90245
(213) 615-0311

INNERLINE
95 W. Algonquin Road
Arlington Heights, IL 60005
(800) 323-1321

INTERACTIVE MARKET SYSTEMS
19 W. 44th Street
New York, NY 10036
(212) 869-8810
(800) 223-7942

ITT DIALCOM
1109 Spring Street
Silver Spring, MD 20910
(301) 588-1572

MANAGEMENT SCIENCE ASSOCIATES,
  INC.
5100 Centre Avenue
Pittsburgh, PA 15232
(412)683-9533

MEAD DATA CENTRAL
LEXIS, LEXPAT, NEXIS
POB 933
Dayton, OH 45401
(513) 865-6800
(800) 227-4908

MERRILL LYNCH TIME SHARING
MERRILL LYNCH ECONOMICS, INC.
1 Liberty Plaza
New York, NY 10080
(212) 637-6200

NEWSNET
945 Haverford Road
Bryn Mawr, PA 19010
(215) 527-8030
(800) 345-1301

ON-LINE RESEARCH, INC.
200 Railroad Avenue
Greenwich, CT 06830
(203) 661-1395

ORBIT SEARCH SERVICE
SDC INFORMATION SERVICES
2500 Colorado Avenue
Santa Monica, CA 90406
(213) 453-6194

PROPRIETARY COMPUTER SYSTEMS
CISINETWORK CORP.
PCS DIVISION
16625 Saticoy Street
Van Nuys, CA 91406
(213) 781-8221

RAPIDATA DIVISION
NATIONAL DATA CORP.
20 New Dutch Lane
Fairfield, NJ 07006
(201) 227-0035

THE SOURCE
1616 Anderson Road
McLean, VA 22102
(800) 336-3366

STSC
2115 E. Jefferson Street
Rockville, MD 20852
(301) 984-5000

TRW INFORMATION SERVICES DIV.
BUSINESS CREDIT SERVICES & CREDIT
  DATA SERVICE
500 City Parkway West, Suite 200
Orange, CA 92668
(714) 937-2000

UNI-COLL
SCIENCE CENTER
PA 19104
387-3890

UNITED INFORMATION SERVICES, INC.
20 N. Clark Street, Suite 1400
Chicago, IL 60602
(312) 782-2000

WARNER COMPUTER SYSTEMS, INC.
605 Third Avenue
New York, NY 10158
(212) 986-1919

WEST PUBLISHING CO.
WESTLAW
50 W. Kellog Blvd
POB 43526
St. Paul, MN 55164
(800) 328-9352

KINDS OF INFORMATION AND SERVICES AVAILABLE

This is a relatively brief list of online databases and information services, but it typifies the kinds of information and services available, which run the gamut.

Most of the services listed here are primarily information resources: they have many different databases—and "many" can mean hundreds and hundreds, in some cases—and can provide subscribers access to these, either directly (to databases installed in their own computers) or indirectly (to databases installed in other people's computers, but available over a commercial communications network. Some, however, offer other kinds of services, such as the use of their own large computers on a timesharing basis. (This enables the owner of a microcomputer that is too small for a given program or project to gain access to a larger computer.) Some also offer a large library of computer programs that the subscriber can run on the larger computer—can have the use of, that is, by this indirect means.

All those listed here are commercial systems—they make charges for their use. Some charge an initiation fee to enroll you as a subscriber, plus connect time (charged by the minute or by the hour/fraction of an hour), and if they require long-distance telephone connections, you have to pay for the telephone service, too. (Some are tied to a network, such as Ethernet, which makes charges for connect time, but usually costs less than the long-distance tolls you would otherwise pay the telephone company.) Others charge only connect time, with no initial fee. Some have a "prime time" rate, during normal business hours, but a lower rate after business hours and on weekends. Most have some minimum monthly charge, also. The rate for 1200-baud communication is generally higher than that for 300-baud communication, as well, although it is usually an economy, especially when downloading information.

In many cases, the initial fees and standard connect-time charges do not apply to all the services and/or databases offered, and there are extra charges for some of the services. The Source, for example, offers some "free" game programs, but it turns out that they are free only to view onscreen, and a charge is made to download—copy—them and record them in your own system.

Many of these organizations can provide access to a number of databases, while some specialize. In some listings, different databases are identified. Mead Data Central, for example, lists three legal databases, LEXIS, LEXPAT, and NEXIS. The following descriptions should illustrate some of that wide range of diversity. Note, however, that the following is little more than a set of notes, and is far from being complete information about any of the systems listed. For complete information it is necessary to communicate directly with the system at the addresses and telephone numbers given.

Nielsen. Produces Neilsen Retail Index, a database of retail activity in cosmetics, alcohol, food, drug, health, and other consumer commodities.

ADP. Offers diverse business data.

Boeing. Financial and economic information.

Business Computer Network. A special service that offers subscribers access to many other databases/services listed here.

BRS. Offers a broad variety of business information and lists a separate system for off-peak-hours subscription. Offers many databases on a wide variety of subjects—taxation, law, finances, industry, sciences, and other.

BRS/Wiley. BRS is the user interface here through which you can gain access to Wiley's four databases, including summaries of management and business articles from 600 periodicals, and the full text of others.

CBD Online. This is the electronic version of the government's

Commerce Business Daily, which enables you to review the bidding opportunities the day they are printed in the CBD, rather than several days later, when the U.S. Postal Service gets around to delivering your copy.

Chase. Historical and forecast data on a variety of business, financial, investment information.

Citishare. Economic/financial databases, including stock market reports.

CompuServe. One of the early entrants into the online commercial database business, offering a variety of data for a range of types of subscribers, and with two types of subscriptions— for business executives and for private individuals.

The Computer Company. Access to industry-specific databases, especially those for banking, transportation, and energy.

Comshare. Demographic data and 5-year forecasts of consumer spending.

Control Data Corp. Marketing, financial, other business information.

Cornell. Economic data on various industries.

Data Resources. Financial/economic/business data.

Delphi. Data on travel, stock quotes, finances, investments, securities.

Dialog. Hundreds of databases available on a wide variety of business subjects. Knowledge Index is for after-hours subscribers.

Dow Jones. 27 databases, covering various aspects of financial, investment, and business topics.

Dun & Bradstreet. Subscribers can use D&B's computer facilities online, use the system to search for companies matching a given set of specifications, get financial data on specific companies, among the many services available.

Edunet. Educational data.

General Electric. Offers teleprocessing, computer timesharing, access to and use of many programs.

GML. Databases about the computer industry itself, organized in terms of different classes/kinds of computers and related equipment.

Infonet.   Business/industrial/securities databases.

InnerLine.   Databases for the banking industry.

Interactive.   Databases providing access to media, including Neilsen Retail Index.

ITT.   Databases for Fortune 100 companies—stock market, business, other.

Management Science.   Databases compiled on consumer/retail market activity.

Mead.   Legal and patent research services (LEXIS and LEXPAT) and general news services (NEXIS).

Merrill Lynch.   Historical and forecast data on several industries.

NewsNet.   Investments and related information.

On-Line Research.   Various data files via access to other organizations' data, such as Frost & Sullivan.

ORBIT.   Over 70 databases on management, business, and news coverage by several major newspapers.

Proprietary.   Economic and financial databases of U.S. and foreign exchange.

Rapidata.   Information utility for economic and financial data, including projections.

The Source.   Another old-timer in this industry, geared to investors and private individuals, more than to business firms.

STSC.   Time series on American economy, with demographic and geo-related economic data.

TRW.   Credit information/reporting service, on both business firms and individuals.

Uni-Coll.   Accesses Wharton econometric databases.

United.   Author's Program, allowing software writers a distribution/marketing facility.

Warner.   Financial databases.

Westlaw.   Business, financial and legal data, with orientation toward law firms.

CHAPTER 13

TIPS AND IDEAS FOR BEGINNERS AND VETERANS

A varied list of gems garnered over the years and from a great many sources, presented in no particular order.

FILMS AND OTHER AUDIOVISUAL PRESENTATION AND MARKETING AIDS

Many public libraries have stock films and slides that can be rented for small fees and even free of charge, in some cases. Moreover, this is not the only source: many government agencies also have films and other aids available for loan or rental. Check with the nearest Federal Information Center or the nearest Government Printing Office bookstore for a government publication listing these.

Collect as many publisher's catalogs as possible, too. (Most publishers will send you a copy on request.) These will help you locate useful books when you are researching something. Also ask the Government Printing Office to put your name on their mailing list for their "Selected Publications" mailer. All of these are useful to help you in your presentations, especially in presenting seminars and training programs, but they are also useful when you are writing a proposal or making a sales presentation, to back up your proposed program with specific detail. (On one occasion, these resources were most helpful in writing a proposal that won an $8.7 million government contract for training programs.)

Here are a few other sources to try for audiovisuals and printed materials that can be helpful in your presentation and your marketing:

AMERICAN MANAGEMENT
 ASSOCIATIONS (AMA)
135 West 50th Street
New York, NY 10020

BNA COMMUNICATIONS, INC.
9417 Decoverly Hall Road
Rockville, MD 20850

ROBERT J. BRADY CO.
Routes 197 & 450
Bowie, MD 20715

DARTNELL
4660 Ravenswood Avenue
Chicago, IL 60640

MARILYN VAN DERBUR
MOTIVATIONAL INSTITUTE
1616 Champa Street
Denver, CO 80202

MEETING MAKERS, INC.
215 Lexington Avenue
New York, NY 10016

MOTIVATION MEDIA
1245 Milwaukee Avenue
Glenview, IL 60025

NATIONAL PARK SERVICE
DIVISION OF AV ARTS
Harpers Ferry Center
Harpers Ferry, WV 25425

MAKING CUSTOMERS INSTEAD OF MAKING SALES

Since it costs so much money to win each sale, it's important to get more than one sale from each new client, even though some clients have a policy of not using the same speaker again—at least, not until a long lapse of time. One way to win multiple sales is to offer a program which is made up of a series of presentations, and another is to offer a kind of package deal, in which you sell the client a consulting service, including speaking, writing, and advisory services, among other consultative functions. This is particularly appropriate to training programs for small companies, where the client has no in-house capability, and needs a total set of services, such as the initial needs or task analyses, program design and development, and presentation. A few such clients, signed up on a long-term basis, and you have a foundation on which to base your entire enterprise.

SUPPORTING BUSY ORGANIZATIONS

One common mistake many make is to assume that when an organization has an in-house capability there is no use trying to sell them your own competitive services. (Why would they buy from a competitor?) For example, suppose you find a company in your area that has a large and well-staffed training department. That means that there is no chance for you to get work there, right? Wrong. Experience shows clearly that frequently it is just that kind of situation that is most fruitful. Any organization that already has its own permanent capability to do what you do is a *special marketing opportunity*. Here's why:

First of all, the existence of a large and well-staffed training department demonstrates that the company has a continuing training need and does a lot of training. The company is training-oriented, obviously *believes* in training. You don't have to sell them on training; only on *using you* to support and aid their training programs. Excellent prognosis.

Secondly, it is all but certain that any organization that does enough training to keep a permanent, fully staffed training department runs into overload situations—more training requirement than the staff can handle, for the moment; training that requires specialized talent not currently available in-house; one or more of the staff ill, on vacation, on special assignment, or otherwise unavailable when needed; and/or perhaps even a policy of using guest lecturers. (The "outside expert" syndrome, in which the in-house experts are somehow less highly regarded by the trainees than the out-of-house experts, the latter somehow commanding respect which the former cannot. More than once I have been called in to do seminars the marketing man or proposal leader could have done as well, but I was the "outside expert," the consultant, and automatically commanded more respect from the trainees.)

Make contacts with the training people here, and stay in touch. Get to know the managers. Make it clear that you understand that "outside expert" syndrome. Keep reminding them that you are ready and able to support them—back them up—in any emergency and on short notice. Eventually, the emergency will arise, and if they remember you—it's your responsibility to see to it that they *can't* forget you—they'll call, and you'll have your foot in the door.

Keep an eye open for such situations. With the right effort, they almost always pay off eventually.

TRADING UP

Always try to expand the sale. When a client engages me to do a seminar for their staff, I inquire as to the total number of people they would like to train eventually and the total number of branch offices they have. On some occasions I am able to schedule several sessions, with a new group each time, when the company wants to have perhaps a hundred or more people trained. (I recommend not more than between 30 and 40 people per session.) And on some occasions I have managed to arrange sessions for each of several branch offices. Offer the client some inducement to make this kind of deal, such as a reduced price or discount for a mass booking.

ON PRICING

Some people tend to price themselves out of the market by being too high. But the mistake of pricing oneself out of the market by being too low in price is probably more common. Check out the competition—your contemporaries—and see how high they go— successfully—for *first-class* presentations. Make sure that you, too, can and do make a first-class presentation, and *charge a first-class price* for it. "High" prices will never price you out of the market if they are competitive for first-class work and that work is, in fact, first class in quality. On the contrary, many people will judge quality by the price asked, and a low price will be the kiss of death, in that case. To many, especially those who judge quality by the price and who are aware of what others charge, a low price is an admission of low quality. On the other hand, if you want to cut prices under that of the competition, for some reason, make it a "special" of some sort and give the prospect good reason to believe that it is a bargain and not the regular price. (In fact, there are many successful businesses that never charge a "regular" price, but always offer "bargain" rates. Sales and special discounts are their regular, normal way of doing business. The public, it seems, never gets tired of "bargains" and never refuses to believe in bargains.)

WHERE TO GET HELP

Many successful speakers are also lecture agents, consultants, publishers, and trainers of speakers. Some conduct seminars for experienced speakers, where even these veterans of the platform can get guidance to help them increase their success. The following are among the many who offer products and/or services of one sort or another. (Some of these names and addresses will be found again in a listing to be presented later of lecture bureaus and other such services.) The names are presented in no particular order, and without comment. The best approach is to write to each and inquire about services and products of interest to you as a speaker and/or consultant. Make your interest clear in writing. (Of course, if you are a prospective client, make that clear, too; they will love hearing from you in any case.)

DOTTIE WALTERS
18825 Hicrest Road
Glendora, CA 91740
(818) 335-8069

BOB MONTGOMERY
12313 Michelle Circle
Burnsville, MN 55337
(612) 894-1348

NIDO QUBEIN, CPAE
Creative Services, Inc.
POB 6008
High Point, NC 27262
(919) 889-3010

ART FETTIG, C.S.P.
GROWTH UNLIMITED, INC.
31 East Avenue
Battle Creek, MI 49017

MIKE FRANK
SPEAKERS UNLIMITED
POB 27225
Columbus, OH 43227
(614) 864-3703

LOU HAMPTON
Hampton Communication Strategies
4200 Wisconsin Avenue
Washington, DC 20016
(202) 363-4941/363-5575

ED LARKIN
SPEAKERS GUILD, INC.
93 Old Kings Highway
Sandwich, MA 02563

FRAN SLOTKIN
LECTURE CONSULTANTS, INC.
POB 327
Mineola, NY 11501

ASSOCIATIONS

There are a number of speakers associations. Here are several you should know about:

INTERNATIONAL PLATFORM
   ASSOCIATION (IPA)
2564 Berkshire Road
Cleveland Heights, OH 44106
(216) 932-0505

TOASTMASTERS INTERNATIONAL, INC.
POB 10400
Santa Ana, CA 92711
(714) 542-6793

NATIONAL SPEAKERS ASSOCIATION
   (NSA)
5201 N. 7th Street, Suite 200
Phoenix, AZ 85014
(National Headquarters: see listing of
   local chapters.)

NATIONAL SPEAKERS ASSOCIATION LOCAL CHAPTERS

Following is the current listing of the various local chapters of the National Speakers Association and the names of the contact person (chapter president) given for this listing.

ARIZONA CHAPTER

MORT UTLEY
7063 East McDonald Drive
Scottsdale, AZ 85253
(602) 998-4665

CAROLINAS

DAVID WARF
105 Glencrest Drive
Gaffney, SC 29340
(803) 489-3405

GOLDEN VOICE (L.A. AREA)

CHUCK SALISBURY
10201 Coral Tree Circle
Villa Park, CA 92667
(800) 854-5955

METRO NEW YORK

LOLA GREEN
Lattingtown Road
Glen Cove, NY 11542
(516) 671-5150

**FLORIDA SPEAKERS
  ASSOCIATION**

GAYLE CARSON
2957 Flamingo Drive
Miami Beach, FL 33140
(305) 534-8846

**GEORGIA SPEAKERS
ASSOCIATION**

KAY HERMAN
2057-A Powers Ferry Road
Marietta, GA 30067
(404) 952-4499

**GULF COAST SPEAKERS
ASSOCIATION**

NEAL SHAW
4814 Willow
Bellaire, TX 77401
(713) 661-5902

ILLINOIS CHAPTER

BILL HAYDEN
1105 Linden Lane
Mt Prospect, IL 60056
(312) 398-2455

INDIANA CHAPTER

FRANK BASILE
POB 40321
Indianapolis, IN 46240
(317) 844-0719

**NORTHERN CALIFORNIA
  CHAPTER**

BERT DECKER
999 Sutter Street
San Francisco, CA 94109
(415) 775-6111

NORTH TEXAS

JOHN KOSANKE
7070 Skilman, Suite 2007
Dallas, TX 75231
(214) 341-3035

OHIO SPEAKERS FORUM

E. LARRY MOLES
1940 Eleda Road
Lima, OH 45805
(419) 228-1204

SAN DIEGO CHAPTER

JEFF LAYNG
657 Pacific View Drive
San Diego, CA 92109
(714) 270-5138/276-0977

NATIONAL CAPITAL (DC)

ART GLINER
8521 Grubb Road
Silver Spring, MD 20910
(301) 588-3561

LIBERTY BELL

SUZY SUTTON
253 G Shawmont Avenue
Philadelphia, PA 19128
(215) 487-2920

WISCONSIN CHAPTER

ROBERT JANSEN
7918 Harwood Avenue
Wauwatosa, WI 53213
(414) 258-5720

THINGS YOU SHOULD READ AND USE

There are a great many excellent publications which will help you in many ways with ideas, trends, opportunities, and speaking techniques. This book makes no real effort or pretense of being able to teach you how to be a more effective or "better" speaker; there are hordes of such books available, written by people far better qualified than I to teach that subject. Here are a few that will give you more help than I can in how to speak well. I and others have found these most useful:

Sharing Ideas!, published by Dottie Walters at address given. This is bimonthly, generally runs on the order of 30 pages, is the bible of the industry, for many readers. It will keep you posted on what's happening, in addition to giving you lots of ideas, tips, and inside information from other professionals. It's one way to get in touch with the professionals in this business and stay in touch with what's going on. Few know the business better than Dottie does, and no one commands more respect and affection from professional speakers everywhere. You'll feel as though you had acquired a new family when you begin to read this warm bimonthly.

Communicate Like a Pro, by Nido Qubein, published by Prentice-Hall, Inc. Words of wisdom on public speaking, offered by a leading light of the industry, past president of NSA, highly regarded by the professionals of the industry, and a respected figure in his chosen profession. Information given in this book that you will find nowhere else and, best of all, based on the author's personal experience and personal successes. Available from Nido directly. Write him at address given.

How to Hold an Audience in the Hollow of Your Hand, by Art Fettig. One of his many books. Loaded with valuable and exclusive ideas, priceless insights. Includes many one-liners you can use, if you can stop laughing long enough to read them all. Write Art at the address cited earlier.

Meetings & Conventions, a monthly slick-paper trade journal, published by Ziff-Davis, One Park Avenue, New York, NY 10016, (212) 503-5700.

Writer's Digest, a monthly magazine, in existence for many years, the bible for many professional writers. (I have been reading it since 1937.) You can find it on your newsstand, but you may want to write to the magazine at 9933 Alliance Road, Cincinnati, Ohio 45242, 1-800-543-4644.

The Writer's Yearbook, an annual of the *Writer's Digest*, published every Spring, usually, worth reading. Full of useful articles, guides, directories.

The Writer's Market, published by the book publishing division of the magazine, an annually revised and updated guide to markets for writers.

How to Succeed as an Independent Consultant, by Herman Holtz, published by John Wiley & Sons, Inc. My own effort to guide others to success in the consulting field. Deals with the nuts and bolts how-to of consulting, especially with marketing, has been thrice a book-club selection, back to press for reprintings a dozen times in slightly more than a year.

The Computer Phone Book, by Mike Cane, a Plume Book published by New American Library. A directory to online databases, electronic bulletin boards, and similar facilities and resources.

How to Hold Your Audience with Humor, by noted comedy writer Gene Perrett, published by Writer's Digest books. (Foreword by Bob Hope, for whom Perrett has written.)

Omni Online Database Directory, Macmillan Publishing, 866 Third Avenue, New York, NY 10022.

Microcomputers for Lawyers, by J. Stewart Schneider and Charles E. Bowen, published by TAB Books, POB 40, Blue Ridge Summit, PA 17214.

MULTIPLYING CIRCULATION OF YOUR DIRECT MAIL

When you send out direct mail, whether it's a sales letter and accompanying brochures or a newsletter you use for promotional purposes, you face the problem of how to address it so that it lands on the right desk in the addressee organization. One way that has worked well for me has been the use of a routing box printed directly on the letter, generally in the upper right corner. (see Figure 8). The advantages of doing this are several: It suggests to the mail clerk (who may be the one who opens mail that has no individual's name in the address) who ought to get the piece. It also suggests to anyone who does wind up with it that perhaps there will be others interested in seeing it.

The result is that the piece usually winds up being circulated among several people in the organization, vastly improving the probability of "finding a home"—landing on the desk of someone who becomes interested in talking to you about your offer.

You begin by imprinting the functional titles of those you think to be the most likely targets, but be sure to leave several blanks also, because you don't know exactly what functions exist and titles are used in organizations. Note, too, that room is left to write

```
┌─────────────────────────────────────────────────────┐
│                                                       │
│   ROUTE TO:                                           │
│                                                       │
│   [ ] Marketing Director:_____      │
│                                                       │
│   [ ] Training Director:_____       │
│                                                       │
│   [ ] Program Director:_____        │
│                                                       │
│   [ ] _____       │
│                                                       │
│   [ ] _____       │
│                                                       │
│   [ ] _____       │
│                                                       │
└─────────────────────────────────────────────────────┘
```

Figure 8   A typical routing box.

in actual names and check-off boxes are provided to enable everyone seeing the piece to know who else has already seen it.

By using this device you have an excellent chance of tripling or even further multiplying the complete circulation of your direct-mail pieces—a mailing of 5000 pieces may easily be seen by 25,000 people!

MEETING/CONVENTION PLANNERS AND CONSULTANTS

Conventions and conferences—major conclaves of people associated with each other on either a long-term, permanent basis or on a short-term, special occasion basis—are big business today, running to billions of dollars annually. They represent an industry in themselves, an industry that supports not only speakers and entertainers, but also many service organizations—lecture bureaus and agents, sellers of audiovisual and other needed equipment, exhibit designers, planning consultants, conference managers, production companies, and sundry others.

Those support organizations, including lecture bureaus, planning consultants, and convention managers, are all potential sources of business for speakers because many of them are assigned the responsibility of engaging speakers for the events, as well as providing other services. A list of some of those organizations describing themselves as planning consultants and/or convention and conference managers is offered here. Some duplication with other lists will be noted, since some of the convention consultants and planners are also lecture agents and lecture bureau operators, and some are, themselves, speakers.

A & B BUSINESSWORKS, INC.
529 Bay Avenue
Point Pleasant Beach, NJ 08742

ACA ATLANTIC CONVENTIONS
POB 891
Cherry Hill, NJ 08003

A.V.P.S. CORP.
225 E. 45th Street
New York, NY 10022

SOL ABRAMS ASSOCIATES
331 Webster Drive
New Milford, NJ 07646

ADELLE COX CONVENTION SERVICES
  & CONSULTANTS
POB 69-4770
Miami, FL 33169

ATLANTIC CONVENTION
  ASSOCIATES
POB 2285
Ventnor, NJ 08406

ATLANTIC EXHIBIT SERVICES
62 W. 45th Street
New York, NY 10036

BANNISTER & ASSOCIATES
6130 Sunbury Road
Westerville, OH 43081

MIKI BELL & ASSOCIATES
4664 Cedar Park Drive
Stone Mountain, GA 30083

BESTCONVENTIONS, INC.
401 Euclid Avenue
The Arcade, Suite 465
Cleveland, OH 44114

MARSHA BLACK & ASSOCIATES
POB 11037
Memphis, TN 38111

RAY BLOCH PRODUCTIONS, INC.
230 Peachtree Street, NW
Atlanta, GA 30303
& 1500 Broadway
New York, NY 10036

BOSTROM MANAGEMENT CORP.
435 N. Michigan Avenue
Tribune Tower, Suite 1717
Chicago, IL 60611

LEE BOYAN & ASSOCIATES
11813 Crawford Road, W
Minnetonka, MN 55343

HELEN BRETT ENTERPRISES, INC.
6 E. Monroe Street
Chicago, IL 60603

BUSINESS INCENTIVES, INC.
POB 1610
Minneapolis, MN 55440

BUSINESS PROGRAMS, INC.
87 Greenwich Avenue
Greenwich, CT 06830

CCR, INC. CONVENTION SERVICE
1130 E. Missouri, Suite 210
Phoenix, AZ 85014
& 2625 East Third Avenue
Denver, CO 80206

CMC MANAGEMENT SERVICES
5224 Riverhills Drive
Tampa, FL 33617

CMR/LTD.
801 Knightsbridge Lane
Schaumburg, IL 60195

CALIFORNIA ASSN. OF MEETING
  PLANNERS
888 Airport Blvd.
Burlingame, CA 94010

CALIFORNIA LEISURE
  CONSULTANTS, INC.
2760 E. El Presidio Street
Long Beach, CA 90810
& 3714 Fourth Street
San Diego, CA 92103

GAYLE CARSON PRESENTS
2957 Flamingo Drive
Miami Beach, FL 33140

GANN CARTER CONVENTION
  SERVICES
261 E. Tahquitz
McCallum Way
Palm Springs, CA 92262

CITY WELCOME CORP.
100 Jericho Quadrangle, Suite 212
Jericho, NY 11753

COMMUNICATIONS CONNECTION, INC.
1723 W. Devon
POB 60276
Chicago, IL 60660

CONFERENCE CONSULTANTS
  INTERNATIONAL
700 Diplomat Pkwy
Hallandale, FL 33009

CONFERENCE MANAGEMENT CORP.
17 Washington Street
Norwalk, CT 06854

CONFERENCE RESOURCES, INC.
1821 E. Fairmount Avenue
Baltimore, MD 21231

CONFERON, INC.
1727 Forest Cove Drive, Suite 203
Mt. Prospect, IL 60056

CONVENTION & CONFERENCE
  CONSULTANTS
644 Timber Lane
Lake Forest, IL 60045

CONVENTION CONSULTANTS OF
  SAVANNAH DELTA, INC.
117 W. Perry
Savannah, GA 31401

CONVENTION ENTERTAINMENT
  PRODUCTIONS
1645 River Road
Des Plaines, IL 60018

CONVENTION MASTERS, INC.
1011 E. Touhy Avenue
Des Plaines, IL 60016
5852 Hubbard Drive
Rockville, MD 20852,
& 350 Fifth Avenue, Suite 3304
New York, NY 10001

CONVENTION PLANNERS, INC.
200 E. Delaware Place, Suite 11A
Chicago, IL 60611

CONVENTION SERVICE ASSOCIATES
3050 Biscayne Blvd, Suite 100
Miami, FL 33137

CONVENTION SERVICES INTERNATIONAL
139 S. Beverly Drive
Beverly Hills, CA 90212

THE HAL COPELAND CO., INC.
3924 Royal Lane, Suite 201
Dallas, TX 75230

CREATIVE COMMUNICATIONS
  ASSOCIATES
16126 Lomacitas Lane
Whittier, CA 90601

CREATIVE CONVENTION CONSULTANTS
18 John Street, Suite 1503
New York, NY 10038

CREATIVE MEETING MANAGEMENT,
    INC.
6501 Mineral Pt. Road
Madison, WI 53705

CUSTOM CONVENTION SERVICES OF
    HOUSTON
2616 S. Loop W, Suite 330
Houston, TX 77054

STEPHEN ARTHUR DERRY, P.E.
7700 Coquina Drive
N. Bay Island
Miami Beach, FL 33141

DETAILS
1750 Pennsylvania Avenue, NW,
Suite 1208
Washington, DC 20006

HELEN R. DIETRICH, INC.
333 St. Charles Avenue, Suite 1221
New Orleans, LA 70130

EGR INTERNATIONAL MEETINGS AND
    INCENTIVES, INC.
290 Madison Avenue
New York, NY 10017

EASTERN U.S. SHOW PRODUCTIONS,
    INC.
121 Chestnut Street
Philadelphia, PA 19106

THE ENTERTAINMENT DESIGNERS
3470 Crews Lake Drive
Lakeland, FL 33803

THE EVENTORS, INC.
213 W. Institute Place
Chicago, IL 60610

EVENTS ALIVE, INC.
222 W. Adams, Suite 1200
Chicago, IL 60606

EXPERIENCE CONFERENCES, INC.
835 Glen Elm Drive
St. Louis, MO 63122

JOE M. FLAKE & CO.
1050 Northgate Drive
San Rafael, CA 94903

FRANK & ASSOCIATE
Speakers Unlimited
POB 27225
Columbus, OH 43227

DONNA J. FRASER & ASSOCIATES, LTD.
336 133-9 Avenue, SW
Calgary Alb T2P 1J9
Canada

G&G MANAGEMENT ASSOCIATES
3656 Beverly Ridge
Sherman Oaks, CA 91423

DR. ART GARNER & ASSOCIATES
2519 Lovitt Drive
Memphis, TN 38138

GELCO CONVENTION SERVICES
924 Sligh Blvd.
Orlando, FL 32806

GEORGE GILL ASSOCIATES
12231 NE 13th Court
Miami, FL 33161

GLAHE INTERNATIONAL, INC.
1700 K Street, NW
Washington, DC 20006

GLOBAL ENTERPRISES, INC.
Westlake Place, Suite 100
Austin, TX 78746

GROUP CONSULTANTS,
    INTERNATIONAL, LTD.
9 Northern Blvd.
Greenvale, NY 11548

HDO PRODUCTIONS, INC.
627 Hazel Street
Glendale, CA 91201

SANDY HAMER ASSOCIATES, INC.
15 Lewis Street
Hartford, CT 06103

HARRISON-BERKALL PRODUCTIONS,
INC.
527 Madison Avenue
New York, NY 10022

AUDREY HOFFMAN ENTERPRISES
12 Prospect Terrace
Albany, NY 12208

IMPACT COMMUNICATORS
1061 N. Shepard, Unit D
Anaheim, CA 92806

IMPACT INTERNATIONAL, INC.
John Hancock Center
Chicago, IL 60611

IN-TRA-PROMO, INC.
22 W. 23rd Street
New York, NY 10010

INTERNATIONAL CONFERENCE GROUP,
INC.
51 E. 42nd Street
New York, NY 10017

INTERNATIONAL ENTERTAINMENT
BUREAU
3612 N. Washington Blvd.
Indianapolis, IN 46205

INTERNATIONAL LANGUAGE &
COMMUNICATIONS CENTER
33 N. Dearborn, Suite 1300
Chicago, IL 60602

ISAACS ENTERPRISES, INC.
Old Route 17
Harris, NY 12742

JORDAN ENTERPRISES
SUCCESS LEADERS SPEAKERS SERVICE
Lenox Square, Box 18737
Atlanta, GA 30326

JORDAN LEISURE OF HAWAII
2222 Kalakaua Avenue
Honolulu, HI 96815

KNS PROMOTIONS, INC.
325 E. 41st Street
New York, NY 10017

KELLOG COMMUNICATIONS CORP.
26 W. Dry Creek Road
Littleton, CO 80121

KEN-DELL PRODUCTIONS, INC.
111 Valley Road
Wilmington, DE 19804

ERNIE KERNS & ASSOCIATES
2555 E. 55th Place, Suite 201
Indianapolis, IN 46220

KEYNOTE ASSOCIATES, INC.
250 W. 57th Street, Suite 1527
New York, NY 10019

LADDIN & COMPANY, INC.
2 Park Avenue
New York, NY 10016

HOWARD LANIN PRODUCTIONS, INC.
59 E. 54th Street
New York, NY 10022

MACMANNES, INC.
5104 MacArthur Blvd, NW
Washington, DC 20016

MANAGED EVENTS, LTD.
POB 14249
Atlanta, GA 30324

MARKETING COMMUNICATIONS
EXECUTIVES INTERNATIONAL
412 Ocean Avenue
Sea Bright, NJ 07760

MARKETING CONCEPTS, INC.
Two Pennsylvania Plaza
New York, NY 10121

MARKETING INNOVATORS
INTERNATIONAL, INC.
9701 W. Higgins Road, Suite 610
Rosemont, IL 60018

R. J. MARTIN CO.
321 Commercial Avenue
Palisades Park, NJ 07650

MCCOLLUM MANAGEMENT &
MEETINGS
POB 10523
Tallahassee, FL 32302

MCRAND, INC.
210 E. Westminster
Lake Forest, IL 60045

MEETING CONCEPTS, INC.
511 11th Avenue, S, Suite 261
Minneapolis, MN 55415

THE MEETING MARKET
2025 Eye Street, NW, Suite 507
Washington, DC 20006

MEETING MASTERS, INC.
4000 MacArthur Blvd, Suite 3000
& 260 Newport Center Drive, Suite
360
Newport Beach, CA 92660

MEETING MEDIA ENTERPRISES, LTD.
3330 Dundee Road, S-1
Northbrook, IL 60062

MEETING PLANNERS, INC.
433 Hanover Street
Boston, MA 02113,
501 Madison Avenue
New York, NY 10022,
& 6005 Overbrook Avenue
Philadelphia, PA 19131

MEETING SERVICES & CONVENTIONS
CONSULTANTS
95 Whiteridge Road, Suite 401
Nashville, TN 37205

MEETINGS UNLIMITED
POB 5052
Westport, CT 06881

ARTHUR MERIWEATHER, INC.
1529 Brook Drive
Downers Grove, IL 60515

BRUCE MERRIN ORGANIZATION
Warner Center
6400 Canoga Avenue, Suite 311
Woodland Hills, CA 91367

MICHAELJAY, INC.
10383 Oak Street
St. Petersburg, FL 33702

MONGRANDI-VARINA MANAGEMENT
888 7th Avenue, Suite 400
New York, NY 10106

L. MOONEY, INC.
5804 W. 86th Terrace
Overland Park, KS 66207

MULTI-ENTERTAINMENT, INC.
JERRY MARSHALL MUSICAL
ENTERPRISES, INC.
1110 NE 163rd Street, Suite 219
N. Miami Beach, FL 33162

BURT MUNK AND COMPANY
666 Dundee Road, Suite 503
Northbrook, IL 60062

NATIONAL SALES SEMINARS
POB 2007
Buellton, CA 93427

NEW ORIENT MEDIA
103 N. Second Street
W. Dundee, IL 60118

FRED A. NILES COMMUNICATIONS
CENTERS
1028 W. Washington Blvd
Chicago, IL 60607

OMNI MEETING PLANNERS
One Crossroads of Commerce
Rolling Meadows, IL 60008

OMNICON PRODUCTIONS, INC.
4700 Ardmore
Okemos, MI 48864

OMNIGROUP, INC.
9350 Baythorne
Houston, TX 77041

ON THE SCENE WITH ELEANOR WOODS
& ASSOCIATES
505 N. LaSalle Street
Chicago, IL 60610

ORGANIZATION MANAGEMENT, INC.
1121 L Street. Suite 500
Sacramento, CA 95814

P.A.M. COMMUNICATIONS
POB 142
Willowdale, North York
Ontario M2N 5S8 Canada

PR SERVICES CO.
1472 Broadway
New York, NY 10036
888 7th Avenue
New York, NY 10106

PASSKEY ASSOCIATES, INC.
425 Park Avenue
New York, NY 10022

KEN POST COMMUNICATION SERVICES,
INC.
33 W. 87th Street
New York, NY 10024

PRINCE & COMPANY
White Flint Mall
Kensington, MD 20895

PROFESSIONAL MEETING ORGANIZERS,
INC.
POB 141423
Coral Gables, FL 33114

PROFESSIONAL SPEAKERS BUREAU
POB 2007
Buellton, CA 93427

THE PROGRAM PEOPLE
POB 1426
Oak Brook, IL 60521

PROGRAM SUPPORT SPECIALISTS
POB 15464
Phoenix, AZ 85060

PROMOTIONAL PLANNING, INC.
502 Hulmeville Avenue
Langhorne Manor, PA 19047

PROMOTIONS FOR INDUSTRY, INC.
6545 Carnegie Avenue
Cleveland, OH 44103

QUETRAD ENTERPRISES, LTD.
2055 Rue Bishop
Montreal, Quebec
H3G 2E8 Canada

DONNA RAY ASSOCIATES
3050 Biscayne Blvd., Suite 100
Miami, FL 33139

RECEPTION ONTARIO
200 Ronson Drive, Suite 606
Rexdale, Ontario
M9W 5Z9 Canada

RED CARPET ASSOCIATES, INC.
19 E. 57th Street
New York, NY 10022

DEANNE ROSENBERG, INC.
28 Fifer Avenue
Lexington, MA 02173

ROUND HILL-IVC, INC.
89 Erickson Drive
Stamford, CT 06903

ST. LOUIS SCENE, INC.
8600 Delmar
St. Louis, MO 63124

SALUBRIS, INC.
69 Fairway Avenue
Verona, NJ 07044

SANDIDGE & SANDIDGE
Communications Bldg.
103 N. Second Street
W. Dundee, IL 60118

SANDY CORP.
1500 W. Big Beaver Road
Troy, MI 48084

SAXTON COMMUNICATIONS GROUP,
LTD.
605 Third Avenue
New York, NY 10158

SUSAN SCHELL ASSOCIATES
330 South Street
Morristown, NJ 07960

SHARON ENTERPRISES
3611 Mossville Court, #103
Houston, TX 77068

SHOW MARKETEERS, INC.
4508 Third Street, Suite 20
La Mesa, CA 92041

SHOWCASE ASSOCIATES, INC.
The Benson East, Suite A-200
Jenkintown, PA 19046

SHOWMAKERS, CONVENTION
ENTERTAINMENT SPECIALISTS
1702 Irvine Blvd., Suite 208
Tustin, CA 92680

JOE SNYDER & CO., LTD.
155 W. 68th Street
New York, NY 10023

SOCIETY & ASSOCIATION SERVICES
CORP.
4720 Montgomery Lane
Bethesda, MD 20814

SPECIAL SERVICES
7 N. 7th Street
St. Louis, MO 63101

STAFF DEVELOPMENT, INC.
1411 W. Olympic Blvd.
Los Angeles, CA 90015

SUNSHINE INTERNATIONAL LTD.
1100 17th Street, NW, Suite 601
Washington, DC 20036

TELECONCEPTS IN COMMUNICATIONS,
INC.
145 E. 49th Street
New York, NY 10017

TELESPAN, INC.
50 W. Palm Street
Altadena, CA 91001

ROGER TIERNEY ASSOCIATES, INC.
2955 McCall Street, #201
San Diego, CA 92106

TOGETHER, INC., MEETING PLANNERS
2016 E. 11th Street, Box 52528
Tulsa, OK 74152

TRAINING SERVICES, INC.
130 Orient Way
Rutherford, NJ 07070

TRANSAMERICA CONVENTION
SERVICES, INC.
POB 2921
Houston, TX 77252

THE TRI COMPANIES
1313 Boylston Street
Boston, MA 02215

UNIVERSAL MODELS & CONVENTION
SERVICE
953 E. Sahara Avenue
Bldg 28-B, Suite 207
Las Vegas, NV 89104

UNIVERSAL TRAVEL
Meeting & Convention Division
425 S. Mill Avenue
Tempe, AZ 85281

VIDEOMEETINGS
2636 Walnut Hill Lane, #110
Dallas, TX 75229

VIEWPOINT INTERNATIONAL
20 E. 53rd Street
New York, NY 10022

ROBERT P. WALKER ENTERPRISES, LTD.
63 Atlantic Avenue
Boston, MA 02110

WEDGEWOOD PRODUCTIONS, INC.
POB 440
Crownsville, MD 21032

WELCOME ABOARD
29 Church Street
Ramsey, NJ 07446

RALPH WHITENER & COMPANY
POB 17413
Dulles International Airport
Washington, DC 20041

JOHN WOLFE INSTITUTE
12335 Boheme
Houston, TX 77024

WOODBINE ASSOCIATES
90 Bagby Drive, Suite 222
Birmingham, Al 35209

CHAPTER 14

LECTURE BUREAUS
AND AGENTS

A directory, organized in geographic/alphabetic order for convenience in finding the bureaus/agents nearest your own home base.

A DIRECTORY

Do not expect any lecture bureau operator to fall joyously into your arms when you announce that you are or wish to become a public speaker. Neither the bureaus nor the clients are waiting to welcome you. Quite the contrary, they both have a wide and varied assortment of experienced and excellent speakers to choose from; you will have to *work* at gaining acceptance as a professional.

This list is not, therefore, offered to you to start bombarding those listed here with demands that they book you immediately at the top rates. It would be a profound mistake for you to go about using this list in that manner. But there are ways to use this list beneficially.

As a starter in using this list, you would probably do best to select those agents or bureaus nearest you, call a few on the telephone, and visit with those who can spare the time and are willing to give you some guidance (hopefully, for your mutual benefit). Go then and discuss your ambitions, what you have to offer, and what you must do to help the agent to help you.

ARIZONA

Roy B. McLaren, CPA
Associated Financial Planning
    Center of America, Inc.
500 West Southern, Store #25
Mesa, AZ 85202

The DeGreen Corporation
13444 N. 32nd Street, Suite 19-B
Phoenix, AZ 85032

National Speakers Association
5201 N. 7th Street, Suite 200
Phoenix, AZ 85014

Plaza Three Talent Agency
4343 N. 16th Street
Phoenix, AZ 85016

Summit Enterprises
3928 E. Corrine Drive
Phoenix, AZ 85032

Sun Safari Tours, Inc.
7500 E. McCormick Pkwy, #33
Scottsdale, AZ 85258

John D. Hammond
8216 N. 54th Street
Scottsdale, AZ 85253

Flair Parisienne
3451 East Speedway Blvd.
Tucson, AZ 85716

Booking Sun West Seminars, Inc.
4023 East Grant Road
Tucson, AZ 85712

CALIFORNIA

George Colouris Productions
1782 West Lincoln, Suite J
Anaheim, CA 92801

A. BYRON PERKINS & ASSOCIATES, INC.
1201 W. Huntington Drive, Suite 102
Arcadia, CA 91006

VERNE BENNOM GRIMSLEY
Int'l Broadcaster, WBN
Box 347
Berkeley, CA 94701

CONVENTION SERVICES INTERNATIONAL
139 S. Beverly Drive
Beverly Hills, CA 90212

TEMPLE BERDAN II
NAT'L REAL ESTATE SALES SEMINAR
PROFESSIONAL SPEAKERS BUREAU
Box 2007
Buellton, CA 93427

ROU DE GRAVELLES
SUCCESS RALLIES
225 Carnation Avenue
Corona del Mar, CA 92625

MAX SACKS INT'L.
888 N. Sepulveda Blvd., Suite 1060
El Segundo, CA 90245

DAVE GRANT PRODUCTIONS
17000 Ventura Blvd., Suite 220
Box 273
Encino, CA 91316

MAXIME MCINTIRE
4725 Rustic Road
Fair Oaks, CA 95628

MIKE HADER
HAPPI
Chapman at Lewis Street
Garden Grove, CA 92640

DOROTHY M. WALTERS
18825 Hicrest Road
Glendora, CA 91740

BARRY BRODY
2530 Manhattan Avenue
Hermosa Beach, CA 90245

CHET LACKEY
UNITED SPEAKERS ASSOCIATES
2120 Main Street, Suite 255
Huntington Beach, CA 92648

JEANETTE MILLER
18931 Via Messina
Irvine, CA 92715

CHERI MARSHALL & ASSOCIATES
3502 Lotus Avenue
Irvine, CA 92714

TONY LEASE TOURS
305 N. Coast Blvd.
Laguna Beach, CA 92651

BOBBIE GEE
ORANGE COUNTY SPEAKERS BUREAU
31781 National Park Drive
Laguna Niguel, CA 92677

PAT PERKINS
TERRY-COLE WHITTAKER &
    ASSOCIATES
Box 2454
La Jolla, CA 92038

CINDY BRYCE
UNIVERSITY OF SOUTHERN CALIFORNIA
COLLEGE OF CONTINUING EDUCATION
RAN 348 University Park
Los Angeles 90007

TEDDI SANFORD
M & T Assoc., Media Trainer
8217 Beverly Blvd.
Los Angeles, CA 90048

ROBERT SEAL
UNIVERSITY OF SOUTHERN CALIFORNIA
COLLEGE OF CONTINUING EDUCATION
Leadership Education &
    Development
Los Angeles, CA 90007

STAFF DEVELOPMENT, INC.
1411 W. Olympic Blvd.
Los Angeles, CA 90015

SHOW COMPANY INTERNATIONAL
8687 Melrose Avenue
Los Angeles, CA 90069

BRUCE MERRIN ORGANIZATION
9000 Sunset Blvd.
Los Angeles, CA 90069

VIRGINIA M. THOMAS
WEST COAST SPEAKERS BUREAU
3500 S. Figueroa, Suite 108
Los Angeles, CA 90007

DORIS NIEH ENTERPRISES
1415 N. Bronson Avenue
Los Angeles, CA 90028

JACQUELINE GREEN, PUBLIC RELATIONS
8326 Kirkwood Drive
Los Angeles, CA 90046

MARKETING ASSOCIATION SERVICES,
   INC.
9911 Pico Blvd.
Los Angeles, CA 90035

SRI INTERNATIONAL
333 Ravenswood Avenue
Menlo Park, CA 94025

MASTERS OF CEREMONIES
POB 390
Monrovia, CA 91016

DEAN HOWARD
SUCCESS SEMINARS
1539 Monrovia Avenue, Suite 14
Newport Beach, CA 92663

MEETING MASTERS, INC.
4000 MacArthur Blvd., Suite 3000
Newport Beach, CA 92660

DELLA CLARK
D. L. Clark & Associates
2295 N. Tustin, #4
Orange, CA 92665

THE PROGRAM EXCHANGE
SUE CLARK
1245 E. Walnut Street, Suite 104
Pasadena, CA 91106

RAY CONSIDINE
25 WEST WALNUT STREET
PASADENA, CA 91103

DARLENE ORAM
J.E.O. MARKETING
Box 60719
Sacramento, CA 95819

SAN JACOBI STAR PRODUCTIONS
4000 Mission Blvd., Suite 3
San Diego, CA 92109

THE PODIUM
(Women speakers only)
Sandra Schrift & Jill Henderson
3940 Hancock Street, Suite 207
San Diego, CA 92110

DAVID BELENZON MANAGEMENT
Box 15428
San Diego, CA 92115

SAMUEL WESTERMAN
4062 Camintito Dehesa
San Diego, CA 92107

PAULA SULLIVAN
542 5th Avenue
San Diego, CA 92101

DAVE WAGEMAKER
4620 Zion, Suite 22
San Diego, CA 92120

KATHLEEN BRENNER
460 Mission Valley Center West
San Diego, CA 92108

FRANK MATTAROCCI
2658 Worden Street, #223
San Diego, CA 92110

RUBY WRIGHT
CONVENTION & CONFERENCE
   CONSULTANTS
Box 19519
San Diego, CA 92115

FRANCISCO HOST, INC.
The Hearst Bldg.
Market & Third Streets
San Francisco, CA 94103

JAYNE TOWNSEND & ASSOCIATES
30 Hotaling Place
San Francisco, CA 94111

WESTERN EXIBITORS, INC.
2181 Greenwich Street
San Francisco, CA 94123

DOROTHY SATIR
CREATIVE PROGRAMS
265 Valdez Avenue
San Francisco, CA 94127

CAPPA & GRAHAM, INC.
59 Eastwood Drive
San Francisco, CA 94112

WAYNE SHORT LECTURE MANAGEMENT
WORLD KNOWLEDGE FILM SPEAKERS
1736 Stockton Street
San Francisco, CA 94133

MARJ HORN
CALIFORNIA SPEAKERS BUREAU
1517 Andreas Avenue
San Jose, CA 95118

FRANK DEMUTH
247 N. Gassey
San Pedro, CA 90731

JANE LEE HAWKINS
FULL SERVICE SPEAKERS BUREAU &
   ADVERTISING AGENCY
2001 East First Street
Santa Ana, CA 92705

MR. PUT ONS
PUT ONS PRODUCTIONS
415 Alan Road, Dept M
Santa Barbara, CA 93109

SARAH W. COOLEY RESEARCH SERVICE
104 Walnut Avenue
Santa Cruz, CA 95060

LAURA SHIELDS
ASSOCIATIONS COMMUNICATIONS
225 Santa Monica Blvd., Suite 202
Crocker Bank Bldg.
Santa Monica, CA 90401

DOLORES ROGERS, DIRECTOR
EXECUTIVE ASSOCIATES
15015 Ventura Blvd.
Sherman Oaks, CA 91403

JOYCE AIMEE
AIMEE ENTERTAINMENT ASSOCIATES
14241 Ventura Blvd., Suite 104
Sherman Oaks, CA 91423

CHARLES WELLER
WINNEY ASSOCIATION
Box 855
Tustin, CA 92680

DONNA HOFFNER
MARKET CONSULTANT
Continuing Education Corp.
17291 Irvine Blvd., Suite 262
Tustin, CA 92680

JOHN LUMBLEAU
LUMBLEAU REAL ESTATE SCHOOLS
6633 Van Nuys Blvd.
Van Nuys, CA 91405

PRO SPORTS PRODUCTIONS
6 Avenue 29, Suite 3
Venice, CA 90291

BRUCE MERRIN ORGANIZATION
Warner Center
6400 Canoga Avenue, Suite 311
Woodland Hills, CA 91367

CREATIVE COMMUNICATIONS
   ASSOCIATES
16126 Lomacitas Lane
Whittier, CA 90603

COLORADO

BILLY JACK LUDWIG
Box P
Basalt, CO 81621

RICKIE HALL & ASSOCIATES, INC.
930 Poplar
Boulder, CO 80302

BOULDER INSIGHTS
1245 Pearl, Suite 205
Boulder, CO 80302

MANAGEMENT RESEARCH CORP.
1200 Pearl Street
Boulder, CO 80302

HIGH FLIGHT FOUNDATION
202 East Cheyenne Mountain Blvd.
Suite 1
POB 1387
Colorado Springs, CO 80901

MCBRIDE SPEAKERS BUREAU
870 Quail Lake Circle, Suite 101
Colorado Springs, CO 80906

RON KAUFFMAN
DIRECTOR ROCKY MOUNTAIN
  SPEAKERS BUREAU
800 Metrobank
Denver, CO 80202

COLORADO CONVENTION &
  RESERVATIONS
1665 Grant Street, Suite 9
Denver, CO 80302

JIM MELTON
Box 6461
Denver, CO 80206

EVERETT PETERSON
DENVER EXECUTIVE CLUB
409-410 Republic Bldg.
Denver, CO 80202

JOHN HECKMAN ENTERPRISES
Box 15577
Lakewood, CO 80215

INTERNATIONAL SPEAKERS BUREAU
100 Everett Street
Lakewood, CO 80226

CONNECTICUT

CONFERENCE & EXPOSITION
  MANAGEMENT CO., INC.
Box 844
Greenwich, CT 06830

CONNECTICUT SPEAKERS BUREAU
91 Reservoir Road
Newington, CT 06111

CONFERENCE MANAGEMENT CORP.
17 Washington Street
Norwalk, CT 06854

MASTER TALENT
993 Farmington Avenue
W. Hartford, CT 06107

DISTRICT OF COLUMBIA AREA

WASHINGTON SPEAKERS BUREAU, INC.
201 N. Fairfax Street, #11
Alexandria, VA 22314

RALPH WHITENER & CO.
DULLES INTERNATIONAL AIRPORT
Box 17413
Fairfax, VA 20041

R. JOSEPH ADVERTISING, INC.
8201 Corporate Drive
Landover, MD 20785

ALAN L. FREED & ASSOCIATES, INC.
Box 304
McLean, VA 22101

RALPH ANDRES
POB 1093
Tappahannock, VA 22560

AMERICAN SOCIETY OF ASSOCIATION
EXECUTIVES
1101 16th Street, NW
Washington, DC 20036

CONFERENCE SPEAKERS INT'L, INC.
1055 Thomas Jefferson Street
Suite 300
Washington, DC 20007

WEDGEWOOD PRODUCTIONS, INC.
Box 440
Crownsville, MD 21032

POTOMAC SPEAKERS, INC.
3001 Veazey Terrace, NW, #1625
Washington, DC 20008

FREEDS SPEAKERS BUREAU
927 15th Street, NW
Washington, DC 20005

INT'L DIPLOMATIC SOCIETY
National Press Bldg.
Washington, DC 20045

INT'L LECTURERS ASSOCIATION
National Press Bldg.
Washington, DC 20045

INT'L STOCK EXCHANGE
INFORMATION & DEVELOPMENT ASSN.
National Press Bldg.
Washington, DC 20045

INT'L ASSOCIATION OF PROFESSIONAL
BUREAUCRATS
1032 National Press Bldg.
Washington, DC 20045

STULL LECTURE BUREAU
National Press Bldg.
Washington, DC 20045

THE LOBBYIST FEDERATION
National Press Bldg.
Washington, DC 20045

NATIONAL PRESS BLDG.
Washington, DC 20045

NATIONAL SPEAKERS FORUM
1629 K Street, NW
Washington, DC 20006

JANET S. DOVE
AMERICAN PETROLEUM INSTITUTE
2101 L Street, NW
Washington, DC 20037

MYSTOR-RUNION & ASSOCIATES
4545 42nd Street, NW
Washington, DC 20015

FLORIDA

THE ALIVE INSTITUTE, INC.
2757 NW 42nd Avenue
Coconut Creek, FL 33066

PROFESSIONAL MARKETING
ORGANIZERS, INC.
Box 141423
Coral Gables, FL 33134

IDA MCGINNISS SPEAKERS BUREAU
2500 East Hallandale Beach Blvd
Hallandale, FL 33160

AL HEYDRICK ASSOCIATES
2830 NE 29th Avenue
Lighthouse Point, FL 33064

BUREAU FOR SPEAKERS & SEMINARS
POB 37
Maitland, FL 32751

JAMES ARCH & ASSOCIATES
POB 37
Maitland, FL 32751

ADELE COX CONVENTION SERVICE &
CONSULTANTS
321 NW 186th Street
Miami, FL 33169

STEPHEN ARTHUR DERRY, P. E.
7700 Coquina Drive, N. Bay Island
Miami Beach, FL 33141

MULTI-ENTERTAINMENT, INC.
JERRY MARSHALL MUSICAL
   ENTERPRISES, INC.
1110 NE 16 Ord Street, Suite 219
N. Miami Beach, FL 33162

GERRY & ROLAND TAUSCH
3530 Pine Valley Drive
Sarasota, FL 33579

McCOLLUM MANAGEMENT &
·   MEETINGS
POB 10523
Tallahassee, FL 32302

PEG McCOLLUM
THE PROGRAM PEOPLE
I I A OF GREATER TAMPA
POB 270334
Tampa, FL 33688

GEORGIA

RAY BLOCH PRODUCTIONS, INC.
230 Peachtree Street, NW, Suite 1417
Atlanta, GA 30303

JORDAN ENTERPRISES
SUCCESS LEADERS SPEAKERS SERVICE
Lenox Square Box 18737
Atlanta, GA 30326

STEVE BROWN
4675 N. Shallowford Road, Suite 200
Atlanta, GA 30338

SPEAKEASY, INC.
400 Colony Square, Suite 1130
Atlanta, GA 30361

RALPH ANDRES, VP
INT'L ASSN. OF SPEAKERS & SALES
   TRAINERS
Box 3309
Augusta, GA 30904

CONVENTION CONSULTANTS OF
   SAVANNAH DELTA, INC.
117 W. Perry
Savannah, GA 31401

ILLINOIS

VIP PRODUCTIONS, INC.
750 West Algonquin Road
Arlington Heights, IL 60005

BURNS SPORTS CELEBRITY SERV.
230 N. Michigan Avenue
Chicago, IL 60601

THE CONTEMPORARY FORUM
2528A W. Jerome Street
Chicago, IL 60645

CARLETON ROGERS, JR.
EXPO MANAGEMENT, INC.
The Apparel Center, Suite 1
Chicago, IL 60654

IMPACT INTERNATIONAL
John Hancock Center
Chicago, IL 60611

NAT'L ASSN. OF BANK WOMEN
111 East Wacker Drive
Chicago, IL 60601

ON THE SCENE WITH ELEANOR WOODS
   & ASSOCIATES
505 N. LaSalle Street
Chicago, IL 60610

BESTROM MANAGEMENT CORP.
435 N. Michigan Avenue
Chicago, IL 60611

INT'L LANGUAGE & COMMUNICATIONS
   CENTER
33 N. Dearborn, Suite 1300
Chicago, IL 60602

CONVENTION & CONFERENCE
   CONSULTANTS
Box 313
Deerfield, IL 60015

CONVENTION ENTERTAINMENT
  PRODUCTIONS
1645 River Road, Suite 12
Des Plaines, IL 60018

PROGRAMS UNLIMITED
515 N. Main Street
Glen Ellyn, IL 60136

DON BRYANT
3049 Godfrey Road
Godfrey, IL 62035

CHERYL L. MILLER
SPEAKERS INTERNATIONAL
1015 W. Woodland, Suite 1A
Lake Bluff, IL 60044

NATIONAL SPEAKERS BUREAU, INC.
222 Wisconsin Avenue, Suite 309
Lake Forest, IL 60045

JANE MARKS
The Program People
Box 1426
Oak Brook, IL 60521

DAVIS MARKETING GROUP, INC.
1550 N. Northwest Hwy, Suite 40
Park Ridge, IL 60068

BRADLEY BARRAKS
Speakers Corner
2018 29th Street
Rock Island, IL 61201

THE SANFORD ORGANIZATION, INC.
4300-L Lincoln Avenue
Rolling Meadows, IL 60008

CMR, LTD.
524 Chatham Road
Roselle, IL 60712

MIDWEST MEETING SERVICES, INC.
Box 9412
Schaumberg, IL 60194

FRED J. YOUNG
516 Provident Avenue
Winnetka, IL 60093

INDIANA

CATHRINA BAUBY
RR 4/306
Elwood, IN 46036

PROGRAM DYNAMICS
2229 Forest Glade
Fort Wayne, IN 46825

RENEE NIPPER
MIDWEST PROGRAM SERVICE
BANE-CLENE CORPORATION
4533 Millersville Road
Indianapolis, IN 46205

BILL CARSON
HOME BUILDERS ASSN. OF INDIANA
143 W. Market, Suite 204
Indianapolis, IN 46204

KANSAS

NAT'L ASSN. OF SALES EDUCATION
POB 12222
Overland Park, KS 66212

PEGGY M. NULL KANSAS MEDICAL
  SOCIETY
AUXILIARY SPEAKERS BUREAU
1318 Marymount Road
Salina, KS 67401

THE ASSOCIATED CLUBS
One Townsite Plaza
Topeka, KS 66603

LOUISIANA

TALBOT, TALBOT & BERLIN, INC.
9441 Common Street, Suite C
Baton Rouge, LA 70809

CUSTOM CONVENTIONS
1739 Julia Street
New Orleans, LA 70113

HELEN R. DIETRICH, INC.
333 St. Charles Avenue, Suite 1221
New Orleans, LA 70130

MASSACHUSETTS

THE FORUM CORPORATION
84 State Street
Boston, MA 02109

LORDLY & DAME, INC.
51 Church Street
Boston, MA 02116

ROBERT P. WALKER ENTERPRISES, INC.
63 Atlantic Avenue
Boston, MA 02110

THE HANDLEY MANAGEMENT
51 Church Street
Boston, MA 02116

K & S ASSOCIATES
308 Brookline Street
Cambridge, MA 02139

AMERICAN PROGRAM BUREAU
850 Boylston Street
Chestnut Hill, MA 02167

SHERMAN EXPOSITION MANAGEMENT
1330 Boylston Street, Suite 209
Chestnut Hill, MA 02167

SPEAKERS GUILD
93 Old Kings Hwy.
Sandwich, MA 02563

UNIVERSAL SPEAKERS AGENCY, INC.
235 Bear Hill Road, Suite 203
Waltham, MA 02154

FROTHINGHAM MANAGEMENT
HELSEY FROTHINGHAM
384 Washington Street
Wesley, MA 02181

MICHIGAN

GROWTH UNLIMITED
31 E Avenue S.
Battle Creek, MI 49017

MARK GREENBURG BUREAU, INC.
Box 358
East Detroit, MI 48021

CHERI VEAKEY
1326 McKay Tower
Grand Rapids, MI 49503

CONVENTION SERVICES INT'L
494 Lake Shore Lane
Grosse Pointe, MI 48236

ALTERNATIVES IN MOTIVATION
BILL SANDERS
10031 Handel Street
Portage, MI 49081

MINNESOTA

R. L. MONTGOMERY ASSOCIATES, INC.
12313 Michelle Circle
Burnsville, MN 55337

J. WARREN BURKE
MIDWEST PROGRAM SERVICE
5309 Vernon Avenue
Edina, MN 55436

LEOPOLD HAUSER, III
PERSONAL DYNAMICS INSTITUTE
5186 West 76th Street
Minneapolis, MN 55436

LIEMANDT'S TOUR & CONVENTION
    SERVICE
1010 Second Avenue
Minneapolis, MN 55403

MICHAEL PODOLINKSY
KEY SEMINARS
5912 Newton Avenue
Minneapolis, MN 55419

NORTH CENTRAL SPEAKERS BUREAU
One Corporate Center, Suite 445
401 Metro Blvd.
Minneapolis, MN 55435

MEETING CONCEPTS, INC.
511 11th Avenue S, Suite 261
Minneapolis, MN 55415

MIDWEST SPEAKERS BUREAU
6440 Flying Cloud Drive, Suite 205
Minneapolis, MN 55344

MISSOURI

JUDY HORNSEY
SYNERGETIC SYSTEMS
3214 Halliday
St. Louis, MO 63118

NEVADA

RICHARD STULL
SPEAKERS BUREAU INTERNATIONAL
POB 19442
Las Vegas, NV 89119

UNIVERSAL MODELS & CONVENTION
  SERVICE
953 East Sahara Avenue
Bldg. 28-B, Suite 207
Las Vegas, NV 89104

NEW JERSEY

JR ASSOCIATES
263 New Street
Belleville, NJ 07109

THE LYONS CO., INC.
309 South Street
Murray Hill, NJ 07974

UNCONVENTIONAL CONVENTIONS
8 Park Road
Paterson, NJ 07514

LEIGH BUREAU
49-51 State Road
Princeton, NJ 08540

TRAINING SERVICES, INC.
130 Orient Way
Box 388
Rutherford, NJ 07070

SUSSEX BUSINESS COMMUNICATIONS,
  INC.
Box 585
Summit, NJ 07901

HOW TO CREATE INCREDIBLE EDIBLES
21 Almroth Drive
Wayne, NJ 07470

NEW YORK

RAINBOW LECTURES
31 Nottingham Terrace
Buffalo, NY 14216

NEW YORK CITY AND AREA

A. SHEEN MANAGEMENT
2703 Batchelder
Brooklyn, NY 11235

THALHEIM EXPOSITIONS, INC.
98 Cutter Mill Road
Great Neck, NY 11021

ALAN CIMBERG
83 Tilrose Avenue
Malverne, NY 11565

LOIS FENTON
721 Shore Cares Drive
Mamaroneck, NY 10543

CMR, LTD.
524 Latham Road
Mineola, NY 11501

FRAN SLOTKIN
PROGRAMS & PROMOTIONS FOR
  BUSINESS & INDUSTRY
POB 327
Mineola, NY 11501

RICH KEEGAN ASSOCIATES
524 Latham Road
Mineola, NY 11501

ROYCE CARLTON, INC.
866 United Nations Plaza
New York, NY 10017

CHARLES R. ROTHSCHILD
  PRODUCTIONS
330 East 48th Street
New York, NY 10022

LEIGH BUREAU
1185 Avenue of the Americas
New York, NY 10036

THE BOOKERS—SPECIALISTS IN TEL/
  RADIO PRESS INTERVIEWS
200 West 51st Street
New York, NY 10019

THE CONFERENCE BOARD
845 Third Avenue
New York, NY 10022

EASTER EAGLES ASSOCIATION
305 East 24th Street
New York, NY 10010

BUILD POWER, INC.
2090 7th Avenue
New York, NY 10037

R. E. DELANEY ASSOCIATES
1270 Avenue of the Americas
New York, NY 10020

WINTHROP EPSTEIN INT'L, LTD.
366 5th Avenue
New York, NY 10018

RICHARD FULTON, INC.
101 West 57th Street
New York, NY 10019

MARTIN V. GALLATIN, PH.D.
80 East 11th Street
New York, NY 10010

WILL JORDAN
435 West 57th Street, Apt 10F
New York, NY 10019

BLANCHE ROSS
ROSS ASSOCIATES
515 Madison Avenue, Suite 1225
New York, NY 10022

HARRY WALKER AGENCY
Empire State Bldg, Suite 3616
350 5th Avenue
New York, NY 10018

DOROTHY SARNOFF'S SPEECH
  DYNAMICS
111 West 57th Street
New York, NY 10019

MARKETING CONCEPTS, INC.
Two Pennsylvania Plaza
New York, NY 10001

AMR INT'L, INC.
1370 Avenue of the Americas
New York, NY 10019

MATTGO ENTERPRISES, INC.
185 East 85th Street
New York, NY 10028

PHILIP NOLAN
134 West 58th Street
New York, NY 10019

NATIONAL EXPOSITIONS CO., INC.
14 West 40th Street
New York, NY 10018

NEW YORK MANAGEMENT CENTER,
  INC.
360 Lexington Avenue
New York, NY 10017

NEW YORK UNIVERSITY/PUBLIC
  RELATIONS SOCIETY OF AMERICA
BUSINESS & MANAGEMENT PROGRAMS
310 Madison Avenue, Rm 1412
New York, NY 10017

PASSKEY ASSOCIATES, INC.
425 Park Avenue
New York, NY 10022

RAY BLOCH PRODUCTIONS, INC.
1500 Broadway
New York, NY 10036

AMERICAN MANAGEMENT
  ASSOCIATIONS
135 West 50th Street
New York, NY 10020

LARIMI CO.
151 East 50th Street
New York, NY 10022

GEORGE LITTLE MANAGEMENT
LITTLE BROTHERS SHOWS
261 Madison Avenue
New York, NY 10016

SELEXOR DISPLAYS, INC.
1916 Park Avenue
New York, NY 10037

JOE SNYDER & CO., LTD.
155 West 68th Street
New York, NY 10023

STEVEN K. HERLITZ, INC.
850 Third Avenue
New York, NY 10022

PENTON LEARNING SYSTEMS
420 Lexington Avenue, Suite 2846
New York, NY 10017

RUSSELL FLAGG, INC.
103 East 84th Street
New York, NY 10028

HARRISON-BERKALL PRODUCTIONS,
  INC.
527 Madison Avenue
New York, NY 10022

IMG SPORTS SPEAKER & PROGRAM
  CENTER
767 5th Avenue, Suite 601
New York, NY 10022

INT'L CONFERENCE GROUP, INC.
51 East 42nd Street
New York, NY 10017

INT'L EXPOSITION CO.
200 Park Avenue
New York, NY 10017

INT'L TRADE SHOWS
545 5th Avenue
New York, NY 10017

EGR TRAVEL INTERNATIONAL, INC.
290 Madison Avenue
New York, NY 10017

EXECUTIVE ENTERPRISES, INC.
10 Columbus Circle
New York, NY 10019

HOWARD LANIN PRODUCTIONS, INC.
59 East 54th Street
New York, NY 10022

SAXTON COMMUNICATIONS GROUP,
  LTD.
605 Third Avenue
New York, NY 10158

CHARLES SNITOW ORGANIZATION
331 Madison Avenue
New York, NY 10017

COMMUNISPOND, INC.
485 Lexington Avenue
New York, NY 10017

LIFEFORCE INT'L PROGRAM BUREAU,
  INC.
2 Washington Square Village,
Suite 6-T
New York, NY 10012

NINA LITTLE PRODUCTIONS, INC.
527 Madison Avenue, Suite 1406
New York, NY 10022

GROUP CONSULTANT INT'L, LTD.
70 Glen Cove Road
Roslyn Heights, NY 11577

PROGRAM CORP. OF AMERICA
595 West Hartsdale Avenue
White Plains, NY 10607

NORTH CAROLINA

CENTER FOR CONTEMPORARY
   MANAGEMENT& EDUCATION
3215-H Calumet Drive
Raleigh, NC 27610

OHIO

TOURCRAFTERS, INC.
3 East 4th Street
Cincinnati, OH 45202

CENTER FOR FAMILY BUSINESS
POB 24268
Cleveland, OH 44124

BESTCONVENTIONS, INC.
401 Euclid Avenue, The Arcade
Cleveland, OH 44114

BANNISTER & ASSOCIATES
50 West Broad Street, Suite 1331
Columbus, OH 43215

WEBER & ASSOCIATES, INC.
3200 Valleyview Drive
Columbus, OH 43204

FRANK & ASSOCIATES
POB 27225
Columbus, OH 43227

GLAMOUR MODEL AGENCY
140 N. Main Street
Dayton, OH 45402

BONNIE MARSHALL, RN
HOLISTIC COMMUNICATIONS
   CONSULTANTS
4162A Indian Run Drive
Dayton, OH 45415

KENNETH L. BARTER
100 Executive Drive
Marion, OH 43302

OFFINGER MANAGEMENT COMPANY
1100 Brandywine Drive
Zanesville, OH 43701

OKLAHOMA

SEYMOUR DAVIS
Box 75171
Oklahoma City, OK 73107

GREATER LIFE RALLIES
GAINEY ARCHARD & PAUL BOSTON
2907 E. 51st Street S., Suite G
Tulsa, OK 74135

OREGON

DONALD J. MOINE
3040 Harris Street, Nob Hill
Eugene, OR 97405

ROB FUSSELL
PEOPLE POTENTIAL SPEAKERS BUREAU
3560 Lancaster Drive, NE
Salem, OR 97303

PENNSYLVANIA

THE RUFFLES CO.
Box 47
Bushkill, PA 18324

SHOWCASE ASSOCIATES, INC.
The Benson East, Suite A-200
Jenkintown, PA 19406

LB ASSOCIATES
231 Hay Avenue
Johnstown, PA 15902

DR. BERNARD B. GOLDNER
4026 MacNiff Drive, POB 279
Lafayette Hill, PA 19444

EASTERN U.S. SHOW PRODUCTIONS
121 Chestnut Street
Philadelphia, PA 19106

SHEA MANAGEMENT, INC.
1326 Freeport Road
Pittsburgh, PA 15238

SHOWCASE ASSOCIATES, INC.
173 Fernbrook Avenue
Wyncote, PA 19095

TENNESSEE

JOHN GOODBARD
SUCCESS SYSTEMS, INC.
1600 East 25th Street
Chattanooga, TN 37404

JOHN R. HANDICK
PERSONAL DEVELOPMENT ENTERPRISES,
  INC.
2114 Seton Place
Germantown, TN 38138

DR. ART GARNER & ASSOCIATES
2519 Lovitt Drive
Memphis, TN 38138

MEETING SERVICES & CONVENTION
  CONSULTANTS
4515 Harding Road, Suite 110
Nashville, TN 37205

DR. CHARLES EDWARD SMITH
139 Holly Forest Drive
Nashville, TN 37221

CANDACE BARR
CELEBRITY SPEAKERS BUREAU
50 Music Square West
Nashville, TN 37203

TEXAS

TECHNOLOGY FEATURES, INC.
2200 Guadalupe
Austin, TX 78705

WOMEN IN COMMUNICATIONS, INC.
NATIONAL HEADQUARTERS
Box 9561
Austin, TX 78766

GARUTH MANAGEMENT CONSULTANTS,
  INC.
2715 Peachtree
Carrollton, TX 75006

RICHARD RUSSELL
4342 Sexton Lane
Dallas, TX 75229

ED BERNET
7027 Twin Hills Avenue
Dallas, TX 75231

BILLY JACK LUDWIG
8330 Meadow Road, #130
Dallas, TX 75231

JOAN FRANK PRODUCTIONS
9550 Forest Lane, #101
Dallas, TX 75243

VERBAL COMMUNICATIONS, INC.
12700 Preston Road, Suite 170
Dallas, TX 75230

RAY BLOCH PRODUCTIONS, INC.
6060 North Central Expressway
Dallas, TX 75206

PARKER CHIROPRACTIC RESEARCH
  FOUNDATION
DR. WILLIAM D. BROWN
Box 40444
Fort Worth, TX 67140

JOHN WOLFE INSTITUTE, INC.
12335 Boheme
Houston, TX 77024

CONTEMPORARY PROGRAMS, INC.
3136 Lafayette
Box 25101
Houston, TX 77005

SCL GROUP & CONVENTION SERVICE
10521 S. Post Oak, Suite 101
Houston, TX 77035

JANUELL TEAGUE
PEOPLE PLUS
5701 71st Street
Lubbock, TX 79424

BILLY JACK LUDWIG
4537 Fremont Lane
Plano, TX 75075

WASHINGTON

GEORGE CARLSON & ASSOCIATES
WESTERN LECTURE/ENTERTAINMENT
  BUREAU
113 Battery Street
Seattle, WA 98121

R. E. DELANEY ASSOCIATES
15259 Wedgewood Station
Seattle, WA 98115

WISCONSIN

PROJECT P, INC.
448 Edgewood Drive
Neenah, WI 54956

CANADA

ENTERTAINMENT ASSOCIATES
2828 Bathurst Street
Toronto, Ontario
Canada M6B 3A7

GEORGE KING ENTERTAINMENT
  SERVICE
404 Huron Street
Toronto, Ontario
Canada M5S 2G6

P.A.M. COMMUNICATIONS
POB 142 Willowdale
North York, Ontario
Canada M2N 5S8

NORMAN K. REBIN
WINOVATIONS
Box 1240
Almonte, Ontario
Canada K0A 1A9

BERNARD SEARLE, INC.
SPEAKERS UNLIMITED AGENCY
2079 Marine Drive
West Vancouver, BC
Canada V7V 1K1

MURRAY BLACK CONVENTION
  ENTERTAINMENT, INC.
POB 131
Place Bonaventure
Montreal, Quebec
Canada H5A 1A6

ENGLAND

PROMOTIVATION-MORRIS MAIN
  EVENTS LTD.
32 Neal Street, Covent Garden
London WC2H 9PS England

JAPAN

BERNICE CRAMER
TRAC ONE, INC.
Room 1075, Hotel New Japan
2-12-8 Nagata-Cho-chiyoda-Ku
Tokyo, Japan 1000

AUSTRALIA

CHRISTINE A. MAHER
Suite 1102, Northside Gardens
168 Walker Street
North Sydney NSW 2060
Australia

═══ CHAPTER 15 ═══════════════

MISCELLANEOUS AND USEFUL GLEANINGS

A potpourri of miscellaneous ideas, checklists, do's and don'ts, musings, and sundry other information that defies orderly classification, but appears worth keeping near at hand on the shelf.

WHERE DO MAILING LISTS COME FROM?

Mailing lists are not sold normally; they are rented, with a fee for each use. Renters "salt" the list with control names to detect any cheating—using the list again without paying again for the use.

Rates vary widely, according to the perceived value of the list. Some run as little as $25 to $35 per 1000 names (the usual unit of sale), while rates also range up to $75 to $100 per 1000 names. And in many cases the lists can be rented only in minimum quantities of 3000 to 5000 names.

The lists are usually those acquired, over years, by periodicals, mail order dealers, and others who do business by mail and so acquire long lists of both inquirers and buyers. In some cases, the list owners do their own marketing of these lists. Dun & Bradstreet does so, for example, because it is a "natural" business for them. In fact, it would be strange if they failed to turn the assets of their business lists to their direct use. But most others choose not to get into the list rental business, when there are so many list brokers—they prefer to call themselves "list managers"—who will handle the marketing of the lists on a commission basis. (There are exceptions, in which list brokers own some lists of their own—"house" lists—and in which list users use a mix of rented lists and their own—again—"house" lists.)

Many of the list managers freely advertise the sources of their lists in such publications as *DM News*, a monthly tabloid read by members of the industry. (Write to Circulation Department, DM News, 19 West 21st Street, New York, NY 10010, for subscription information.)

Here are a few—and only a few—of the many list brokers offering their wares to the public:

NCRI List Management
30 East 42nd Street
New York, NY 10017
(212) 687-3876

Names & Addresses, Inc.
3605 Woodhead Drive
Northbrook, IL 60062
(312) 272-7933

Potentials in Marketing Magazine
731 Hennepin Avenue
Minneapolis, MN 55403
(800) 328-4329

List Services Corp.
890 Ethan Allen Hwy
POB 2014
Ridgefield, CT 06877
(203) 438-0327

Hayden Direct Marketing Services
10 Mulholland Drive
Hasbrouck Heights, NJ 07604
(201) 393-6384

The Kleid Company, Inc.
200 Park Avenue
New York, NY 10166
(212) 599-4140

Qualified Lists Corp.
135 Bedford Road
Armonk, NY 10504
(212) 409-6200
(914) 273-3353

Texas Direct
5100 Rondo Drive
Fort Worth, TX 76106
(817) 625-4221/429-4120
(800) 433-7750

The List House
130 Lyons Plain Road
Weston, CT 06883
(203) 227-6027

American List Counsel, Inc.
88 Orchard Road
Princeton, NJ 08540
(800) 526-3973

Ed Burnett Consultants, Inc.
2 Park Avenue
New York, NY 10016
(212) 679-0630

Chilton Direct Marketing & List
  Management Company
1 Chilton Way
Radnor, PA 19089
(800) 345-1214
(215) 964-4365

R. L. Polk & Co.
3030 Holcomb Bridge Road
Suite F
Norcross, GA 30071
(Send for catalog; Polk
has offices throughout U.S.)

Seminars
525 N. Lake Street
Madison, WI 53703
(608) 251-2421

TIPS ON DIRECT-MAIL COPY

Here are a few reminders, as a checklist or "do's and don'ts" list
to refer to when preparing diret-mail copy:

☐ Always make things as easy as possible for the customer, as
for example:

1. Make it easy to understand what you are saying. Use short
   words, short sentences, short paragraphs. One thought in
   a sentence, one subject and one main point in a paragraph.
   (Be sure first that you yourself fully understand the main
   point.)

2. Make it easy for the customer to order, ask for more information, or otherwise reveal interest by providing a return card, telephone number, or other convenient means for responding.

3. Make it easy for the customer to understand what you want him or her to do by *telling* the customer what to do. A great many sales are lost by advertisers who fail to tell the customers what they want the customers to do.

☐ A direct-mail cliche (which is nonetheless a truism) is "The more you tell the more you sell." Don't stint on copy. Be sure to include a letter, a brochure or flyer of some sort, and a response device (envelope and/or order form) as an absolute minimum, and there is no harm in enclosing even more. The experts claim that three-quarters of the response results from the letter, and that a good circular or brochure can increase response by as much as one-third. My own experience bears this out quite emphatically.

☐ Don't tell it all in the letter. Split the copy up among the various enclosures, or at least provide additional details in the various enclosures. Make it clear that additional information/details are to be found elsewhere in the enclosures. Give the reader good reason—inducements—to read everything, if you want maximum impact.

☐ Geography makes a difference. Prospects who are nearby tend to respond better than those at a distance. Know nearby zip codes, and use these. But do test, for there are always exceptions. Example: when it comes to consulting and speaking services, there is some appeal, even a kind of mystique, to the expert from a distant place, especially if you are mailing from a major industrial or business center, such as New York, Chicago, Washington, or another major metropolitan area. If you are, take advantage of it, somehow, by giving it prominence in your copy.

☐ If you use envelope copy—advertising and sales messages on the outside of the envelope—do two things:

1. Use both sides of the envelope. If you are going to make a bulletin board of the envelope, you might as well get full

use of it; copy on both sides pulls better than copy on one side only if the copy is powerful.

2. Now that you've served notice that the envelope contains advertising matter, why pay first-class postage? You might as well save money by using bulk mail or, at least, something less expensive than first class.

For more help—for a stream of direct-marketing ideas every month from a team of experts, for example—you might try subscribing to Galen Stilson's newsletter, *Mail Order Connection.* You can reach Galen at P.O. Box 1075, Tarpon Springs, Florida 34286-1075, (813) 938-1555 for more details.

Another source of useful information is *Personal Selling Power*, a tabloid published by Gerhard Gschwandtner at 1127 International Pkwy, Suite 102, POB 5467, Fredericksburg, Virginia 22405, (703) 752-7000. In fact, Gerhard welcomes material from anyone with something to say, and you may be able to promote some useful publicity here by contributing an article to this publication. In any case, you'll always be in good company reading this thought-provoking publication, for Gerhard manages to persuade some of the most prominent personalities of the speaking and marketing industries—Norman Vincent Peale and Zig Ziglar, for example—to contribute to his periodical, and they usually have impressive and helpful ideas to pass along.

Be sure to read as many trade papers as possible. Unexpected opportunities arise. For example, the issue of *DM News* that is on my desk at the moment—it was in this morning's mail—has an article in it headlined:

SPEAKERS BEING SOUGHT FOR NEW YORK DM DAY

The story explains that the program committee for next year's Direct Marketing Day event in the big city is "looking for 'new faces and ideas'," and tells readers where applicants may apply.

SOME BIBLIOGRAPHIC
RECOMMENDATIONS

Although several books and periodicals have been introduced and referred to in earlier chapters, here are a few others that should be of some help also, especially for marketing purposes. However, never overlook the truth that as a speaker you are in the information and communications field, and it is essential that you keep up with what's going on in the world generally and in your own and related professionals especially, while you also recharge your batteries regularly by such reading. It has been observed many times that no one is selling what they sold 10 years ago, and anyone who is still selling precisely what they sold even five years ago is probably verging on obsolescence already, so rapidly are things changing today.

On Consulting

Despite all that has been written on the art of public speaking, almost nothing has been written before about the practical aspects of establishing a career/enterprise in public speaking. Perhaps that is because so few public speakers are speakers exclusively. You may have noted earlier that Dottie Walters was quoted as estimating that probably 90 percent of public speakers have other career interest and activities. Whatever the case, it is necessary to turn to other, often related fields for useful information. One of these other fields is that of consulting.

The majority of successful consultants are also effective speakers. The ability to speak well is more than an asset to a consultant; it's virtually a necessity, an obligatory skill in consulting. So it is not surprising that a great many speakers are also consultants. However, there has been, at least until recently, almost as great a paucity of useful publications about consulting as a career and enterprise as about speaking. But that has begun to change, probably because consulting has been growing, as a profession and as an industry (now estimated by *INC.* magazine as currently a $30 billion business). Among the publications that should therefore be of some interest to you is the bimonthly newsletter, *Consulting*

Opportunities Journal, published by J. Stephen Lanning, P.O. Box 17674, Washington, DC 20041. I also unblushingly recommend my own *How to Succeed as an Independent Consultant*, published by John Wiley & Sons, Inc., 605 Third Avenue, New York, NY 10158.

On Writing

The books on writing that are in print today are a library in themselves. There is hardly an aspect of writing that has not been itself the subject of at least one book, and usually several books. (Of course, it should not be a surprise that writing is one of the favorite subjects of writers!) Every month's edition of *Writer's Digest* alone carries an impressive list of writers' books sold by the Writer's Digest Book Club, with many of the books published by Writer's Digest Books, their own book publishing division. There are, however, some special and useful publications which are not advertised widely and which you may therefore not have heard of. One of these is a newsletter, *The Inkling*, published by Inkling Publications, Inc., P.O. Box 128, Alexandria, Minnesota 56308.

Directories

Hendrickson Publishing Co, Inc., 79 Washington Street, Hempstead, NY 11550, publishes a monthly magazine, *World Convention Dates*, which lists and describes upcoming conventions, trade shows, meetings, and related news.

Gale Research Company, The Book Tower, Detroit, Michigan 48226, publishes a number of useful directories, including an *Encyclopedia of Associations*, which lists some 7000 such organizations in nearly 1700 pages.

R. R. Bowker Company, 205 E. 42nd Street, New York, NY 10017, publishes several directories and periodicals, notably *Publisher's Weekly*, the annual *Literary Market Place*, listing book publishers, agents, and related services; and another annual, *Ulrich's*

Guide to Periodicals, which lists magazines and newsletters world-wide.

A directory to federal government markets is my own *Directory of Federal Purchasing Offices*, published by John Wiley & Sons, Inc. (address given previously).

INDEX